Democratizing Texas Politics

Number Forty
Jack and Doris Smothers Series in Texas History, Life, and Culture

Democratizing Texas Politics

Race, Identity, and Mexican American
Empowerment, 1945–2002

BY BENJAMIN MÁRQUEZ

University of Texas Press ◆ *Austin*

Publication of this work was made possible in part by support
from the J. E. Smothers, Sr., Memorial Foundation and the
National Endowment for the Humanities.

♾ The paper used in this book meets the minimum requirements of ANSI/NISO
Z39.48-1992 (R1997) (Permanence of Paper).

Library of Congress Cataloging-in-Publication Data
Márquez, Benjamin, 1953–
    Democratizing Texas politics : race, identity, and Mexican American
empowerment, 1945–2002 / Benjamin Márquez.
      pages   cm
    Includes bibliographical references and index.
    ISBN 978-0-292-75384-6 (hardback)
    ISBN 978-1-4773-0215-6 (paperback)
    1. Mexican Americans—Texas—Politics and government.   2. Texas—
Politics and government—1951–   I. Title.
    F395.M5M367   2014
    976.4′063—dc23

                                              2013019910

doi:10.7560/753846

To Julia Márquez

Contents

Acknowledgments

In the course of writing this book, I have been assisted by many colleagues. Over the years a number of scholars were kind enough to offer feedback and encouragement on this project. Henry Flores, Sandy Magana, Michael Olivas, Luis Fraga, Melissa Michelson, David Canon, and Yoi Herrera commented on various parts of the manuscript. I especially want to thank those who read the manuscript in its entirety and offered their thought-provoking comments: Booth Fowler, Valerie Martinez, and Francisco Scarano. I am grateful for the support that I received from Graham Wilson and John Coleman.

I am indebted to my students at the University of Wisconsin who worked as researchers: Sudha Rajan, Aaron Swerdlow, Bryce Nyeggen, Natasha Lewis, Kathryn Hall, and Katherine Grace Mendez. I want to thank Jack Edelson for his help with the charts and figures. I deeply appreciate the assistance of Alexander Dunn, who was a terrific editor and critic.

I thank the many archivists and librarians who guided me through my research, especially those at the Dolph Briscoe Center for American History, University of Texas at Austin: Allison Beck, Amy Bowman, and Brenda Gunn. Special thanks go to Evan Hocker for his tireless assistance and good humor. Tom Kreneck and Grace Charles of the Charles Mary and Jeff Bell Library at Texas A&M University–Corpus Christi provided invaluable assistance as I researched the Dr. Hector P. Garcia Papers. I am also grateful for the assistance of Darlene Mott, Lynda Young, and Lisa Meisch of the Sam Houston Regional Library and Research Center.

Thanks also to Cecilia Arnos Hunter and Sandra Rexroat of the South Texas Archives at the James C. Jernigan Library at Texas A&M University–Kingsville; Irene Gonzales at the Austin History Center; Robert Tissing at the Lyndon B. Johnson Library; Margo Gutiérrez at the Nettie

Lee Benson Latin American Collection; and Sergio Velasco at the Texas State Library and Archives Commission. I am also grateful to Charles Schultz of the Cushing Library at Texas A&M University, who helped me with the William P. Clements Jr. Collection. I thank the library staff at the University of Texas at El Paso, the Houston Public Library, and Rice University. Claudia Rivers, head of Special Collections at the University of Texas–El Paso Library, gave me invaluable and timely assistance with this project. I gratefully acknowledge the financial aid that I received from the American Philosophical Society, Lyndon Baines Johnson Foundation, and University of Wisconsin Graduate School.

This book would not have been brought to fruition without the support of Theresa May at the University of Texas Press. Her assistance and the aid of the anonymous reviewers have greatly improved this book. Kathy Lewis did a wonderful job with the final edit. Finally, I am most grateful to my wife, Lolita, and my children, Carlos, Carina, and Antonio, who gave me unwavering support over the time it took to complete this book.

Introduction

This is a book about Mexican American incorporation into Texas electoral politics after World War II. It is a study of social change in a state with a long and often violent history of racial conflict (Montejano 1987; Johnson 2003). The transformation of Texas politics is evidenced by the increase in Mexican American elected officials. In the 1940s the state had virtually none, even at the local level; but by the turn of the twenty-first century descriptive representation reached virtual parity in Texas and other southwestern states. By 1967 ten members of the Texas legislature were Mexican Americans, with one serving in the Senate (Grebler et al. 1970: 561). Although race relations in Texas were arguably worse than in other southwestern states, it was second only to New Mexico in the number of Mexican American state representatives. Though the larger Texas legislature allowed more opportunities for representation than in other states, a racial breakthrough was clearly taking place in a relatively short period (Grebler et al. 1970: 561). In 1975 Texas had 298 elected and appointed Mexican American officials. By 1984 it had 1,427. In that same year 3 of the 27 members of the Texas congressional delegation and 18 of the 150 members of the Texas House of Representatives were Mexican American (Davidson 1990: 249). In 1994 Texas had 2,215 Mexican American elected officials, representing a full 8 percent of all Texas elected officials. By 2003 Mexican Americans constituted 20 percent of the Texas legislature but only 18 percent of the general population. This change was not just a function of demographics but a result of intense Mexican American political activism. My question is, how did they do it? Which organizations and individuals were the most influential? Given the long list of problems facing Mexican Americans, which policy solutions received serious consideration and why? How did their adversaries and allies shape or reconfigure this ethnic insurgent movement?

The following chapters demonstrate that the increased participation of Mexican Americans in Texas party politics and the accompanying rise in formal representation have their roots in the culmination of six interrelated forces. First, activists developed a strong organizing capacity from their long history of political organizing to challenge racial exclusion in all areas of life. These organizations mobilized community resources and nurtured a cadre of leaders who articulated the politics of equal opportunity and engaged in the difficult work of desegregating the state's representative institutions. Second, Mexican Americans became a significant proportion of the voting-age population, large enough to constitute John F. Kennedy's margin of victory in Texas during the 1960 presidential election. The growing influence of the ethnic vote gave organizers a greater ability to negotiate with Anglo leaders at the state and local level. Third, the Democratic Party adopted policies during the late 1960s stipulating increased representation of women and minorities at state and national conventions. These changes, imposed by the national party, gave minority activists the ability to force concessions from entrenched interests. Fourth, the Republican Party emerged as a viable alternative for conservative voters in the South, thereby weakening resistance to racial reform within the Democratic Party. Fifth, civil rights legislation passed at the national level during the 1960s gave Mexican American activists the legal tools for dismantling unfair voting practices in Texas. Finally, a coalition of Mexican American and Anglo liberals enabled the transition to a more representative two-party system.

Mexican American activists changed the racial composition of Texas party politics, but they did it in a context where Anglo leaders and economic interests were alert to and hoped to shape the course of ethnic integration. The result was ethnic representation decoupled from its traditional mooring of group solidarity to representation more closely based on class, occupation, and ideology. During the fifty years after World War II descriptive representation increased to the point where Mexican Americans achieved parity in elected office relative to their numbers in the population. Their participation in party affairs became the norm. This study of racial transition and how it was negotiated over the years provides new insight into the structure of representation and power-sharing that replaced the old racial order. It offers additional new insights into the potential of minority social movements to change social institutions and how those movements were changed in the process.

Race and Social Change

Three theoretical approaches inform my analysis of social change in Texas. The first is the work on assimilation and acculturation. In the classic text *Assimilation in American Life*, Milton Gordon (1964) argued that the power of ethnicity to influence an individual's attitudes and behavior was determined, in large part, by the degree to which its members are socially and economically assimilated into the larger society. Immigrant groups in the United States have a long history of creating political organizations to fight against discrimination and preserve their cultural distinctiveness. However, a considerable body of literature predicts that ethnically based politics declines as immigrants achieve economic mobility and adopt the language and mores of U.S. society. As a group overcomes discriminatory barriers, the major cliques, clubs, and institutions of the host society are integrated and the economic and cultural distinctiveness that originally set the group apart disappears. Once the link between ethnicity and socioeconomic status is broken, each succeeding generation will become more like the majority in their beliefs and political behavior (Dahl 1964; Lieberson and Waters 1990; Waters 1990). If Mexican Americans are following the classic pattern of social and economic assimilation set by white ethnic immigrants, the gradual breakdown of differences between the ethnic subculture and the broader society over time should be accompanied by a dilution of ethnic identity and its power to influence political behavior.

First, I argue that the assimilation framework, when applied to the increase in minority elected officials and party activists, is an important though imperfect interpretive tool (Alba and Nee 2003). Its utility lies in the attention that it draws to the ability of evolving cultural practices, individual mobility, and changing attitudes to elevate a group's status through successive generations. Second- and third-generation Mexican Americans experience considerable income and occupational mobility, as well as an increased tendency to intermarry with Anglo Americans (Murguia 1982; Fuchs 1990; Lee and Bean 2007). Assimilation theory rests on the capacity of U.S. society to incorporate successive waves of immigrant groups into the major institutions of the host society, including partisan affairs. Assimilation theory offers some help in explaining the change that took place after World War II, but the model has serious shortcomings. Mexican American racial status and group history differ significantly from those of white ethnic immigrants. A legacy of conquest and persistently high levels of discrimination make the direct comparison to white ethnic immigrants problematic (Montejano 1987; Portes and Rumbaut 2001).

Mexican Americans have a history of responding collectively to racism and segregation that extends far longer through time than models of social assimilation predict (Ignacio García 1989; Mario García 1989). Even those most integrated into society's dominant institutions utilized ethnic identity as a basis for political mobilization (Macias 2006). Recent evidence of stagnation in economic and occupation mobility even among multigenerational residents limits the model's predictive utility (Portes and Rumbaut 2001; Telles and Ortiz 2008).

A major shortcoming of any straight-line assimilation framework is that it does not account for the conditions under which incorporation takes place or the role of ethnic mobilization in creating change. The political process model offers important insights in this regard by linking the economic changes taking place after World War II to civil rights activism. In this view, political and economic realignments, independent of the protest group's efforts, create opportunities for social movement organizations to press for change. Based on the African American civil rights movement, the political process model argues that transformative economic changes left political institutions open to challenge from subordinated groups. The mechanization of southern agriculture destroyed the system of sharecropping and made it possible for millions of African Americans to migrate to urban areas in the North (Piven and Cloward 1979). Urbanization allowed for more organizing possibilities and rendered political and economic structures vulnerable to the politics of protest and disruption. A rapid growth in the South's industrial base added to the disruption of social relations there. Industrialization throughout the South ushered in an economic and political elite whose interests resembled those of their northern counterparts rather than those of the old agricultural aristocracy, whose power depended on racial repression. The new elite and their political representatives were more amenable to negotiating an integrated political regime in exchange for a more stable social order (Bloom 1987; Marx 1998; Luders 2010). As demonstrated in the following chapters, economic and demographic change in Texas bolstered the possibilities for social change. These forces created conditions favorable to social reform by raising income as well as occupational and educational opportunities, resources that could in turn be tapped by social movement organizations. The profound changes of the postwar era also contributed to a greater willingness to participate in politics by rendering the possibilities for change more discernible. The historical record shows that Mexican Americans were aware of and inspired by the transformation that they witnessed in Texas and urged others to join them in the struggle. Consciousness raising was an important element in the creation of an effective social movement. As Douglas McAdam (1982: 34) found, changing circumstances facilitated activism by black people during the civil rights movement by revolutionizing their worldview, taking them from a state of "hopeless submission to oppressive conditions to an aroused readiness to challenge those conditions."

The political process model does not predict the course of social change but identifies opportunities and helps explain the emergence of new and effective challenges to racial exclusion. It does not tell us which tactics will be most successful or the organizational form that challenges are likely to assume. After World War II the list of grievances that Mexican Americans lodged against U.S. society was long: a wide range of individuals and organizations were engaged in remedying those problems. Labor unions, liberal civil rights groups, mutual aid societies, and women's organizations worked to advance their vision of social justice, but not all had the same prospect of achieving their objectives. Those struggling for integration into existing structures of authority were more likely to secure tangible gains than those with broader, diffuse goals. In other words, individuals and groups seeking accommodation and compromise enjoy far more success than those working to displace their antagonists (McAdam 1982, ch. 8; Jenkins 1985). Groups and individuals whose ideas are closer to groups in power have an advantage over those who initiate aggressive challenges to authorities and institutions. Indeed such challenges have often provoked harsh repressive measures (Vigil 1999; Haney-López 2003).

During the 1960s minorities were too few in number and too oppressed by a powerful set of forces to break the shackles of racial domination alone (McCarthy and Zald 1973). Critics argue that this approach neglects community-generated resources and overemphasizes the impact of white support during the civil rights movement (Morris 1984). This is certainly true in the Texas case. Prior to the end of World War II Mexican Americans had a long record of political organizing to achieve equality before the law, decent wages, better working conditions, and political representation. Their demands were articulated through community-supported civil rights organizations, labor unions, or mutual aid societies, often without the aid or sympathy of Anglo Americans (Mario García 1989; Márquez 1993; Márquez and Jennings 2000). Still, inequalities in power and resources, the underpinning of Mexican American discontent, meant that they needed allies in order to realize their objectives. Hence Mexican Americans were compelled to forge a working relationship with the Anglo majority. The history of liberalism in Texas party politics is the story of this tortured alliance.

To understand how the interaction between the races influenced political outcomes in Texas electoral politics, I draw from the literature on race and identity politics. Political identities are the constructed result of a process where practical interests, political beliefs, and moral values are brought into the political sphere. The literature on identity construction emphasizes asserted identities, the claims that activists make for themselves via ethnic symbols, group history, and cultural affinity (see Márquez 2003; Martinez-Ebers 2009; Beltran 2010; Fraga et al. 2010). In this study I find that ethnic representation in party politics was the result of the tension between asserted and ascribed identities. Mexican American activists asserted an ethnic identity when working to integrate the electoral process, but differences over the goals and strategies contained within that identity were a significant point of contention. Anglo power holders capitalized upon these differences. Every time Mexican American demands for change could no longer be ignored, their movement was engaged and redirected by an Anglo-dominated party apparatus, Anglo politicians, and Anglo voters. The structure of race relations was vulnerable to change, but entrenched political and economic elites carefully monitored this challenge in order to protect their interests, understanding the risks of a strong ethnic insurgency. As J. Craig Jenkins (1985) observes, electoral coalitions between polity members and excluded groups create opportunities and restrictions: "Liberal democratic rules rationalize the struggle for power by converting it into a series of routinized electoral contests between contending factions supported by voting coalitions of polity members. Political elites may temporarily lift the institutional controls conventionally used to keep the excluded in check and may even sponsor insurgent organizations" (17).

The confluence of racial, individual, and institutional interests rewrote the ethnic script in party politics, bringing about genuine concessions and greater inclusion in an important arena of public life. These accomplishments can be attributed in part to Mexican Americans' racial identity in Texas. The literature on white identity theorizes that European immigrants' acquisition of a white racial status was facilitated by the centrality of discrimination against African Americans in the United States. Immigrant groups like the Irish and Italians distanced themselves from blacks, fought nativism, and embraced a white identity (Ignatiev 1995; Jacobson 1999; Roediger 2006, 2007). Mexican Americans were not white, and few active in partisan politics asserted a white identity beyond the 1950s.

Their complex racial status, however, gave them some respite from the harsh and oftentimes violent racism practiced against blacks. Discrimination kept Mexican Americans from having an effective voice in state politics. But when they fought to eliminate racial barriers they did not encounter a massive wall of resistance. For Mexican Americans, partisan politics was porous and access to the ballot box open. They were in a much better position to turn conflicts between liberals and conservatives in the Democratic Party to their advantage.

Coalition building was an essential part of racial reform, and Mexican Americans looked for ways to join forces with Anglo liberals, other minorities, and blue-collar workers. Such an alliance brought benefits for all parties involved. Liberals could capitalize on the growing Mexican American electorate by helping remove impediments to voting and participation in party politics. A larger liberal bloc could then wrest control from conservatives so that the state party's platform and policies would more closely approximate those of the national Democratic Party. Liberal Anglo Democrats found the logic of an alliance including the poor, blue-collar workers, and racial minorities compelling—in theory. In practice the nascent alliance was hobbled by Anglo prejudices and a fear that close association with minorities would provoke a racist backlash. After a protracted and difficult struggle Mexican Americans won the right to participate in Texas party politics, but the kind of representation they achieved was the result of negotiations between Mexican American and Anglo politicians. These negotiations took place over a long period and involved many people and organizations. Rather than ask which organizations or individuals most faithfully represented Mexican American interests, it is more useful to understand the characteristics of those that succeeded and the circumstances under which they broke the color line.

Mexican Americans knew they faced difficult choices. Democratic Party membership obligated them to support their party's nominees and platform, a reoccurring problem for activists dependent upon community support. In the years immediately after World War II Mexican American Democrats saw the potential for social progress through partisan solidarity but had little evidence to support their optimism. Even during the 1960s conservatives still dominated the Texas Democratic Party and offered them few opportunities for meaningful participation. As the following chapters show, the doctrine that Mexican American interests were best served through the Texas Democratic Party drew harsh criticism from the beginning. In the 1950s community activists like George I. Sánchez argued vehemently against compromise with Democratic governors or party officials, all of whom they held responsible for preserving systems of discrimination and segregation. In the 1960s longtime Democratic Party activists like Albert Peña were encouraged by the rising power of liberals at the national level, but they later left a state party that they believed was beyond reform. During the mid- and late 1960s a virulent strand of ethnic nationalism rejected the two-party system altogether. José Ángel Gutiérrez led an electoral revolt under the banner of La Raza Unida Party, a Chicano third party that rejected both the Democratic Party and the Republican Party.

The angry rejection of the Democratic Party and the politics of ethnic nationalism faded after the 1970s. Part of the reason for its demise was the steady incorporation of Mexican Americans into Texas party politics, leaving little room for angry, ethnic-based challenges. Mexican Americans demanded their right to party membership; but the more they succeeded in penetrating the party's governance structure or were elected to public office, the less credible were charges of racial discrimination. The income and occupational attainment gap that spawned the confrontational politics of La Raza Unida Party quickly lost traction. The most successful Mexican American activists were those who conformed to the demands and accepted the promise of social reform through party membership. In other words, racial grievances were further moderated by incorporation itself, further boosting the political fortunes of those who spoke the language of incremental change and compromise.

Mexican Americans were slowly assimilated into the state's socioeconomic and political structure. This absorption had its roots in an economic transformation that dismantled the foundation of semifeudal race relations in the state's agricultural sector and shored up an ethnic power base in its cities. Economic and demographic trends favored change, and Mexican American organizers strove to capitalize on these new opportunities. However vulnerable the structures of racial and ethnic relations may have been, incorporation did not take place in a direct linear fashion. Rather, change was uneven, halting, and filtered through existing structures and imperatives. Mexican Americans eventually achieved descriptive representation in elective office and party politics, but whether or not they achieved effective ethnic representation remains a question without a definitive answer. Mexican American elected officials and party operatives navigated a maze of campaigns, elections, institutional procedures, and countless meetings while pursuing a mix of personal and political goals. Over time, committed partisans superseded hard-line critics like George Sánchez, Albert Peña, and José Ángel Gutiérrez, who were isolated and marginalized by their more moderate colleagues. As ethnic participation in electoral politics became the norm, discontent was funneled into legitimizing channels. Gubernatorial appointments, party procedures, and individual ambition further moderated the voice of ethnic insurgency and favored those who put their faith in social assimilation and government to produce change.

The issue is not whether Mexican Americans were incorporated into mainstream electoral politics after the civil rights movement—they were. Racial change took place in Texas politics because Mexican American activists took advantage of the breakdown of long-standing processes and structures in southwestern politics. By the 1960s Texas's one-party system was in decline. The arrival of the Republican Party as a challenger, continuing unrest in the streets, and the growing Mexican American voting bloc created an unprecedented opportunity for change. Accompanying the rising tide of activism was a contentious debate over what constituted ethnic solidarity and loyalty in the electoral sphere. Critics of incorporation were frustrated with the pace of change, given the asymmetry of power and privilege between the races. They also questioned the utility of partisan solidarity, a commitment that bound the Mexican American voter to conservative and often racist Anglo politicians. They encouraged voters to support Democratic Party candidates and attacked the emerging Raza Unida Party. The influx of Mexican Americans into Democratic Party politics swelled the ranks of liberals, hastened the defection of Anglo conservatives, and in the process ended the Democratic Party's history of racial exclusion.

Data Sources

In addition to personal interviews and readily available historical and electronic resources, I have gathered data from all major archived collections in Texas. These include the archives of Hector Garcia (Texas A&M University, Corpus Christi); Henry B. González (Dolph Briscoe Center for American History, University of Texas at Austin); Arcenio A. García, the Mexican American Democrats of Texas, Albert Peña, José Ángel Gutiérrez (University of Texas at San Antonio); Carlos Truan, Irma Rangel (Texas A&M University, Kingsville); Alicia Chacon (personal); Tati Santiesteban (personal); Richard Moya (Austin History Center, Austin Public Library); Al Bustamante, Joe Bernal (Benson Latin American Collection, University of Texas at Austin); Leonel J. Castillo, and Hector García (Houston Metropolitan Research Center). The personal papers of Joe Belden, founder of the Texas Poll, were made available to me by his daughter, Nancy Belden. University of Texas librarian Margo Gutiérrez kindly shared her collection of newsletters and other materials on the Mexican American Democrats. I have also examined the papers of all Texas governors since the end of World War II: Allan Shivers (Dolph Briscoe Center for American History, University of Texas at Austin); John Connally (Lyndon Baines Johnson Library, Austin); Preston Smith (Southwest Collection/Special Collections Library, Texas Tech University); Dolph Briscoe, Ann Richards (Dolph Briscoe Center for American History, University of Texas, Austin); Bill Clements (Texas A&M University, College Station); Mark White, and George W. Bush (Texas State Library and Archives, Austin). Other gubernatorial archival sources that I used include the papers of Allan Shivers (Sam Houston Regional Library and Research Center, Liberty), Price Daniel's papers (Texas State Repository in Liberty), and the Lyndon B. Johnson archives (LBJ Library, Austin). The Lyndon Baines Johnson Library at the University of Texas at Austin contained important documents on Mexican Americans in Texas politics. I found numerous journalistic accounts of Texas politics in the Texas Observer Records, 1952–1990 (Dolph Briscoe Center for American History, University of Texas at Austin) in addition to the articles indexed in *Texas Observer Index, 1954–1970* and *Texas Observer Index, 1971–1981*. I researched the papers of early liberal Democratic Party activists Creekmore Fath (Southwest Collection/Special Collections Library, Texas Tech University); Frankie Randolph, Walter Gardner Hall, and Billie Carr (Woodson Research Center, Rice University). I used the vertical files of newspaper clippings at the Dolph Briscoe Center for American History at the University of Texas, Austin, in addition to the Southwest Vertical Files and the El Paso Vertical File (El Paso Newspaper Index) at the El Paso Public Library.

Data Collection Issues and Problems

Most of the archived collections researched for this project contain vast amounts of material. For example, the collected papers of former Texas governor Dolph Briscoe (1973–1979) consist of over 1,045 linear feet of policy statements, speeches, pictures, financial records, and newspaper clippings. Although they are well organized and come with a reasonably accurate finder's guide, I found that only a fraction of Governor Briscoe's communications with his constituents, party officials, elected officials, staff, and community groups divulged his racial attitudes or strategies for dealing with minority group demands. The equally massive collected papers of former governor Price Daniel Jr. (1957–1963), however, contain a great deal more information on his racial attitudes and those of his contemporaries. After carefully examining these collections, I believe it is unlikely that either governor purged his materials of any documents relating to race. Governor Daniel spoke frankly about his racial attitudes and his intention to circumvent every federal effort to integrate the public schools. His public pronouncements and acts as governor recorded in the press corresponded well with the documents in his archives. Similarly, Dolph Briscoe's collection appears to be complete. It contains duplicate copies of many documents, careful documentation of his work, and, in one instance, a box filled with old office supplies and the remains of geckos that lived there during storage at Governor Briscoe's home. Provocative documents on race and ethnicity may have been removed from the collection, but what remains compares well with what the press and other observers reported.

Establishing an accurate historical narrative was my first challenge. With the exception of seminal texts like Ignacio García's books *United We Win* and *¡Viva Kennedy!* or Chandler Davidson's *Race and Class in Texas Politics*, little has been written about the role that Mexican Americans played in the development of the American two-party system. The gaps and silences on race in Texas governors' materials would have been impossible to decipher if it were not for the archived papers of activists like Albert Peña Jr., Eugene and Sylvia Rodriguez, Dr. Hector Garcia, and Texas congressman Henry B. González. The archived documents of Anglo liberals like Billie Carr, Creekmore Fath, and Walter Hall were invaluable in putting together the pieces of a complex puzzle. I am grateful to individuals like Alicia Chacon and Nancy Belden for sharing their personal documents with me. The observations of journalists contained in clipping files and the *Texas Observer* archives also clarified and contextualized the evolving story.

The final task was interpreting politically charged historical documents. As I argue, the rise in urbanization, income, educational, and occupational levels for Mexican Americans and the state's industrialization set the stage for progress in electoral politics. I found that Mexican and Anglo American activists in the first three decades of the postwar era understood the political implications of these shifts and often reflected on the significance of these changes. Understanding the interaction between asserted and ascribed identity politics was more difficult. Actors engaged in the politics of identity are aware of its power and strive to manipulate the symbols of race, ethnicity, and class. I reconstructed the decades-long exchange between Mexican American and Anglo activists by examining their interactions and assessments of elections, politicians, and organizations. The record shows that they occasionally spoke directly with one another but often did not; at other times Anglo politicians circumvented racial confrontations by responding proactively. Complicating this historical interaction were the strategic calculations made by Mexican Americans themselves. From the start, disagreements over short- and long-term goals and strategies characterized the campaign for racial incorporation. This interracial dialogue was a struggle for power where ambition and ideology were complicating factors, but it was not a contest between equals: racism structured interactions and outcomes from beginning to end.

Understanding the fundamental economic changes that created an opportunity for social activism to break barriers is straightforward. Changes in the productive process, urbanization, and rising socioeconomic status paved the way for changes in other arenas. During the transition to an integrated two-party system, numerous players were involved on both sides. On occasion Mexican American and Anglo activists recorded the substance of their interactions through correspondence or other public outlets. More often Mexican American civil rights activists would make their values and preferences known by issuing demands, criticizing party leaders, or reporting to their organization's members. Anglo party leaders sometimes responded directly, offering the researcher insight into the calculations made by power holders when dealing with an ethnic voting bloc. Rebuffs as well as concessions and alliance building can be readily documented and placed in historical context. At times political exigencies elicited responses that were oblique, noncommittal, or nonexistent. Still, Mexican Americans were fighting to remove racial barriers, and the responses they received contain important insights into the severity of racial conflict and the process of change. For this project most documentation concerning ongoing negotiations over power sharing was recorded during election years. The election cycle gave Mexican Americans opportunities to raise their grievances anew and press party leaders for concessions. Not coincidentally, election years were also periods when all parties were likely to generate documentation currently available to scholars.

When examining historical documents, I looked for materials relating to two issues that have historically been most important to Mexican American social movement organizations: racial representation and socioeconomic equality. In the early years most Mexican American activists were members of various social movement organizations, outsiders to the electoral process, who pressured the Texas Democratic Party to adopt policies greatly expanding the scope of government services and civil rights protection. The unity of purpose on these two broad goals offers a good analytical point from which to judge the tactical choices that they made when pressuring the state party to change. It also sheds light on the relative ease with which the Republican Party later appropriated the themes of racial representation and equality. The difficult tactical choices that Mexican American activists made when they became part of the Democratic Party help explain the declining role of community organizations in the realm of electoral politics. As Mexican Americans made inroads into the Democratic Party, electoral politics became a distinct realm of politics. The rules, factions, governance structure, and alliance building called for activists willing to specialize and engage in the frustratingly slow pace of electoral change. By the 1960s old-guard civil rights organizations like the League of United Latin American Citizens (LULAC) and the American GI Forum were no longer the leading force behind electoral politics. Instead doors opened for a new set of actors working almost exclusively as party activists, functionaries, or candidates for public office.

CHAPTER 1

Mexican Americans and Social Change

During the 1950s Mexican Americans in Texas were marginalized in almost every respect. Discrimination was rampant in housing, education, and employment (Montejano 1987: ch. 4). Of the five southwestern states, Texas had the worst Anglo–Mexican American education and income differentials (Briggs et al. 1977: 20, 61). Turnout was low, and in rural areas of the states the Mexican American vote was manipulated through intimidation by law enforcement agencies or machine politics (Weeks 1930). Civil rights organizations and labor unions struggled for reform in an atmosphere permeated by racism (Mario García 1989). At the national level, racial inequality was further cemented as the Democratic Party scaled back its commitment on civil rights legislation in an effort to prevent itself from fracturing along racial lines (Katznelson 2005: 50).

The most important development was a postwar economic boom that erased the economic gap between the American South and the rest of the nation. At the beginning of World War II 40 percent of the workforce in the South was employed in the agricultural sector, twice the rate of the rest of the nation. By 1990 that figure had dropped to 1 percent (Shafer and Johnston 2006: 12). The mechanization of agriculture and rapid industrialization that enabled this transformation of labor disproportionately affected Mexican Americans. Between 1947 and 1956 manufacturing employment greatly expanded in Texas, more rapidly than in the country as a whole. From 1940 to 1956 about 1.25 million people migrated from rural Texas to the state's major cities. Because Texas experienced little migration from other states, this remarkable demographic shift was almost exclusively a movement of native Texans leaving the farm and taking up manufacturing employment (Long 1968: 50–52). The old

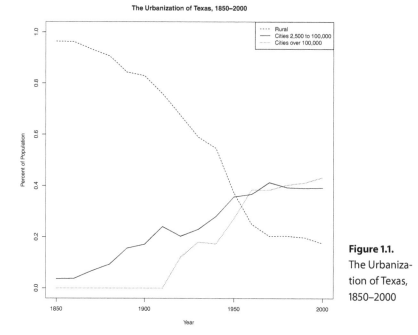

Figure 1.1.
The Urbanization of Texas, 1850–2000

agricultural sector dependent on manual labor disappeared, replaced by a modern industrial economy.

The occupational shift was driven by a reorganization of the Texas economy. Like the rest of the South, Texas was rapidly industrializing, with its agricultural sector becoming mechanized. The result was increasing employment opportunities in urban areas accompanied by a drop in demand for manual labor in rural areas. Mexican Americans were particularly affected by the migration from rural to urban areas (fig. 1.1). Mechanization, herbicides, and fertilizer use were on the rise. Tenant farmers became increasingly rare, and the demand for manual labor dropped. Texas agriculture became more efficient and productive with fewer laborers.

The industrialization of the state, the mechanization of agriculture, and the movement to urban areas were accompanied by increases in educational and occupational attainment (see figs. 1.2–1.6). The political process model predicts that dramatic social dislocations such as these create new opportunities. The break from agricultural work undermined rural political machines and ideological systems of justification that kept Mexican labor in bondage. It did not guarantee that they would disappear, instead raising the possibility that they could be eliminated (especially in

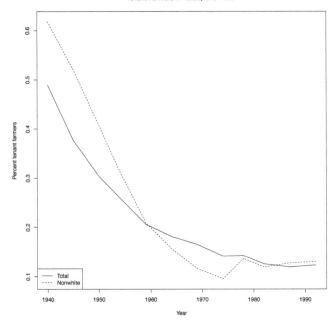

Figure 1.2.
Tenant
Farmers
in Texas,
1940–1992

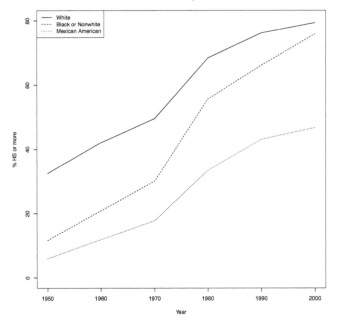

Figure 1.3.
The Education
Gap in Texas,
1950–2000

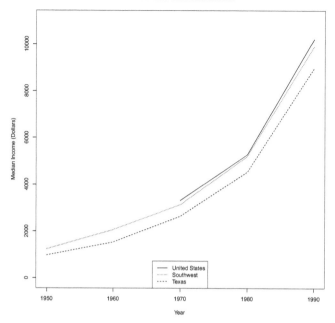

Figure 1.4.
Mexican
American
Median
Incomes
in Texas,
1950–1990

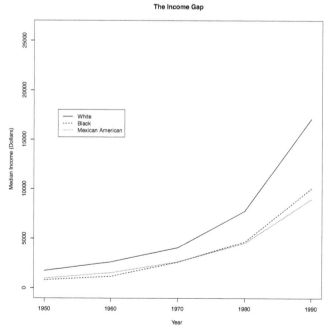

Figure 1.5.
The Income
Gap in Texas,
1950–1990

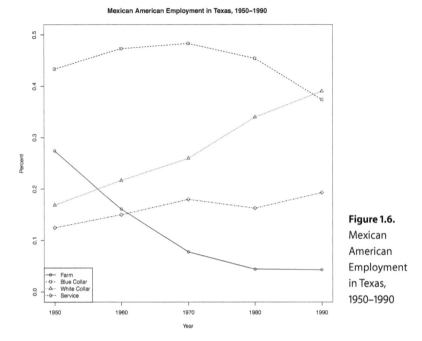

Mexican American Employment in Texas, 1950–1990

Figure 1.6.
Mexican
American
Employment
in Texas,
1950–1990

urban centers). Urban residence allowed for a pooling of Mexican American community resources that could be used for political purposes. Cities provided activists greater anonymity and lowered the prospect of economic or physical retribution for their activities. Finally, the large-scale movement of Mexican Americans into higher-paying nonagriculturally based occupations helped generate a larger class of educated and higher-income individuals more capable of engaging and challenging political exclusion.

The state's unique demographic trends bolstered the prospects for political empowerment, especially in the electoral arena. As early as 1960 the overwhelming majority of Mexican Americans were citizens. A full 86 percent of all Mexican Americans in Texas were born in the state (Grebler et al. 1970: 107). They were all living in well-established urban communities in a state that led all southwestern states in the naturalization of Mexican immigrants (Grebler et al. 1970: 559). From 1950 to 1960 the percentage of foreign-born Spanish-surnamed people in Texas dropped from 18 percent to 14 percent, a function of natural growth and an outflow of immigrants to California (Browning and McLemore 1964: 8). The urbanization rate for Mexican Americans in Texas was second only to California and higher than that of Texas Anglos (Grebler et al. 1970: 113).

By 1960 almost four out of five Mexican Americans lived in urban areas, a higher number than for Anglos and blacks (Browning and McLemore 1964: 18). All of these trends pointed to a growing urban population poised to make a strong claim as long-term residents and citizens for increased representation in governmental affairs.

After World War II the Texas rural population was in rapid decline, driven by agricultural modernization and a drop in the need for manual labor on the state's farms and ranches. The dwindling rural population was further depleted by employment opportunities created as a result of government spending on defense production plants and military installations as well as an increase in the state's manufacturing base. In 1940 about 45 percent of the population was urban; by 1950 the figure had risen to 60 percent, an average exceeding that of the country as a whole (Mathis 1968: 131–132). Houston emerged as a large metropolitan city; but Dallas, San Antonio, Forth Worth, and El Paso, cities with large Mexican American populations, grew into important production and distribution centers (Mathis 1968: 109, 120–121). Not only were the vast majority of Mexican Americans in Texas native born, but in large urban areas like San Antonio their voter registration rate was higher than that of the general population (Grebler et al. 1970: 565). During the 1960s the voter registration rate in predominantly Mexican American counties exceeded that of the state as a whole in all but one election (McCleskey and Merrill 1973). Between 1965 and 1970 Mexican Americans slowly increased their employment in white-collar occupations and professional, managerial, and clerical groups. Accompanying that rise in higher-status occupations was a decline in the number of Mexican Americans classified as laborers and farmworkers. Their wages lagged behind those of their Anglo counterparts, but the occupational shift for Mexican Americans took place among youthful entrants into the job market, whose incomes rose sharply over time (Briggs et al. 1977: 75–77).

Conclusion

Prior to World War II farmers and ranchers who depended on a large pool of farm laborers dominated Texas's economy. Control of Mexican American agricultural workers was achieved through an ideology of social inferiority, social customs, and brute force. For their part, Mexican Americans had few resources and little or no access to government at any level through which they could effectively challenge their inferior status.

That would soon change as economic and demographic trends undermined the foundations upon which the state's racial hierarchy rested. In short, the modernization of the Texas economy set the stage for political engagement.

Racism and subordination did not disappear with industrialization and agricultural mechanization. Rather, the number of Mexican Americans under the control of semifeudal regimes in rural Texas dropped dramatically, with migration and natural population growth in cities where incomes were higher, public schools were more accessible, and it was easier to organize political resistance. For those who remained in the agricultural economy, farm employment continued to be difficult, low-paying work. Texas became a center of farmworker organizing in the 1960s and 1970s. By that time the population shift was complete, however, and Mexican Americans were overwhelmingly urban, as were their politics. Industrial employment, higher levels of education, and a larger urban population further increased their capacity for political action—a new era of organizing was underway. The old order's legacy of social inequality and poverty remained in place, but the economic changes unfolding in postwar Texas rendered discrimination and exclusion vulnerable.

The gradual increase in occupational status, income, and other indicators of mobility was a product of this demographic shift, allowing Mexican Americans to take advantage of greater, albeit limited, opportunities. Assimilation theory predicts a gradual process of social and economic incorporation into civic clubs, political associations, and government. This study demonstrates that incorporation in party politics did indeed take place, but it was uneven and marked by reversals. The process was neither impersonal nor mechanistic. Rather, the elimination of racial injustices and greater social acceptance were accomplished through the work and skill of an emerging political class, who negotiated directly with Anglo power holders. Individuals who assumed leadership positions in the community soon after World War II often commented on the changes that they witnessed and the ways in which they hoped to capitalize on a fluid social terrain. An empowered political class emerged as a result of these structural shifts, but the individuals who represented Mexican American interests also changed as a result of their group's entry into the political sphere. Those articulating Mexican American interests in the state's electoral politics—those who won a seat at the negotiating table—were themselves the product of struggle and negotiation with Anglo-dominated institutions. By confronting the barriers to equal participation, Mexican American activists set in motion a dynamic that continues to this day.

CHAPTER 2

The 1950s—A Decade in Flux

I guess World War II was mostly responsible for ending a lot of the discrimination, the boys became pretty rough on places that denied service, especially in South Texas, this later spread north, and also the many court cases fought by Albert Peña, Gus Garcia, Carlos Cadena and others on school segregation that progressed the [end] of discrimination in public places.
ALBERT FUENTES (CA. 1963)

The decade after World War II was a time when economic and demographic changes made viable the first Mexican American challenge to racial exclusion in Texas party politics. As theories of assimilation and incorporation predict, Mexican Americans began to participate in party affairs in greater numbers. The population was largely urban. The overwhelming number of voting-age Mexican Americans were citizens, inflating their potential as a voting bloc. But the first steps toward incorporation took place because Mexican Americans extracted them through strategic action, negotiations, and persuasion. The integration of the party system was neither smooth nor welcomed by Texas Anglos. The Democratic Party felt no urgency to reach out and incorporate the growing Mexican American electorate. Change came to the Texas Democratic Party because Mexican Americans demanded it. This chapter is about how ethnic mobilization wove its way through an Anglo-controlled Democratic Party and how its leaders contended with politicians, internal factions, and racial discrimination.

Mexican American political leaders in the 1950s could not force the Democratic Party to change but could lay the groundwork for doing so by seeking out liberal allies within the party who shared their policy preferences. They proceeded by demonstrating the importance of the minority electorate to the liberal coalition through community organizing and get-out-the-vote drives. At every opportunity, whether at the precinct, county, or state level or even during face-to-face interactions, they lobbied for a new identity for themselves in Texas politics based on citizenship and equality before the law. This chapter examines the process of identity negotiation between Mexican Americans and Anglos in a deeply divided Democratic Party. Mexican American activists fought for inclusion but also wanted to align the state party's policies more closely with those of the national Democratic Party. Their natural allies in this campaign were Texas liberals, a faction that had long fought for greater representation and state allegiance to the policies of the national Democratic Party. Mexican American activists readily supported the liberal cause in the Texas Democratic Party and reasonably expected their Anglo colleagues to reciprocate. When Mexican Americans sought such an alliance, however, they found that Anglo liberals were willing to accept their presence and votes but reluctant to accept them as equal members of a coalition.

The question of integrating the Democratic Party's liberal wing assumed new importance in the 1950s because of an increasingly bitter conflict between Anglo liberals who supported the economic and social policies of the national party and conservatives who resisted those changes (Key 1984: ch. 12). The divide created an opportunity for Mexican American activists to fight the state party's indifference to minority issues, which is precisely what they did. O. Douglas Weeks (1953) found that minorities in the early 1950s were playing an increasingly important role in the liberal or "loyalist" movement within the Democratic Party (Weeks 1953: 76). The most visible first steps took place in cities like San Antonio, where Mexican Americans were a large portion of the population and had a long history of community activism. These were the same cities where Loyal Democrats organized against Democratic governors who supported Republican presidential candidates ("The Democratic Women of Bexar County" n.d.). As Weeks noted, the "politically conscious Negroes . . . [and] . . . Latin-American leaders with urban working and lower middle class followings" were working in the state Democratic Party and seizing opportunities as they emerged (Weeks 1953: 29).

Minority activists wanted to influence the outcome of the conflict between competing factions because they had the most at stake. Liberals in Texas supported New Deal policies like banking regulation, Social Security, unemployment insurance, public works projects, home mortgage guarantees, and welfare measures to cushion workers from the impact of poverty and an unrestrained market. They sought legislation to protect consumers, establish a minimum wage, impose taxes on the oil and gas industry, equalize the state's funding of public schools, increase access to higher education, and create an array of protections for the health and safety of working people. The most progressive liberals also fought for racial equality. They worked to abolish the all-white Democratic primary, desegregate schools and neighborhoods, guarantee equality before the law, and change voting laws and practices that hampered minority participation (Davidson 1990: 28). Longtime activist Billie Carr concluded that there was a clear link between Texas liberalism and minority interests:

> We worked with labor to obtain their rights to organize and for the right of collective bargaining. We marched side by side with African Americans to protest segregation in schools on buses, in stadiums, neighborhoods, restaurants and in the workplace. We marched with Hispanics in the valley and from the valley to Austin to see the governor. We didn't eat grapes or lettuce and we supported Caesar [*sic*] Chavez and the farm workers. We marched against the war in Vietnam in 1963 when it was un-American! We supported Women's Rights and the Equal Rights Amendment was passed in the Texas Legislature. We passed pro-choice laws in Texas. We climbed trees and refused to come down so they would not be cut down. We worked against pollution and for clean air and water. We declared that we were friends of Gays and Lesbians. (Carr ca. 2001)

The 48-year veteran of Democratic Party politics wanted to remake the party into one that "protects women and minorities from exploitation; free enterprise from monopoly and fraud in the marketplace; the environment from degradation; and working people from the misery of unemployment and substandard wages" (Carr ca. 1979a).

Billie Carr claimed solidarity with racial minorities, but others in the liberal caucus wavered during the 1950s. Anglos and Mexican Americans shared many policy goals and an interest in moving their party to the left, but racism and a fear of close association with the most demonized groups in the Democratic Party hampered coalition building. White liberals hesitated even as the party's leadership undermined their work at every turn. In 1952 the State Democratic Convention urged party members and instructed the governor and all state officials to support the Republican Party ticket because of the national party's support for racial equality. Governor Allan Shivers called civil rights legislation "hate breeding and trouble making" (Shivers 1952b). The party's 1952 platform of principles condemned the "exploitation of minority groups through advocacy of federal hate-breeding, class legislation under the labels of 'civil rights' and 'fair employment practices.'" It further denounced "the proposal that the federal government should invade the states with a new bureaucracy, even more prying and vicious than any heretofore created, to impose its arbitrary and arrogant will upon the people if the states do not take legislative action in this field to its liking" (Texas Democratic Party 1952d: 114).

The message from conservatives was ominous. The Democrats' 1950 platform commended the people of Texas for the great strides made in relations "between English speaking and people speaking Spanish of this state [*sic*]." The Democratic Party went on record supporting racial segregation and warned of dangerous forces "within and without the colored race" threatening to disrupt a "time tested" system (Texas Democratic Party 1950). The party later warned that a civil rights platform was "but one more step to enslave the states in the foolish attempt to impose and enforce tolerance and brotherhood by compulsion of law" (Texas Democratic Party 1952d). State officials openly sided with Republican Party national candidates, while Democratic governor Allan Shivers campaigned for Dwight D. Eisenhower in 1952 and again in 1956. Despite the presence of fellow Texan Lyndon B. Johnson on the Democratic presidential ticket, Governor Price Daniel refused to campaign for John F. Kennedy in 1960. He openly opposed key provisions of the national party platform like minimum wages for farmworkers and expanded civil rights protection for racial and ethnic minorities ("The Demos' Platform for Texas" 1960).

The strongest incentive for Anglo liberals fully to incorporate people of color into their ranks and endorse racial equality was the prospect of successfully opposing conservative repression. For example, liberals were denied the opportunity to participate in the 1954 State Democratic Convention when the party's state committee did not assign hotel rooms to liberal delegates and did not allow them to hold a caucus meeting during the convention. When they tried to meet in a local park, the police threatened them with arrest. They were not allowed to speak from the floor during the convention, and the keynote speaker referred to them as Communists (Carr 1976). Anglo liberals were disinclined to embrace the cause of civil rights but had no other way to build an effective coalition against the state's conservatives, who were in open revolt against the national party. When Governor Shivers campaigned for Eisenhower in 1952, he urged his fellow conservative Democrats to do the same. The Democrats, he argued, had abandoned individual and states' rights, were blind to the problem of world communism, and took a paternalistic attitude on race relations (Shivers 1952a). The governor campaigned for Richard Nixon in 1960, deriding Kennedy's promise to solve problems of discrimination in housing, education, and employment through an expansion of the federal government's social programs. Shivers declared that Nixon was a superior candidate because of his ardent anticommunism and belief in a small government that avoided regulation of the market and "social problems" (Shivers 1960a, 1960b). As the decade wore on, it was clear that conservatives would not abide by the policies of the national party or relinquish their control of the Texas Democratic Party. Moreover, they were not going to leave the state party. In 1958 Governor Daniel rejected the idea of switching his party identity. Conservatives' real power base, he maintained, was the Democratic Party, so they had no reason to surrender its structure to liberals (P. Daniel 1958c; Sheldon 1958).

The political crisis in the Democratic Party was intensified with the 1954 Supreme Court *Brown v. Board of Education* decision declaring school segregation unconstitutional. This galvanized Texas conservatives to resist the integration of the public schools in Texas. Governor Price Daniel, an avowed segregationist, defended the practice as a state right and asserted that Texas segregation laws nullified federally mandated integration orders. To demonstrate popular support for segregation, Daniel called for a referendum on the issue during the 1956 Democratic Party primary (Shivers 1956; Badger 1999). White Citizens' Councils responded to the governor's call, gathering 140,000 signatures to place three pro-segregation propositions on the Democratic primary ballot, all of which were overwhelmingly approved by Texas voters (Weeks 1957: 37). Daniel then called for a special session of the legislature to consider legislation allowing local option elections on segregation, the option to close schools when federal troops were used to enforce desegregation orders, and the option to deny public employment for members of the National Association for the Advancement of Colored People (NAACP). The legislature passed all three acts. For their part, liberals closed ranks but framed their grievances in terms of party loyalty. They charged that Texas conservatives were charting a dangerous, reactionary course and that it was time for them to leave the Democratic Party altogether:

> For decades, the identity of the Democratic Party has been destroyed in Texas by an almost unbelievable laxity about party membership. The minimum principle a political party must have if it is to exist with any meaning is that its essential affairs ought to be limited to its members.

Yet in the most essential event of all our events, the nominating primary, Texas law permits, and unscrupulous Old Guarders encourage, Republicans to infiltrate the Democratic Party. They cross over by the hundreds of thousands and then brag afterwards that they, the Republicans, swung the Democratic nomination to the Dixiecrat. (Democrats of Texas 1957c)

Many of us have long believed that if Republicans would remain in their own party, we would have done [away] with the continuous suppression of liberal principles and candidates. We consider the Democratic Party to be a party of liberals and believe that those who are unwilling to let the majority control it should openly move into the Republican Party where they belong. (Jones 1956)

In spite of these withering criticisms, conservatives rejected any reconciliation with desegregation efforts. The Texas Democratic Party's 1958 platform declared that the state had a right to resist federal attempts to desegregate public schools (Texas Democratic Party 1958a).

Mexican American activists seized upon the struggle between liberals and conservatives to press for greater racial inclusion and to advance the liberal cause. The incorporation process most often appeared as a conversation between races over participation and power sharing, which it was. But the demand for inclusion was also at the intersection of competing understandings of political representation. Mexican American community organizations tended to frame the demand for inclusion in multifaceted terms linking the fate of the individual with the group. Those working within the Democratic Party were more inclined to advocate social change within an electoral and legislative process in concert with their wavering liberal colleagues. Even at mid-century, when race relations were tense, Mexican American electoral activists by necessity and preference framed most issues in nonracial, partisan terms. The individual who embodied this vision was a state senator from San Antonio, Henry B. González. González earned a reputation for civil rights advocacy when the Texas legislature convened to consider the segregation proposals of Governor Daniels. González and his colleague Abraham Kazen launched a thirty-six-hour filibuster against the proposals (Rodriguez 1976: 79–81). They attacked the legislature for its racism and argued that Texas would soon be inundated with other racist bills, all stemming from the "same witch's brew—hate at the bottom" (Brooks and Wood 1957). González won national attention for his courage and eloquence on civil rights, but his political agenda was decidedly race-neutral at its core.

Henry B. González for Governor

González, sales ¿por qué sales?
Para gobernador no podrá ver mejor

González, why do you run?
No one could be better for governor
HENRY B. GONZÁLEZ CORRIDO (MORANTE 1958)

Henry B. González was a veteran civil rights activist from San Antonio, where he built a career in the city that was home to the largest concentration of Mexican American voters in Texas. Elected to the San Antonio City Council in 1953, González won with strong support from the predominantly Mexican American west side that delivered his margin of victory, an achievement that he repeated in his 1956 election to the State Senate (Rodriguez 1976: 75, 77). He personified a renewed challenge to conservative dominance of the Democratic Party, and his ascendancy during the 1950s exposed liberal cravenness on their own principles. González brought his indignation over segregation to the 1958 Democratic primary election by running against sitting governor Price Daniel, thereby becoming the first Mexican American to run for governor of Texas. His quixotic run against a sitting governor was part of the revolt against conservatives and a demand for ideological consistency from liberals.

In 1952 the liberal Democrats of Texas (DOT) railed against their party's endorsement of Republican Dwight D. Eisenhower's presidential bid (Weeks 1953: 17–18). In 1958 Henry González turned the tables on Texas liberals by arguing that their cause was inextricably bound with the interests of racial minorities and the poor. He believed that the ease with which Governor Daniel proposed—and the majority Democratic legislature passed—his segregation laws was an intolerable attack on the Democratic Party's core values. González called for a break with the cult of personality rampant in Democratic politics. He also demanded that all candidates in the primary take clear positions on issues important to liberals, including an expanded social welfare state, civil rights, and integration of the public schools (Banks 1958a; Brooks and Wood 1958; Duncan

Photo 2.1. Henry B. González accompanied by a conjunto campaigns for governor at the Democrats of Texas annual convention, 1958. Courtesy of the Dolph Briscoe Center for American History, University of Texas at Austin. Russell Lee Photograph Collection, di_07909.

1958; "González Enters Governor's Race" 1958; "González for Governor" ca. 1958).

By the end of the decade the liberal caucus of the Democratic Party became a venue where these ideas were circulated and debated. In 1958 two Mexican Americans were elected to the DOT's executive board (Democrats of Texas 1958). One of them was Albert Peña Jr. Like Henry González, Peña broke into the DOT governing structure from a base of support in San Antonio, where he was the first Mexican American elected to the Bexar County Commission. Another prominent DOT member was Hector Garcia, president of the American GI Forum (Stephenson 1967: 25). Also represented in the DOT was the Texas branch of the American Federation of Labor and Congress of Industrial Organizations (AFL-CIO), the NAACP, the Texas Farmers Union, and what one journalist called a "strong Ultra Liberal segment of Latin-American voters" (Wood 1958a).

Henry B. González's run for governor in 1958 tested the viability of this nascent electoral coalition by embarking on a crusade against liberalism's enemies. In his campaign for governor, he endorsed the same programs supported by the Democrats of Texas: aid to the poor, elderly, and infirm as well as an expansion of the state's system of higher education. Like the DOT, González called for new legislation requiring voter declaration of party affiliation when paying a poll tax that would have to be shown for the special or general elections ("Party Vote Bill" 1957).

Photo 2.2. Albert Peña Jr. and Senator John F. Kennedy holding "¡Ole! Adlai" campaign poster at Adlai Stevenson's campaign headquarters, San Antonio, 1956. San Antonio Light Collection, MS 359: L-4880-N, University of Texas at San Antonio Libraries Special Collections from the Institute of Texan Cultures.

Photo 2.3. Albert Peña Jr. and Senator John F. Kennedy at Adlai Stevenson's campaign headquarters, San Antonio, 1956. San Antonio Light Collection, MS 359: L-4880-N, University of Texas at San Antonio Libraries Special Collections from the Institute of Texan Cultures.

Photo 2.4. Henry B. González surrounded by supporters at the 1958 Democratic Party's gubernatorial nomination at the Democrats of Texas annual convention. Courtesy of the Dolph Briscoe Center for American History, University of Texas at Austin. Russell Lee Photograph Collection, di_07910.

González wanted to solidify party lines and prevent movements that he believed were designed to "infiltrate and destroy" the Democratic Party (Duckworth 1957). González voiced, almost word for word, the opinions of DOT leaders who asserted that the state was dominated by a "ruthless, cynical, selfish political machine" (Randolph 1958a).

González attacked Governor Daniel and his reactionary policies while insisting that Anglo liberals affirm their values with action. Addressing the 1958 DOT convention, González declared that he was a "no-handle Democrat" and that he would not apologize for his liberal convictions. He called for greater honesty in the state's party politics and asserted that he had "always run as a Democrat which is more than my . . . opponents can say" (Banks 1958c). He called for increased government spending to stimulate economic growth, unemployment compensation, stronger antitrust laws, separation of church and state, and support for organized labor—a classic liberal democratic platform (Banks 1958b; "Senator

González Cites Roosevelt Leadership" 1958; "González Calls 'Atheism'" 1959). He was often red-baited: some called him a socialist, to which he retorted that Texas conservatives endorsed socialism for "plutocrats" while deriding state support for the poor. He expressed fear that citizens could not depend on the legislature to support their civil liberties and that most legislators were willing to abandon these liberties in pursuit of short-term political goals ("Poll Tax, Hymns, and Henry" 1958). When speaking of his conservative critics, González said that they

> call me the dimpled darling of the liberals, labor and the NAACP. The blasted fools! Don't they know they're givin' [*sic*] me the highest compliment I could ever receive? Since when do we curl up our lips with scorn when we talk of laboring people? Isn't it on the backs of laboring people that democracy has been built? I offer no apologies [for] the free trade union movement. If that costs me an election, I can tell you, my friends, there are worse things than losing an election. (Stephenson 1967: 81)

The *Texas Observer* reported that the DOT audience repeatedly interrupted this speech with raucous applause and in the end "roared their approval." Hundreds of delegates surged up to the platform and then to the convention floor, shaking González's hand and offering encouragement (Stephenson 1967: 81).

González won an unusual amount of attention for a candidate with little money and no experience running for statewide office. He traversed the state in his personal car making speeches anywhere he could find an audience and refusing to submerge issues of race and ethnicity ("González for Governor" ca. 1958). González proudly acknowledged his Mexican roots and traveled with a mariachi band to provide entertainment at his rallies. At the same time he called for a political solidarity that transcended race by pointing to the "fanatical racists" in the state legislature and the danger that they posed for the health of a democratic society ("The Segregation Filibuster" 1957). He told Democrats that the state had a "bigoted racist" in the governor's mansion and that it was time for a change (Dugger 1958). True liberals, he said, are guided by political principles not by ethnic loyalty and can never "compromise with evil" ("González Defends His Liberal Role" 1958). During a campaign swing in South Texas, González recalled an incident when a man came up and "hugged me and said he didn't know anything about me, but he was voting for me because my name is González. Well, I don't see how I could do that man much good" (Beagle 1958).

González's 1958 campaign may have challenged the Mexican American civil rights establishment, but it was a moment of reckoning for Anglo liberals. Noting that neither the Democrats of Texas nor other labor or liberal organizations had asked him to run, González said that it was now time to set aside racial favoritism and rally around the national Democratic Party and leaders like himself (González ca. 1958). His self-initiated crusade put the DOT in a difficult position. If the liberal caucus stood by in silence as he drew large, enthusiastic crowds on his improvised crusade, its members would effectively sanction the policies of a conservative sitting governor and forego an opportunity to advertise their political enemy's hypocrisy ("The González Candidacy" 1958). Racism ran deep in Texas politics, however, and identifying with the flamboyant González would cost the caucus support from white voters. DOT activists knew that Anglo liberals could be rallied both by populist agendas and by racist appeals. As one observer put it,

> What, for example, is the Southern liberal politician to do when his opponent promises to maintain segregation to his dying gasp? The liberal knows that segregation is on its way out, not just in schools, but in all walks of life. What's more, he knows that his opponent knows it too. But the liberal also knows that his opponent's irresponsible pledge will get votes. [Those] . . . who vote time after time . . . are habitually suspicious of Wall Street—these are in large measure the very people who are most rabid on the subject of segregation. ("The Liberal's Dilemma" 1955)

At this point of decision, Anglo liberals chose to equivocate. Instead of endorsing his campaign, the DOT finessed González's call for unity. Walter Gardner Hall, who delivered the keynote address to the 1958 Democrats of Texas state convention, took the opportunity to praise its members as the "shock troops of democracy." Hall's lengthy speech contained just a single indirect reference to Henry González when he criticized the Texas legislature for its preoccupation with "vicious racial hatred bills" (Hall 1958). Hall avoided mentioning González's candidacy for governor, while the DOT insisted that the state party follow the policies of the national party, support all democratic nominees for president, and call for a loyalty pledge as a condition for participation in all Democratic Party affairs (Democrats of Texas 1957b). Hall avoided endorsing González even as he argued for the DOT's substantive policy positions on environmental protection, expanded health care, public housing, an annual minimum wage, a state Labor Relations Act, a graduated income tax, civil rights protections, and food subsidies for the poor (Democrats of Texas n.d.).

This disingenuousness did not pass unnoticed. Henry González faulted white liberals for not realizing the potential of a "natural liberal coalition" including labor, blacks, Mexican Americans, and white liberals. He was deeply disappointed when his campaign did not attract the support of liberal groups, lamenting that white liberals "sat on their hands" when a unique opportunity materialized to strike a decisive blow against a reactionary governor and his allies ("The Only Way" 1959). Albert Peña did not mince words and blamed racism for the stillborn coalition's failure (Ragsdale 1958a; Stephenson 1967: 83). George Sánchez demanded that the DOT purge its ranks of discrimination and rebuild the coalition from scratch. He meditated on the failure of González's campaign, believing that it should have drawn more support from Anglos because activists like "Hector Garcia, Ed Idar, Robert Sánchez, Cris Aldrete and others have shown that the issues can be sold to the Spanish-speaking voter." He added: "[D]oesn't it seem that DOT should take a page or two from their book?" (Sánchez 1958). Despite the vociferous critiques by Peña and others, the Bexar County DOT in San Antonio was the only caucus to endorse Henry González's candidacy. All other county caucuses withheld their endorsements, weakly citing "technical problems" or their desire to keep the governor's office in the hands of the Democratic Party ("Local DOT" 1958).

Peña and Sánchez could not convince the DOT to support González's candidacy, not unlike their failed attempt to get the DOT to strongly endorse the Supreme Court's *Brown v. Education* decision in 1954 ("Bexar's Efforts" 1954). This time, however, aggressive organizing by conservative activists, an ascendant liberal wing of the national party, and an emerging cadre of Mexican American leaders with independent political bases giving them the freedom to act independently prompted a rethinking of the DOT's overly cautious strategy. During González's 1958 campaign, some Anglo DOT activists criticized their organization's inaction by arguing that Henry González was the only true Democrat in the gubernatorial primary with respect to the party's own criteria (Ragsdale 1958b). Albert Peña was one of only three Mexican Americans on the 76-member Democrats of Texas executive board, but he took every opportunity to change the group's behavior on issues of race and civil rights (Democrats of Texas 1959). As in the case of Henry González, his support base was the large Mexican American and liberal vote in San Antonio. The

Bexar County DOT passed resolutions condemning the poll tax and the Bracero Program as well as the state's recently enacted segregation laws and commended González for his filibuster in opposition to those bills (Bexar County Democrats 1958b). The Bexar County chapter of the DOT went a step further by adopting a statement of principles declaring its commitment to stronger civil rights legislation and the racial integration of public schools. It adopted positions on a minimum wage for agricultural workers and the integration of the public schools that were similar to those of the National Democratic Party ("DOT Positions" 1960; Stephenson 1967: 142). Finally, the Bexar County DOT sent 239 delegates to the 1958 Texas Democratic state convention, 48 of whom were Mexican American (Bexar County Democrats 1958a; Democratic Party of Bexar County 1958).

The saga of Henry González's filibuster and subsequent campaign for governor offers a window into race and identity politics in Texas after World War II. By asserting the identity of a liberal Democrat, González served as a model of success for a new generation of Mexican American politicians. González was heavily dependent on his ethnic base to be competitive, but he never campaigned as an ethnic candidate and was pleased that he could not have won public office without the support of Anglo voters. The DOT leadership did not come to his aid in the 1958 gubernatorial primary, but many liberals began to understand the potential of an alliance that transcended race because of his principled stand. In this way González's 1958 campaign against Governor Price Daniel helped reshape the foundations of the Democratic Party coalition.

The greatest burden of these protracted negotiations with Anglo Democrats rested on Mexican American activists, who often had little to show for their efforts. González understood the dilemma that minority activists faced, but in the aftermath of the 1958 gubernatorial primary he affirmed his unshakable faith that the American people would remedy the problem of discrimination. He claimed that Texas had a long tradition of equality and fair play rooted in the frontier experience "where every settler was judged by his individual merits as a man and not on how he worshipped his God or the country he or his father came from, or the color of his skin" ("Demos to Hear" 1957). Governor Daniel's race bills, he argued, were an attack on civil society by a small minority of fanatics willing to destroy the public school system in the name of racial superiority (Duncan 1957a). González knew that racism cost him an endorsement from the Democrats of Texas, but he also believed strongly that the majority of people in Texas wanted equality of the races (Knoles 1957;

"Integration Works Fine" 1957; Freeman 1958). He pointed to his own achievements as proof that racial incorporation was key to the success of the liberal agenda. It was also a vitally important point in the case for color-blind policies. Of the 1,317,486 votes cast in the 1958 gubernatorial primary, González received 245,969, second to Governor Daniels's 799,107 votes but still 19 percent of the total and a number that vastly exceeded the 26,000 that he could expect from his ethnic base in San Antonio (Garces 1957; Weeks 1961: 9).

At the time of his gubernatorial campaign, observers believed that Henry González was indeed forging a new coalition of black, Mexican American, labor, and Anglo liberal voters (Duckworth 1958; Duncan 1958). His goals and values were comparable to those espoused by many community organizations like the League of United Latin American Citizens (LULAC) and the American GI Forum. González wanted to remove the ethnic lens from those calculations. In partisan politics, he asserted, most Mexican Americans were best served by identifying as Democrats, the only viable identity in the public sphere. The importance of group attachments and the continuing power of racism were undeniable, but both were counterproductive when building electoral coalitions. Henry González joined his fellow Democrats in this political project and played an active role policing the party's boundaries. Just as Anglo liberals in the Democrats of Texas demanded loyalty pledges from all party members, González demanded that Mexican American voters and activists do the same. It was a difficult commitment for Mexican American activists during the 1950s. All who worked through the Democratic Party were active in community organizations and were themselves members of ethnically defined social networks. Compounding their difficulties was drawing a line between ethnically and ideologically based organizing.

Making the Transition

If a new multiracial alliance was to be the future of Texas politics, it was only in its formative stages during the 1950s. Even as the conflict between "loyalist" and "state" Democrats raged, Mexican Americans working on electoral issues were primarily civil rights activists and thus outsiders to state centers of power. They were dismayed with Anglo liberals for their lack of courage and foresight (Idar 1953b). Ed Idar Jr. claimed that American GI Forum's poll-tax and get-out-the-vote drives resulted in Mexican Americans voting at a rate of ten to one for liberal Democratic candidates;

yet Anglo liberals remained on the sidelines during these efforts (Idar 1955a). In a letter to the chair of the Texas Democratic Organizing Committee, Dr. Hector Garcia argued that Mexican Americans worked diligently for the Democratic Party but were dismayed because their contribution went unrecognized and their issues remained ignored (H. Garcia 1953a).

Ideological appeals and protests drew attention to the Democratic Party's contradictory behavior. But to be effective they had to go hand in hand with electoral power. Activists knew that party bosses and political machines counted on poverty, low levels of education, and devices like the poll tax to suppress voter turnout (American GI Forum 1950). The key was for Mexican Americans to demonstrate their importance as a voting bloc—an idea that animated early get-out-the-vote drives in South Texas (H. Garcia 1950). Mexican Americans were the dominant racial group in the south but had less electoral influence than whites because they did not register to vote in meaningful numbers. To correct the political imbalance in these areas, the American GI Forum launched its first statewide poll tax drive in 1949. Activists traveled across the state holding large outdoor rallies and claimed to have registered 100,000 Mexican American voters ("GI Forum Went 'All Out'" 1949; Idar 1952b). Hidalgo County in South Texas was 70 percent Mexican American, while in Cameron County and Willacy County Mexican Americans were 60 percent of the voting-age population. These super majorities did not translate into electoral strength because Anglos continued to constitute a majority of those registered to vote, but the potential for empowerment was undeniable. A survey conducted by the GI Forum of Mexican American voters in those three South Texas counties in 1950 found that 44 percent of the 46,674 poll taxes issued went to Spanish-surnamed individuals, who, not coincidentally, were also dependable Democratic voters (Garces 1957). Nine out of ten South Texas counties with large percentages of Mexican Americans tended to favor Adlai Stevenson over Dwight Eisenhower, as did twenty-three of twenty-five East Texas counties with large numbers of African Americans (Weeks 1953: 104–105).

However much activists asserted a liberal Democratic identity, they knew that successful incorporation would be achieved via existing ethnic leaders and organizations. When Henry González ran for governor in 1958, he quickly gained support from the civil rights community. The American GI Forum organized a "Friends of Senator Henry B. González" club to raise funds for his reelection campaign to the Texas Senate and had chapters outside his congressional district in Robstown, Bishop, Mathis, Edroy, Driscoll, Alice, Kingsville, Three Rivers, George West, and Corpus Christi, where Hector Garcia served as chief organizer ("Committee 'Friends'" 1960; "Commite para el banquete" 1960). When González ran for an open congressional seat, the Political Association of Spanish-Speaking Organizations (PASO) and the American GI Forum quickly mobilized to raise funds for his election campaign ("Contribución" ca. 1961; H. Garcia 1961). By 1960 the American GI Forum had laid the groundwork for successful campaigns by training community activists and mobilizing the Mexican American vote. For example, at the fourth annual convention of the American GI Forum in 1952, Ed Idar reported that he had traveled seventeen thousand miles organizing chapters of the forum in the previous year. "We have carried the message of our Forum from the southernmost tip of Texas to the Halls of our National Congress and to the President of the United States himself" (Idar 1952b). He proudly added that 1952 would be the first year when Mexican Americans were delegates to the Democratic National Convention. The list included Hector Garcia, Cris Aldrete, Frank Pinedo, Albert Peña, and Ed Idar. This feat was accomplished by "fighting for it all the way from the precinct to the state level" (Idar 1952b).

Idar reported on a significant development in the working relationship between Anglo and minority Democrats, but he failed to mention one thing. Six Mexican American representatives to the Democratic Party convention were part of an unofficial "Loyal Democratic" delegation that traveled to Chicago to challenge the conservative official delegation, which did not include a single Mexican American (Texas Democratic Party 1952b). They were only a tiny fraction of the 1,500 loyalist delegates who walked out of the 1952 Texas state convention. The Chicago protest failed to oust a single Texas delegate to the national convention (Maverick et al. 1952). But Mexican Americans and Anglos joined forces in a very early multiracial alliance, united by a belief that the governor and his allies were "fascists" bent on undermining the basic principles of democracy (Dickson 1952). They believed that this movement constituted the formative steps toward the creation of a party "truly representative of the people of Texas." As its leaders observed:

> On the Maverick Delegation you'll find small bankers, small businessmen, working people, union and non-union. You'll find the 900,000 Negroes of Texas represented, for the first time on any Texas delegation

to a Democratic National Convention. You'll find the 1,500,000 Texans of Mexican ancestry represented on the Maverick Delegation. You'll find three times as many women delegates to the Maverick Delegation as on the Shivers Delegation. ("Democrats vs Dixiecrats" n.d.)

Mexican Americans were loyal to the Democratic cause, but activists knew that they could not rely on the goodwill of the Anglo liberal caucus: they needed an independent power base in the community. American GI Forum founder Hector Garcia visited Mexican American neighborhoods throughout the state extolling the benefits of paying the poll tax and voting, without which they would have little influence over public officials. By voting Mexican Americans would gain the power to negotiate concessions in closely contested elections and threaten uncooperative public officials with retaliation at the ballot box. With a strong voting bloc, roads would be built, antidiscrimination legislation would be passed, and new hospitals and schools would be constructed in Mexican American neighborhoods. Like Henry B. González, Hector Garcia had unwavering faith in the electoral process: "I believe in the American system of democracy. I believe in the American Constitution and the principle of equal representation" and that "a nation's strength is measured by the rights and liberty its minority groups possess" (H. Garcia ca. 1952b). The promise of democracy could be realized through community organizing.

Hector Garcia was cautiously optimistic about the prospects of an expanded democratic participation for two reasons. First, the constitutional structure of the American government was well constructed: if all citizens had equal access to its institutions, the system could produce democratic outcomes. Second, incorporation into the electoral sphere differed significantly from integration in other arenas of social life like housing or education. A republican form of government did not necessitate personal or day-to-day contact between the races. Much of the personal interaction between Anglos and Mexican Americans in party politics took place at public rallies, at conventions, or between political leaders. Practically speaking, electoral politics was an arena of social life where Mexican Americans could successfully negotiate incorporation without igniting fierce opposition from the Anglo majority. From Hector Garcia's perspective, votes mattered more than race in the electoral system: "Politicians don't care who you are. What they want to know is whether or not you have paid your poll tax and how many of your friends have done the same" (H. Garcia ca. 1952b).

Garcia and other activists were confident that America would soon make good on its promise of equality for all, but until then they had to contend with a deeply racist society. The American GI Forum was mobilizing the ethnic vote, and its demands were always coupled with the assertion that Mexican Americans were prepared to fulfill all the obligations of equal citizenship (H. Garcia ca. 1952a). Garcia also made the implausible argument that the American GI Forum was not a civil rights group but a veterans' and family organization promoting good citizenship and civic work (H. Garcia 1954). It was a difficult and frustrating strategy for activists, who encountered hard choices at every turn. In 1959 Archbishop Robert E. Lucey of San Antonio delivered a speech to a meeting of the American GI Forum on the topic of electoral participation and the limited options available to Mexican Americans. He observed that the candidates running for public office were generally incompetent and hostile to people of color, but some were clearly better than others. His advice was to avoid "the idiots and imbeciles" and cast their vote for the "high grade morons" ("GI Forum Thanks LBJ" 1959).

Henry B. González for Congress

The election of John F. Kennedy in 1960 is widely regarded as a watershed event for Mexican Americans. Kennedy's liberalism and Catholicism resonated with the community, as did his targeted campaign for their vote. By 1960 demographic trends and years of mobilizing had made the Mexican American voter an important part of the national Democratic Party's strategy for winning close presidential contests. The Kennedy-Johnson campaign in Texas accelerated their incorporation into party politics, but the actual get-out-the-vote campaign was run by existing organizations and leadership networks. Chairing the Texas ¡Viva Kennedy! campaign was longtime San Antonio activist Albert Peña Jr. GI Forum president Hector Garcia and former LULAC presidents John J. Herrera of Houston and Roberto Ornelas of McAllen were assistant campaign directors (Kennedy Johnson State Campaign Headquarters ca. 1960). Their work on behalf of the Democratic Party contributed to John F. Kennedy's razor-thin victory over Richard Nixon in 1960. Though Mexican American activists remained frustrated by the lack of reciprocity from Texas Democrats, their contribution to the party's success was clear (Weeks 1961: 64–65; "Liberals and the Governor's Race" 1962).

Henry B. González won a congressional seat in a 1961 special election, becoming the first Mexican American from Texas elected to the U.S.

Photo 2.5. Senator Paul Douglas (*left*) accepting membership in the Illinois Viva Kennedy Club from Illinois state chair José Alvarado (*center*). Michigan governor G. Mennen Williams (R), chair of the Nationalities Division of the Democratic National Committee, presents the membership card and button in October 1960. Dr. Hector P. Garcia Papers, Special Collections and Archives, Texas A&M University–Corpus Christi, Mary and Jeff Bell Library.

House of Representatives. González's 1958 campaign gave him the highest stature of any Mexican American politician in the state, he was a sitting state senator, and he ran from San Antonio, with its strong base of Democratic voters and long history of ethnic activism. González received help from President Kennedy and Vice President Johnson, both of whom were anxious to keep the congressional seat in Democratic hands (Duckworth ca. 1961). Kennedy and Johnson made repeated visits to San Antonio in support of González. The Kennedy administration was grateful for González's help during the 1960 presidential campaign and worried that the Democratic Party might lose a congressional seat in the face of the Republican Party's deep inroads in the South (Baskin 1961a, 1961b).

Henry González won, as he did in previous elections, by uniting a liberal coalition of labor unions, Mexican Americans, African Americans, and independent white voters from the north side of San Antonio ("Bexar's Renewed Coalition" 1961). His margin of victory in the congressional primary was higher than President Kennedy's that year. González called his victory proof that a man could be elected to Congress because of his leadership abilities and not because of his race or ethnicity ("González Flies to Help Wagner" 1961; L. Jones 1961; Rodriguez 1976: 95).

Despite his optimism, González knew that race mattered; but from his perspective it was only one element in a complex political coalition requiring constant attention and renegotiation. The Democratic primary contest for his congressional seat was bitter and drawn out. His opponent was fellow liberal Maury Maverick Jr., son of a former San Antonio mayor and head of a powerful local political machine. The campaign for the Democratic Party nomination was filled with racial overtones. But González reminded his Mexican American supporters that it was wrong to support any candidate for public office because of race or ethnicity ("González Flies to Help Wagner" 1961). Maverick also understood that race mattered in Texas elections and worked to mobilize Anglo voters. Although Maverick ran as a Kennedy liberal, the subtext of his message to white voters amounted to what one reporter called an "offensive and repugnant" smear campaign filled with personal attacks and race baiting (Hatefield and Hatefield 1960).

Photo 2.6. ¡Viva Kennedy! rally, September 1960. Courtesy of the Dolph Briscoe Center for American History, University of Texas at Austin. Russell Lee Photograph Collection, di_07907.

Maverick accused González of running as an ethnic candidate and characterized the win as a victory of race over ideas: "Henry wiped me out in San Antonio among the Mexicans where I had been strong and my father was strong. That polished me off from going to Congress" (Maverick 1975). Contrary to Maverick's charge, evidence suggests that González won by implementing a race-neutral strategy, though it is true that González would not have won the Democratic Party primary or the general election without great support from Mexican American and black voters. With over 90,000 votes cast in the general election, González won by only 10,000 votes. Mexican American precincts recorded a higher rate of voting than the city as a whole (75 percent vs. 60 percent), and that turnout gave him 12,000 votes. These precincts were located in the poorest neighborhoods in San Antonio, while wealthy areas of the city voted for his Republican opponent by a six-to-one margin (Rodriguez 1976: 116). In a congressional district where race and political identity paralleled one another, González's fought for and garnered multiracial support for the Democratic Party's liberal agenda. In other words, he mobilized his base.

González's victory in the Democratic primary and subsequent election made history. He became the first Mexican American elected to the United States Congress, defeated the son of a former San Antonio mayor, and destroyed a once powerful political machine in doing so. At the same time the primary contest between González and Maverick was in many ways an ordinary political event that followed a predictable course. The two men were liberal Democrats with outsized personalities but had few policy differences between them (González 1960; Maverick 1960). They coveted their district's congressional seat and worked for years to build alliances within the Bexar County Democratic Party. Both men knew that the various Democratic Party factions supporting either candidate would make amends after the primary and support the winner (Chastain 1958; González 1960; Maverick 1960b). The hard-fought contest for the Democratic nomination between González and Maury Maverick Jr. left both camps angry. But any racial animosities that surfaced during the election were set aside after González won. The Democratic Party closed ranks behind a Mexican American candidate. The party needed a win: Maury Maverick quickly endorsed González, affirming that all "Loyal Democrats" were bound to support its nominee (Benham 1961). Maverick's endorsement was unsurprising. As head of the Democratic Party in San Antonio he campaigned tirelessly for the Kennedy-Johnson ticket in Texas and ten other states ("González Campaigns" 1961). Now he would campaign for González as well. The Republican Party was believed to have amassed a huge war chest of money. Unless Bexar County Democrats were willing to lose a congressional seat, they needed to rally behind González. Maverick was obligated to do everything he could to assure González's election because, in his own words, "I'm a soldier in the ranks of the Democratic Party" (Maverick 1961).

Partisan solidarity helped break a racial barrier in San Antonio but had unintended consequences for Mexican American representation elsewhere in Texas. In areas of the state where Mexican Americans were a large proportion of the voting-age population, candidates like González could capture public office. Where Mexican Americans were outnumbered, partisanship tied them to a conservative state party actively resisting any influence of the national Democratic Party. When responding to demands that the state party bring its policies more in line with those of the national party, State Democratic Executive Committee member John Peace explained that compromise was the price of political power. He argued that the state party was on record supporting the principles of loyalty to the national party and that campaigning for Republican candidates was unacceptable. Peace invited Mexican Americans displeased with the party's leaders or policies to participate in its governing structure but warned that coalitions required cooperation on all sides. He pointed out that it was a "fallacy that one can only be a Democrat if he agrees 100% with me or my idea as to all candidates for public office, and all legislation with which I may be in personal sympathy. It is with an understanding of this fallacy that the State Committee not only recognizes the various complexions of opinion among Democrats, but . . . invites all to operate under and work through the official party organization" (Peace 1957).

On Race

The classic model of assimilation predicts that economic integration goes hand in hand with greater tolerance and racial inclusion similar to that experienced by white ethnic groups. The gains made by Henry González and other Mexican American activists were part of an uneven incorporation process in a racially stratified state. By the late 1950s Mexican Americans had increased their participation in Democratic Party politics and convinced liberal Anglos to start engaging in coalitional politics. Mexican American incorporation did not provoke a strong negative reaction among Anglo voters in the electoral arena, avoiding the specter of black/

white integration. Mexican Americans were victimized by discrimination throughout the state, but racism's power receded enough in population strongholds like San Antonio to elect Henry González to state office and the U.S. Congress. It is important to recognize that Mexican Americans' move toward incorporation resulted in tangible successes. Mexican Americans were integrating a major political institution and would push the process forward in the following decades, as the model of assimilation and acculturation predicts.

Mexican Americans were a marginalized group but did not experience the same force of social exclusion as blacks. Legally they received some protection because federal and Texas state laws classified people of Mexican descent as white, thereby exempting them from legal segregation. Significantly, they were able to vote and participate in the state Democratic Party's white primaries (Goldberg 1983; Guglielmo 2006). In fact their legal right to participate in the Democratic Party primary was affirmed by resolution at the party's 1932 convention and later reaffirmed in a 1934 opinion rendered by Texas attorney general James V. Allred. Allred found that the Texas Democratic Party fully intended to allow Mexican Americans of "mixed Caucasian and American Indian blood" to be considered "white citizens" as promised by the resolution of the Democratic Party convention. He added that members of the Democratic Party "were not ignorant" of the fact that Mexican American voters were allowed to participate in the primaries and would have barred them if it had been their desire to do so. Mexican Americans, he said, were generally understood to be white by the people of the state: "the whole course of racial legislation in this State is predicated upon that proposition" (Allred 1934).

In contrast, attitudes toward blacks were overwhelmingly negative, and their exclusion from the party politics was written into law. In 1905 the state legislature passed the "Terrell Election Law," allowing county committees to prescribe qualifications for voting in primary elections with the intention of giving local officials the power to exclude black voters. In 1923 the legislature enacted another statute stipulating that no "negro" was eligible to participate in a Texas Democratic party primary election. When the law was declared unconstitutional by the U.S. Supreme Court, Texas restored the statute's intent by granting political parties the power to set qualifications for primary participation. The State Democratic Party Executive Committee accepted this invitation to discrimination by claiming that it was a private political association and voting to prohibit blacks from participating in the party and in its primary elections. When the Supreme Court ruled such practices unconstitutional in 1941, the white primary was resurrected by an organization called the Jaybird Democratic Association. This group held a preprimary election, where the winner would run in the regular election and be virtually assured of victory. The Jaybird Democratic Association limited its membership to whites (Cotrell and Polinard 1986: 68–69). This argument withstood legal challenge until 1944, when the U.S. Supreme Court held that exclusion of nonwhites from membership in the Democratic Party was unconstitutional (Keyssar 2000: 198).

The Anglo response to Mexican American activism lacked the hostility that characterized black and white relations. Mexican Americans were the largest minority group in the state, concentrated in areas where effective registration and get-out-the-vote drives could displace Anglo politicians. Their demands for incorporation began at a time when discrimination was, arguably, most pervasive. Yet the lobbying of civil rights groups like the League of United Latin American Citizens, the American GI Forum, and a myriad of individual activists did not provoke the same violent opposition commonly elicited by the black civil rights movement across East Texas and other southern states. Economic and political conservatives opposing Mexican American aspirations were scattered over the state, but the most intensely race-conscious Anglo voters lived in the Black Belt counties of East Texas (Weeks 1953: 9).

In 1955 public opinion polls revealed that 45 percent of all Texans believed that federal laws mandating integration should be evaded or disobeyed ("Texans Divided" 1955). In 1956, two years after *Brown v. Board of Education* (1954), three referenda on race were placed on the Democratic Party primary ballot, allowing segregation of African Americans in the public schools. Democratic voters were asked to express their opinions on "Mixing White and Negro Children in Public Schools," "Intermarriage between Negroes and Whites," and "Interposition" ("Texas Referendum Committee" ca. 1956). Over 78 percent of voters casting a ballot in the Democratic primary voted to keep Texas schools segregated. Some East Texas counties registered 90 percent support for racial segregation among Anglos (Texas Advisory Committee on Segregation 1956: 9–10). In large urban areas like Dallas, voters rejected school integration, intermarriage between blacks and whites, and the principle of federal supremacy by margins of five to one ("Dallas County Returns" 1956). In a 1957 poll 42 percent of white Texans said that they would either disobey the law or find ways to get around it to keep the races separate. White residents of East Texas, where the state's black population was concentrated, consistently showed the strongest resistance. There the Belden Poll found that 84 percent of all Anglo respondents agreed that integration should be fought through extralegal means (Belden 1957).

Belden Polls in the early 1950s found a far lower level of Anglo opposition to integration in Southwest Texas and the Valley, areas with the highest numbers of Mexican Americans. In 1951 the Texas poll revealed that only 30 percent of all Anglos disapproved of interacting with Mexican Americans in public places, such as eating in the same restaurant. They found that the proximity of a large Mexican American population did not necessarily generate sharp negative attitudes. The pollsters also learned that Anglo Texans who actually rubbed shoulders with Mexican Americans were less likely to object to an integrated social space than those living in areas where few of them resided (Belden 1951). These apparently open attitudes among Anglo Texans contrasted with their deep antiblack attitudes. In 1946 half of white Texans would deny blacks the right to vote (Belden 1946). In 1948 two-thirds of all white voters said that black people should not have the same rights as white people. Anglo opposition to civil rights reform was so great that the same polls revealed that any Texas Democrat committed to white supremacy would have a fifty-fifty chance of defeating President Harry Truman in an election (Belden 1948). The Belden Poll on Social Integration found that Anglos in Texas were not ready to accept blacks as social equals as late as 1963 (Belden 1963). The data revealed fierce resistance to integration in public accommodations, schools, social gatherings, and residential areas (Belden 1963). Although opinions moderated over time, large majorities of white Texans continued to reject social mixing of the races even in the late 1960s and believed that the federal government was pushing integration too fast (Belden 1968a, 1969).

In the 1950s Anglo politicians enthusiastically promoted—and were the beneficiaries of—an antiblack political culture. East Texas Democrat Price Daniel had a history of campaigning on a segregation platform as a candidate for the U.S. Senate and Texas governor. His campaign literature claimed that the Brown decision was wrong and that the NAACP was trying to take over Texas politics (Price Daniel for Governor Headquarters ca. 1956). While governor, he rewarded his antiblack supporters by calling a special session to pass three interposition bills discussed earlier in this chapter ("Segregationists' Program" 1957). Despite the lengths to which Daniel went to identify himself as a prosegregation politician, race radicals attacked him for not pursuing an even harder line. Daniels's archives are filled with letters urging him to continue his resistance to federal government desegregation orders. An exchange with one critic offers insight into the governor's thinking and the contours of Texas race relations at the time. Reverend Carey Daniel, Price Daniel's cousin and the leader of a Dallas White Citizens' Council, corresponded with the governor between 1955 and 1958 over the issue and accused his cousin of being "soft" on segregation. He warned that the federal government would soon integrate the entire public school system unless the governor held the line and forced integrated schools to resegregate (C. Daniel 1958). The governor angrily replied that those who questioned his commitment to segregation had "short memories and little understanding of my personal and official connection with the fight to preserve local control of our schools" (P. Daniel 1958a).

The two men were worried first and foremost about black-white integration. The Reverend Carey Daniel described blacks as "physically, mentally, socially, hereditarily, geographically, environmentally [*sic*]" different from and inferior to whites (C. Daniel n.d.). He told the governor that he would never allow his daughter to attend school with "sex crazed Negroes" and that Communist nations would like nothing better than an easily enslaved "mongrelized America" (C. Daniel 1955). Governor Daniel assured his cousin that the threat was minimal because strict residential segregation precluded most efforts to integrate neighborhood schools. Moreover, the state legislature and local school boards would evade all federal segregation orders through token compliance and subterfuge (P. Daniel 1955). The governor was confident that white resistance would quickly reverse any race mixing imposed on the schools. In thinly veiled terms he said that blacks would segregate themselves as they did in Austin, where "about half of the few who attended one of our high schools here last year transferred back to the Negro high school" (P. Daniel 1958b).

Price Daniel's determination on black/white segregation contrasted with his conciliatory attitude toward Mexican Americans, many of whom were anxious to distance themselves from blacks. In the late 1940s, when Daniel was still Texas attorney general, LULAC, GI Forum, and the secretary of the Good Neighbor Commission sought clarification of the state's segregation laws as applied to Mexican Americans. Their lawyers wanted assurance that the state's segregation laws did not apply to ethnic or national groups (Cortez 1947; P. Daniel 1947a; Gus Garcia 1947a, 1947b; Inter-Organizational Committee 1947). As they had hoped, Price Daniel found that the state's racial segregation laws did not apply to Mexican Americans. In a letter to Gus Garcia, Daniel affirmed that the law prohibited "discrimination against or segregation of Latin-Americans on account of race or descent, and that the law permits no subterfuge to accomplish such discrimination" (P. Daniel 1947b). As Texas attorney general Daniel issued a decision that interpreted the state's segregation statutes as applied to higher education barred only blacks from admission to the University of Texas (P. Daniel 1948). He further found that the *Delgado v. Bastrop Independent School District* decision barring segregation of Mexican American children in the public schools would have no effect on segregation suits involving blacks. Litigation involving the two groups was "entirely different," because the U.S. Constitution and Texas statues did not segregate other races or national origin groups (P. Daniel ca. 1948).

The irony of being given a nonblack legal status was that the public schools segregated Mexican American children anyway. Guadalupe San Miguel (1987: 216) called the 1950s an era of subterfuge, where discriminatory practices like the "no Spanish" rule, racist remarks by teachers, and rigid cultural dress codes prevailed. Activists were able to exert pressure on offending school districts, however, with the legal tools afforded by a white racial status. Citing *Delgado*, decisions made by the state superintendent of schools, and rulings by Daniel himself, Mexican American activists contended that this segregation was "in violation of the laws of the state and of the Constitution of the United States." They called upon the attorney general to stop what they characterized as a statewide conspiracy by public officials (Maldonado et al. ca. 1949). Daniel agreed and encouraged them to contact the superintendent of public instruction and the Good Neighbor Commission to challenge the violations in court (P. Daniel 1949). When pressed for a response to the charge of illegal segregation, the superintendent of public schools held that Texas courts and the legislature defined "colored children" to mean only members of "Negro race" or ancestry (Woods ca. 1949).

The advantaged legal and social standing of Mexican Americans in these debates contrasted sharply with the single-minded drive to keep black students out of white schools. In 1955 Governor Allan Shivers created the Texas Advisory Committee on Segregation in the Public Schools to find answers for two questions: how to stop forced integration and whether the state could legally help local school boards resisting integration. The committee found that those issues were most acute in the eastern part of the state, where the bulk of the state's black population lived. South Texas counties expressed fewer and less intense concerns than their eastern counterparts and counties recorded as having less than 1 percent of "colored" students or none (Texas Advisory Committee on Segregation 1956: 24–25). When gauging the strength of popular support for segregation, the committee reported that "the percentage in favor of maintaining our racial mores is generally highest in those areas in which the percentage of the Negro population is the highest." The report went on to say that "as the percentage of Negro population declines, so declines the vote in favor of segregation, for those who have fewer contacts with the other race must by nature have less understanding of the necessity for and advantages of segregation" (Texas Advisory Committee on Segregation 1956: 9).

The success that Mexican Americans experienced in the Democratic Party at this time came in part because they were not black. They were in a better position to negotiate a new political identity without provoking the specter of black integration in the minds of Anglo Texans. Early public opinion polls pointed to a dual system of discrimination whereby Mexican Americans stood outside of a fierce black/white conflict. In Texas counties adjacent to Louisiana and Arkansas, the great majority of white adults were against integration in any form. However, "in Southwest Texas and the Valley . . . which contains the largest number of Latin Americans in Texas, opposition is the lightest" (Belden 1960a). A white legal status did not desegregate the public schools for Mexican Americans, but the dialogue surrounding the issue pointed to an evolving racial schema even as Anglos worked to reinforce African Americans' inferior social position. When Henry B. González threatened a filibuster against the proposed segregation bills, Governor Daniel tried to dissuade him by arguing that none of them applied to Mexican Americans. State representative Oscar Laurel demanded further guarantees against any negative impact on Mexican Americans by amending the legislation forbidding school boards from using national origin or foreign language use to segregate students (P. Daniel 1957). When Texas lieutenant governor Ben Ramsey heard about Henry González's impending filibuster against the governor's segregation bills in 1958, he framed the controversy as a fight that his people had no interest in joining and then asked: "Henry, you're not gonna fight our nigger bills, are ya?" (Dugger 1980a).

The distinction between African Americans and Mexican Americans was more than symbolic. A rigid rule of hypodescent did not apply to Mexican Americans; their racial status was fluid and hinged on local conditions. As David Montejano (1987: 235) found: "in some counties, Mexicans and Anglos were completely separate. In others, there was an easy mingling among them." Race relations were harsh in agricultural regions of the state, but Mexican Americans exercised a greater degree of independence and power in urban areas with significant Mexican American populations. Most observers agreed that discrimination against Mexican Americans was a serious problem in cities but did not rise to the level of outright exclusion. In cities like El Paso, Mexican Americans could eat in restaurants, sit anywhere in theaters, attend public schools not segregated by race, and live in every precinct in the city. No attempts were made to keep Mexican Americans from voting even though the city had a strong tradition of ethnic mobilization, had a Mexican American population that had been in the majority since the turn of the twentieth century, and had elected its first Mexican American mayor in 1957 (United States Department of Commerce 1916; Adams and Adams 1963: 1–9).

The story of the black civil rights movement in Texas was far different. Shortly after the *Brown v. Board of Education* decision, the NAACP was the target of political repression throughout the South. Texas state senator Wardlow Lane said that the organization took its orders from "niggers and foreigners" in New York ("Carr of Lubbock" 1966). Utilizing the legislation, the Texas attorney general enjoined the NAACP from operating in Texas. Its records were seized and its offices closed. District judge Otis Dunagan issued the order closing the NAACP, its legal arm, and all 112 local chapters in Texas and prohibiting the collecting of dues, filing of lawsuits, and any application at any time in the future to enter Texas. The judge denied that the State of Texas was acting in a discriminatory fashion: "This case isn't a case against the nigger race. It don't keep [*sic*] them from filing a lawsuit as individuals. I don't want anybody to think I've got anything against the niggers. I've got a lot of nigger friends" (Dugger 1956). House Speaker Waggoner Carr and fifty to sixty fellow elected officials trumpeted their approval of the new laws at a dinner in Houston honoring Marvin Griffin, Georgia's segregationist governor. A White Citizens' Council in Texas paid for the event and the legislators' expenses ("Carr of Lubbock" 1966).

Mexican American organizations were often harassed but did not suffer these kinds of repressive attacks (Morris 1984). This difference in treatment is significant, because Mexican Americans were a much larger minority group: their demands could have had far-reaching consequences if realized. The same year the NAACP was shut down in Texas, McAllen attorney Robert Sánchez organized a voter registration drive in South Texas. That drive and others like it made Mexican Americans a pivotal voting bloc capable of rearranging the region's power relations (R. P. Sánchez 1956). At one point an Anglo state senator charged that the voter registration campaign fomented "class and racial warfare" and "inharmony" in the Rio Grande Valley (Hager 1955). Governor Shivers joined him, contending that labor unions were paying poll taxes on behalf of others (illegal under Texas law) and asking the attorney general to investigate ("Probe of 'Demo Club'" 1956; "Shivers Asks Probe" 1956). These objections came late: the drive was well underway before either politician registered complaints. The governor was criticized by a Valley newspaper editor for being unaware of political developments in the area and having an unfounded fear of social unrest ("News to Allan" 1956).

The American GI Forum and labor groups made no secret of their plans to register Mexican American voters and overturn the political status quo (Rio Grande Democratic Club ca. 1955). By the mid-1950s cross-racial political alliances were commonplace, especially in the southern part of the state, where Mexican American and Anglo members of the Democrats of Texas conducted fund-raising and poll-tax rallies (Fath 1957; R. P. Sánchez 1957a, 1957b). At one such rally in Brownsville the mayor, the city council, a county judge, and five hundred people gathered to hear New Mexico congressman Joe Montoya deliver a political address—in English and Spanish (Duarte 1957). Once again an organizing drive in the Valley drew the scrutiny of Governor Shivers. He was disturbed that the drive was funded by the American GI Forum, the Texas Federation of Labor, and the United Auto Workers and asked the Hidalgo district attorney to investigate for possible violation of state election laws ("Union Deposit Photos" 1956; Democrats of Texas 1958; Democrats of Texas ca. 1958). When Shivers pressed for this investigation, the local district attorney "laughed the matter off" (R. P. Sánchez 1956).

Racial and political affinities were key to this relatively open attitude toward Mexican American organizing. Civil rights leaders made no secret of their desire to register as many voters as possible in order to increase the number of Mexican American public officials. When they talked about a reconstituted political order, however, their goal was to advance the liberal agenda with more Mexican Americans in elective office under the Democratic Party's auspices. Mexican Americans were also working hand in hand with their Anglo allies in the Democratic Party. One reason why these South Texas registration drives drew the attention of Governor Shivers was because they were part of U.S. senator Lyndon Johnson's bid to wrest control of the state Democratic Party from Shivers ("Angry Blasts" 1956). Johnson was one of the first Democratic Party leaders to reach out to Mexican American voters and was well aware that activists like Dr. Hector Garcia had been able to raise money, conduct poll-tax drives, and mobilize the Mexican American vote. Instead of stifling this new movement, Senator Johnson understood that nurturing this voting bloc could make a critical difference for him in future primary and general elections (R. N. Jones 1949).

The attacks on South Texas organizing were few and lacked the negative attitudes that Anglo politicians had toward the African American vote. Some politicians framed their appeals with this differential status in mind. When liberal stalwart Ralph Yarborough ran against Price Daniel in the 1956 gubernatorial primary, he fought hard for the Mexican American vote in South Texas and circulated Spanish-language literature attacking his opponent ("Translation" ca. 1956). Yarborough advocated New Deal programs like support for old-age pensions, education, and labor protection when speaking to Mexican American audiences. In his Spanish-language radio spots he stated his opposition to the segregation of Spanish-speaking children. He pointed out that state law allowed Mexican American children to be segregated only for "educational reasons." If elected governor, he vowed to put an end to the practice ("Translation" ca. 1956). When campaigning in Anglo neighborhoods, however, he defended segregated schools and opposed "the forced commingling of white and Negro children in the public schools." Reminding Anglo voters that he was the grandson of two Confederate soldiers, he defended states' rights and local control in the name of avoiding "hatred, strife, and dissention" ("Yarborough Gives Progress Plan" 1956).

Ralph Yarborough believed that even a limited outreach to black voters damaged his prospects among Anglos. Campaigning for the Mexican American vote was not only less likely to alienate whites but held the potential to increase his vote total significantly (Yarborough 1982). Yarborough's openness to Mexican American voters while shunning blacks was shared with the segregationist Price Daniel. In his 1956 campaign for governor Daniel enlisted LULAC president Oscar Laurel of Laredo and LULAC legal counsel Phil Montalbo of Houston to broadcast ads in Spanish. The ads reminded voters that as attorney general Daniel had issued his opinion that Texas law guaranteed Mexican Americans equal access to schools, public places, and housing (Daniel Campaign ca. 1956). In the 1958 campaign Price Daniel invoked a bridging identity based on the Texas Revolution that would be employed by liberals and conservatives alike for the next forty-five years. He said that Anglos and Mexicans could trace their political origins to the same source: "it is an often forgotten fact in history that Mexicans fought side by side with Anglos in the Texas War for Independence 122 years ago. They died together at the Alamo, and they shared the victory at San Jacinto. Twenty-four men of Mexican descent were among Sam Houston's heroes at San Jacinto" (P. Daniel 1958d).

It would be a long time before Mexican American activists were accepted as equals, but they were not completely locked out of the state's politics. In contrast, racial bias against African Americans was so strong that some observers believed that they harmed their cause whenever they affiliated with black organizations like the NAACP (S. Wood 1958a). The Democratic Party platform in 1948 declared that Texas Democrats "deprecate discriminatory practices against Latin-Americans" (Texas Democratic Party 1948: 3–4). That statement was hardly a courageous defense of human equality, but the same platform lashed out against African Americans. The Texas Democratic Party reaffirmed its support of states' rights and a racially segregated school system. It further declared that the federal government had no role in state politics because Texas was capable of fulfilling "its responsibilities to the Negro race" (Texas Democratic Party 1948: 7).

Mexican American activists were well aware of their complicated position relative to the black/white binary (Márquez 1993; N. Foley 1997). This understanding made its way into their strategic calculations, with some arguing that the path toward civic equality was facilitated by a white racial status. Manuel Crespo of the GI Forum advised his organization to make an overt claim for a white racial status: "Let's face it, first we have to establish we are white then be on the 'white side' and then we'll become Americans" (Crespo 1956). Many shared his assessment, and some American GI Forum chapters barred African Americans from membership to strengthen their claim to a white identity (R. P. Morgan 1956). When it came to admitting African Americans to the American GI Forum, one official argued that "90% do not want them." He went on to ask: "[W]hat are we to do when we approach merchants and they tell us we can come in, but if Negros [*sic*] come with us then we too will be barred?" (Torrez 1956). American GI Forum founder Hector Garcia agreed. He maintained that Mexican Americans were members of the white race and should not be segregated with "Negroes." To lump Mexican Americans and blacks in the same category not only was contrary to laws governing segregation of the races but was a harmful "slur" against the entire community (H. Garcia 1953b, 1956). They understood that two civil rights movements coexisted in Texas. As one journalist put it, one was in "South and far West Texas with more than a million Latin Americans" and the other was in "East Texas with a million Negroes" (Dugger 1957).

Conclusion

Mexican American activists faced obstacles that would have remained virtually insurmountable without modernization of the state's agriculture, industrialization, and subsequent demographic shifts. As the political process model posits, these changes undermined the foundations of rural servitude and created new opportunities in Texas cities and towns. As long as Mexican Americans were principally a rural population, voter registration would be low and rural political machines would continue to dominate their lives. Job opportunities in cities improved, incomes rose, and community organizations could thrive, thereby rendering long-standing political arrangements vulnerable to attack. The struggle would take years, but activists understood that these structural changes presented an unprecedented opportunity to destroy entrenched white minority regimes (Idar 1955b).

Theories of assimilation predict that blatant exclusion will eventually yield to social acceptance but that formally excluded groups will also change as well. In the 1950s Mexican American activists became members of the Texas Democratic Party, adopting its language and rules even as it remained hostile to minority interests. By doing so, ethnic representation was funneled into institutional modes of change and away from the community-based organizing that made those gains possible. Leading activists like Hector Garcia, president of the American GI Forum, doubted the efficacy of engaging in coalition politics from a position of weakness. He believed that race relations were so bad during the 1950s that the only way to change the state's electoral system was through racial advocacy, at least in the short term (H. Garcia 1953c). Garcia was correct that racism was endemic in Texas politics, but the prospects for leveraging influence in the Democratic Party via ethnic organizing diminished as racial barriers crumbled. Party membership imposed rules, processes, and a leadership structure that tempered ethnic advocacy. Moreover, the era's most influential leader, Henry B. González, forcefully articulated the case for decoupling electoral politics from its traditional ethnic base. He believed that American society was assimilating Mexican Americans as it had waves of white European immigrants. The most effective way to raise Mexican Americans' standard of living was to join with Anglo liberals through an alliance based on class and occupational interests and change the Texas Democratic Party's policies.

Finally, a nonblack racial status facilitated Mexican Americans' ability to negotiate a new position for themselves in state politics. Relative to

African Americans, they experienced more freedom of action and opportunities to lobby government, elect public officials, and work within the Democratic Party structure. Their civil rights organizations were not targeted for state-sponsored repression or subjected to legal segregation or laws of interposition designed to reinforce their inferior status. Public opinion was overwhelmingly antiblack during the 1950s, but the majority views and the attitudes of Anglo politicians moderated when it came to the political rights and social integration of Mexican Americans. Anglos were more prepared to accept a new social and political status for Mexican Americans, at least when it came to voting rights. Mexican Americans were able to mobilize their community without inciting an overwhelmingly negative reaction. Favorable legal opinions exempted them from legal segregation, individuals were elected to public office, the liberal caucus of the Democratic Party was integrated, and Anglo politicians began taking their vote more seriously.

CHAPTER 3

The Dilemmas of Ethnic Solidarity

*An Anglo Democratic activist on La Raza Unida Party, ". . . those dumb
bastards! Why don't they realize? They can't win, but they were willing to
screw us up. How could they?"*
MOLLY IVINS, 1972

BOYCOTT GRAPES, eat watermelon;
BOYCOTT Lettuce, eat celery;
BOYCOTT SAFEWAY. Go somewhere else.
HARRIS COUNTY DEMOCRATS, 1973

The Texas Democratic Party of the 1950s was a formidable barrier to racial
progress. Minorities, labor, and liberals had few representatives on the
State Democratic Executive Committee (SDEC) (Davidson 1990: 165–
166). Conservatives dominated the party structure and liberals were so
excluded that Democratic leaders even in places like San Antonio were
"leery of anything pro labor or pro-Negro" ("Texas Liberals Argue"
1955). The party strongly supported the principle of state's rights and
opposition to racial integration, urging the state's national representatives
to restrict the power of the Supreme Court. Early in the decade the SDEC
did not require loyalty pledges to vote in Democratic primaries or participate in Democratic Party conventions (Texas Democratic Party 1952a).
SDEC members like John Peace invited greater participation by all Democrats but in practice squelched dissent and enforced conformity. Governor
Price Daniel and other conservative leaders threatened the liberal Democrats of Texas with legal action for unauthorized use of the name "Democrats" (Texas Democratic Party 1958b). In the face of this political repression, and to the dismay of Mexican American activists, liberal Anglos in

the besieged Democrats of Texas still hesitated to embrace their minority allies openly. As late as 1959 the caucus still scheduled its meetings in racially segregated facilities and "Whites Only" hotels (Peña 1959).

Racial incorporation proceeded at a slow pace, but ethnic organizing received a boost from the 1960 presidential campaign and rule changes within the Democratic Party later in the decade that increased minority representation. The close 1960 presidential election energized activists because of the important role that they played in winning Texas for the Democrats ("The Harris County PASO" ca. 1962). As South Texas attorney Tony Bonilla recalled, Mexican Americans were galvanized by Kennedy's election and subsequent willingness to appoint civil rights leaders to positions in his administration. Bonilla called the election an incredible achievement that "generated the kind of enthusiasm for expanding our political base, getting more people involved in politics, more people to pay their poll tax, and more people to go out and vote" (T. Bonilla 2007). Along with this movement came a growing realization by white liberals that aligning the state party's politics with those of the national party would not happen without the minority vote. In 1961 leaders from black, Mexican American, and labor organizations began meeting with Anglo Democratic activists to formulate a strategy to unite the liberal base of the Democratic Party in Texas. Two years later their work resulted in the formation of a new liberal group, the Democratic Coalition (DC). The DC was used as a vehicle to evaluate candidates for office and conduct poll-tax and get-out-the-vote drives (A. Draper 1994: 101). The *Texas Observer* claimed that "Texas Latin Americans, Negroes, union people and independent liberals have hooked together a four-group 'Democratic Coalition' that is like nothing that has been tried seriously in the South since Populism in the eighteen nineties" (Dugger 1963: 24).

Anglo activists worked with Albert Peña and black civil rights leader Arthur DeWitty to assemble a new multiracial alliance (Goodwyn 1963c). Albert Peña insisted that the new organization avoid the DOT's mistakes and adopt a strong antiracism, pro–civil rights agenda from its inception (Democratic Coalition 1963). This time Anglo liberals, long relegated to the margins of the Texas Democratic Party, found the argument of mutual interest among Anglos, poor whites, and Mexican American more compelling (Goodwyn 1963e). Instead of shunning association with minority voters, some Anglo liberals believed that it was time to rework their caucus and include minorities in all the deal making and to respond to candidates for public office "without regard to their race" (Dugger 1963: 112). Larry Goodwyn, who managed the day-to-day operations of the new group, vowed to mobilize "200,000 to 500,000 new Negro and Latin-American votes" for the 1964 presidential election (Goodwyn 1963a, 1963b). In his words, the natural coalition among liberals of all races and creeds would finally be realized in Texas: "from this day, let the word go out that liberals of all races will meet together, work together on a year-round basis for the political breakthrough we hold in our very grasp. Let the word go out that for every conservative who leaves the party, we will find two negroes to take his place. Let the word go out that for every Negro who joins our ranks, two Latin-Americans will join with him" (Goodwyn 1963d).

This enthusiasm dissipated almost immediately when it ran up against long-standing racial prejudice. As he canvassed the state testing the new coalition's viability, Goodwyn had great difficulty convincing more minority activists to join the effort, because they distrusted the Democratic Party (Goodwyn ca. 1963). To make matters worse, racism was so entrenched in the Texas labor movement that he could make little progress engaging union members. As much as labor needed allies, C. J. Haggerty, president of the AFL-CIO building and construction trades, was astounded by the degree to which some union leaders had "a strong dislike and contempt for their Negro and Latino brothers" (Draper 1994: 102). The depth of the mutual antipathy was confirmed in the 1963 referendum to repeal the poll tax, a measure that would increase liberal and minority voting strength. The Texas AFL-CIO funded a well-coordinated campaign in sixteen cities, each with a full-time director, but to no avail. Although labor's leadership supported the repeal, individual unions did not; the measure ultimately failed. Some local unions disaffiliated with the AFL-CIO over the poll tax issue or refused to fund coalition activities. Minority members of the coalition retaliated by refusing to support labor-backed candidates in the general election. By the end of 1964 the Democratic Coalition was in shambles (Draper 1994: 101–103).

Although Albert Peña was a founding member of the Democratic Coalition, he had grave doubts about multiracial coalitions from the onset. Without an independent, well-organized ethnic base to back them up, he reasoned, Mexican Americans would be junior partners in any political enterprise. Peña's model of effective political action was the 1960 ¡Viva Kennedy! campaign, an operation that he had chaired in Texas. It combined support of the national party, a mobilization of Mexican American voters, and the disruptive power of a social movement to hold the Democratic Party accountable for its actions. Leaders of the ¡Viva Kennedy! campaign were veteran civil rights activists like American GI Forum resident Dr. Hector Garcia and former LULAC presidents John J. Herrera of

Houston and Roberto Ornelas of McAllen (Kennedy Johnson State Campaign Headquarters ca. 1960). Ed Idar Jr. later recalled that political organizing and communication for the ¡Viva Kennedy! campaign was vibrant:

> Most of us had worked together in the GI Forum, were good personal friends; we trusted each other; we had confidence in one another. We had Gilbert Garcia in Fort Worth. We had Hector Garcia and James DeAnda in Corpus Christi. We had Gregorio Coronado in Lubbock. Myself and Bob Sánchez in Hidalgo County. We had Dr. Fermin Calderon and Cris Aldrete in Del Rio, and in other parts of the state we had developed political leadership by then. (Idar 1969: 24)

Albert Peña's plan was to harness the organizational strength and networking skills that Idar described in order to initiate serious negotiations over power sharing and representation in the Democratic Party ("Political Association" ca. 1962).

It was not long, however, before Peña grew disenchanted with Anglo intransigence and decided to use those networks against the Texas Democratic Party, a tactic that brought him into direct conflict with partisans like Henry B. González. The ensuing debate illuminated a divergence in strategy and vision. González held up his political ascendancy as an example of successful identity bridging and tirelessly attacked anyone using race and ethnicity as an organizing principle. Peña countered that the state was stratified on the basis of race and ethnicity and that it was imperative to attack the problem at its roots. In the course of some remarkable organizing work over the next ten years, Peña helped topple Anglo minority regimes in South Texas and exposed the Democratic Party's continued resistance to racial integration. Tapping ethnic dissatisfaction led to the formation of La Raza Unida Party, a Chicano third party. But for all his successes, the conflict with González over strategy was a fight that Peña was destined to lose. Peña's organizing helped dismantle some of the most blatant racist practices in Texas politics, but by that time incorporation was well underway. Initially the Texas State Democratic Party offered limited but symbolically important opportunities for Mexican Americans to participate in party affairs. Later in the decade the national Democratic Party mandated greater gender and racial representation, thus creating even more pathways to influence the state party. Mexican American elected officials and activists who took advantage of these new opportunities saw themselves as Democrats in the mold of Henry B. González, not as ethnic representatives. By the early 1970s they and their Anglo colleagues in the Democratic Party were united in their condemnation of nationalist politics.

From a historical perspective, the culmination of demographic changes, racial progress at the national level, concessions by the Texas Democratic Party, and growing Mexican American activism within the state party did bring about change. At the time, however, actors like Albert Peña remained unconvinced that the Democratic Party was changing at all. In order to force change on Texas politics, he created a new organization, the Political Association of Spanish-Speaking Organizations (PASO) (Shockley 1979). PASO was the multipurpose ethnic organization favored by Peña. It was a partisan group designed to unite all Mexican Americans into a single political organization with the goal of attaining full citizenship rights in addition to economic progress and preserving culture (G. Sánchez n.d.). Under Peña's leadership, the new organization was soon campaigning against political regimes in South Texas towns where a small number of Anglos controlled all aspects of local politics. PASO bypassed the local Democratic Party organization, mobilized the Mexican American vote, and fielded candidates to dislodge Anglo officials. The group's most celebrated success took place in Crystal City when Peña and other PASO volunteers helped organize La Raza Unida. In 1963 La Raza Unida launched Crystal City's "first uprising" when the city's first Mexican American mayor and city council were elected (Shockley 1979). It was a heady beginning. PASO's rapid formation and membership rolls impressed political observers. At the height of its power, PASO claimed to have chapters in over seventy Texas counties and a membership of 20,000 (Arnold Garcia 2000).

PASO's electoral victories in South Texas convinced its leaders that their strategy of ethnic mobilization was the only way to break the political deadlock in Texas. The problems facing Mexican Americans, they argued, not only were linked to a lack of racial representation in public office but were deeply rooted in a structure of social bias and economic domination. As Albert Peña explained, they would use government to root out institutionalized racism: "we want laws that will raise the wages of farm workers and workers in industry. We want jobs that will pay enough to feed, clothe and house our families, and let us send our children to school. We want equal job opportunities. We intend to have them" (S. Long 1964).

PASO public meetings reinforced the sense of accomplishment. Its first annual convention in 1962 attracted over 200 delegates from 30 counties, most of whom had been active in the ¡Viva Kennedy! clubs. The historic gathering attracted 24 Democratic and Republican candidates for public office. One declared that he had arrived "hat in hand, asking your backing," while others clumsily mingled with the delegates mispronouncing names like González as "Gan-SAIL-ez" or Martínez as "Mar-ti-NEZ." PASO's most important symbolic achievement was a visit by Texas governor Price Daniel, who followed suit by referring to PASO president Albert Peña as Mr. "Piña," the word for pineapple ("Latin Group Split" 1962).

Under Peña's leadership, PASO was a hybrid organization, part social movement and part Democratic Party interest group. Unlike the ¡Viva Kennedy! clubs, however, PASO was an independent organization with an open-ended mandate to articulate Mexican American political interests in the electoral sphere. PASO's 1962 convention was a highly contentious and deeply divided assembly. The members agreed on the problems facing the community, but differences over strategy arose almost immediately. Incumbent governor Price Daniel, liberal challenger Don Yarborough, and John Connally, Lyndon Johnson's former assistant, all appealed to different individuals and factions within PASO. Some activists wanted to endorse Governor Daniel because they had worked with him in the past. Others argued for Don Yarborough, the strong liberal candidate, whose policy preferences aligned more closely with those of the Mexican American voter. Still others endorsed John Connally, the candidate with close ties to Vice President Johnson, thereby providing the state with a direct contact to the White House (Ignacio García 2002: 240–241). PASO members believed that they had a rare opportunity to influence the course of the gubernatorial election, and emotions ran high. After a protracted and bitter fight PASO delegates endorsed conservative Price Daniel, a sitting governor whose past outreach to Mexican American voters was little more than an afterthought.

Endorsing a segregationist governor may have been an optimal political choice for a Democratic Party caucus, but it was an incomprehensible act for a Mexican American social movement organization. In his first campaign for governor in 1956 Daniel invested little time and thought in the minority vote. At one point his Spanish campaign flyers were so poorly written that he was advised to get help from someone familiar with the language (Guerra 1956). Daniel stunned a PASO screening committee by claiming that he was unaware of any inequalities between Anglos and Mexican Americans. He admitted that the state failed to give Mexican Americans equitable representation in state government but said that his administration was willing to reverse the problem if he was reelected

(Cuellar 1969: 47). After receiving PASO's endorsement, he hired a full-time Mexican American campaign worker who kept in close touch with PASO activists, sending them poll lists and voter registration forms for areas where Mexican American voters were concentrated. They were also given 200,000 Spanish-language flyers explaining the link between PASO and candidate Daniel (Daniel Campaign 1962).

A deeply conservative party and the ambitions of the politicians who made their careers in its structure trapped PASO. The group was bound by the need to protect and defend group interests, but what constituted group interests was hotly debated. Some PASO members were dismayed by the group's endorsement of Price Daniel, while others felt that they had no other choice. The most liberal candidate, Don Yarborough, did not even campaign for Mexican American votes, declaring that he could win without them. Vice President Johnson's favored candidate, John Connally, was openly antagonistic toward PASO. Governor Daniel's supporters held that the best strategy would be to gain some recognition by demonstrating their capacity to deliver a huge bloc of voters (G. C. Garcia 1969: 20–23, 26). Their hope was that some concrete benefits would result from supporting Daniel. Ed Idar argued against endorsing the most liberal candidate in the election because it had always failed:

> we had already been supporting the liberal movement in Texas for years. We had started out with Yarborough in '52 and lost with him. We lost with him in '54. We lost with him again in '56 . . . Then Henry González ran in '58 for governor. And we lost with him. We supported Henry again in '61 in the special Senate race . . . and we lost again. So we have been faithful to the liberal movement, but we had lost consistently. We finally decided in '62 we were going to consider everybody—liberals, moderates, and conservatives . . . We figured we might be able to get at least part of the things we hoped to get for our people. (Idar 1969: 25–26)

In the end PASO's gambit came to naught. Governor Daniel lost the Democratic primary election, finishing behind both John Connally and Don Yarborough. PASO did not endorse a candidate in the primary runoff but hoped to recoup some of its credibility by supporting John Connally in the general election (Pycior 1997: 134).

PASO's cost-benefit calculation infuriated activists who wanted the group to function as a civil rights or social movement organization. The most prominent member of this camp was University of Texas professor George I. Sánchez, who stormed out of PASO's 1962 convention in protest when he failed to convince other delegates to support Don Yarborough (Idar 1969). He was angry that an organization representing Mexican Americans would even consider supporting Price Daniel or John Connally, who treated Mexican Americans "like dirt" (Sánchez 1962a). Others echoed this sentiment, pointing out that PASO members "must never forget that we have preached unity on principle, on dignity, on respect, on responsibility. Price Daniel does not have political integrity and honesty and never will" (P. Montemayor 1962).

George Sánchez was further incensed when PASO endorsed the Democratic nominee John Connally in the general election, a man he called "LBJ's stooge." He accused those who supported Connally of a breach of racial solidarity. He pointed out that PASO members represented every civil rights organization in the state and were obliged to form a united front against a hostile Anglo establishment. Sánchez expected disagreements within PASO but believed that ethnic attachments were a beacon, a principled guide to decision making in the political arena (G. Sánchez ca. 1962). He was deeply troubled by the political expediency he witnessed at PASO's convention and the resulting pact with politicians who had long records of animosity toward Mexican Americans (G. Sánchez 1961). Supporting one candidate over another for marginal advantage, he said, made PASO nothing more than another interest group. Connally was a known entity: those who voted to support Connally needed to accept responsibility for what they did. As Sánchez put it, "díme con quien andas y te diré quien eres [tell me what company you keep and I will tell you who you are]" (G. Sánchez 1962d).

Abandoning ethno-racial politics in favor of electoral strategizing struck Sánchez as a dangerous act, given the political and economic injustices suffered by most Mexican Americans. After PASO's endorsement of Price Daniel, Sánchez sent a tersely worded letter to Hector Garcia charging the American GI Forum leader with hypocrisy. He said that the endorsement contradicted everything that the two of them had worked for on behalf of their people. He went on to say that they would probably not "live to see the day when the *Mexicanos* get a square deal in Texas. If we do not, it is going to be in large part because of the mistaken political tactic of going along with the traditional winners. Have you forgotten that you fought these very people because of their neglect of the *Mexicano*?" (G. Sánchez 1962d). Although Sánchez was disturbed by PASO's endorsement of a conservative governor, others were equally frustrated by PASO's lack of political discipline. In defense of the Governor Daniel endorsement, Ed Idar leveled his own charges against activists like Sánchez. Idar asserted that Mexican Americans benefited more from solidarity than from ideological consistency and lamented the possibility that ethnic identity might ultimately deny Mexican Americans a seat at the Democratic Party's decision-making table. He further accused those in Sánchez's camp of blindly following labor and white liberals, who had abandoned Mexican Americans in the past. Idar noted that these were "the same people who would not endorse Henry González for Governor in 1958, who planted Maury Maverick in the special senate race against Henry in 1959 and who killed DOT in 1960" (Idar 1963).

The debate revolved around the question of racial exclusion and whether or not Mexican Americans possessed identities and interests that overlapped with those of the Anglo majority. George Sánchez understood the idea of building alliances and extracting concessions from gubernatorial candidates but did not think that it would work for Mexican Americans. PASO's best strategy, he argued, was to serve as a moral force, a vehicle for articulating ethnic grievances and exposing the gap between the rhetoric of equality and the harsh reality of race relations in Texas. Sánchez's choice for the 1962 Democratic nomination was Don Yarborough, a strong liberal that most observers believed was unlikely to defeat his well-funded conservative opponents. Group interests, he argued, should stand above party loyalty. Sánchez felt that party identification was meaningless and that candidates of either party could serve Mexican American interests: "if a conservative Democrat, or a Republican, gave evidence that he would perform this, I'd be for him" (G. Sánchez 1962a). He believed that it was better to lose with a candidate committed to social change than to win the marginal degree of access that conservatives like John Connally offered (G. Sánchez 1962b). Partisan solidarity was more compelling in theory than in practice for Mexican Americans because they had no standing in the polity. In a letter to PASO's leaders, Sánchez tried to persuade them that falling in line behind a winning candidate yielded little in an atmosphere poisoned by racism:

> You talk about the will of the majority. The will of the majority gave us Pappy Lee O'Daniel, Jester, Shivers, Johnson, ad nauseum. Look at the local politics of predominantly Latin counties or regions. They gave us Rogers Kelly in the State Senate for years, they give us Joe Kilgore in the U.S. Congress. Should I go on? (G. Sánchez 1962c)

Idar thought that this was a reckless position, especially because Sánchez did not offer any practical alternatives. He was just as frustrated with Anglo officials who ignored Mexican American voters and paid little attention to their issues (Idar 1961). He worked for many years to find solutions to segregation, education, wages and salaries, employment, the problems of migrant workers, and other forms of discrimination (Idar 1955b). Idar found Sánchez's failure to face up to the reality of Texas politics exasperating and fired back a letter to the professor charging him with elitism. He pointed out that Mexican Americans faced serious and difficult choices in the political world, where the possible was not the same as the desired. Finally, he pointed out that PASO members worked long hours against formidable opponents and that "only someone deep in the ivory tower can so blithely shrug off the attitude of rule or ruin which you so recently displayed, forgetting years of friendship and accusing old associates of selling out" (Idar 1962).

Idar knew that Anglo liberals had reneged many times on their political debts to the Mexican American voter, but this was not always the case. U.S. senator Ralph Yarborough would have lost his 1964 senatorial race without their support and when in office worked to expand civil rights protection and social service programs in Texas (Pycior 1993). In the forty-three Mexican American precincts canvassed by PASO, Yarborough won by a margin of 24,000 votes. In the 14 black districts Yarborough's margin of victory was 10,000 votes. In Bexar County 29 percent of the voters gave Yarborough 44 percent of the total vote and 12 percent of his victory margin ("New Power" 1964: 4). Here the connection between electoral support for Ralph Yarborough and interest representation was direct, but high levels of poverty and discrimination obscured the link and the progress it represented. The danger in this scenario was that Mexican Americans could be persuaded to vote against their interests via irrational ethnic appeals articulated by people like George Sánchez (Idar 1960/1961). Gus Garcia struggled with the same ethno-ideological conundrum but believed that at the end of the day the Democratic Party held the key to social progress. He wrote in a letter to Senator Yarborough:

> I firmly believe that with a complete victory of liberalism in Texas, the problems of the little people will be solved; therefore, the Mejicano's problems will be solved and my twenty years of fighting for the Mejicano will be [rewarded]. I am a liberal Democrat first and a Mejicano second! Still, I am concerned about your future political campaign, because there are a number of our Mexican-American leadership in Texas who are Meji-

canos first and loyal Democrats second. As you probably know, there is a tremendous effort being made by the opposition to corral the emerging "Sleeping Giant" and it is up to you, me, and others like us to help him get his bearings and sort of guide him in the right direction. If we fail this giant will crush us all. (Gus Garcia 1963)

Gus Garcia and Ed Idar knew that liberalism could generate change but worried that the "sleeping giant" would be influenced by ethnic dema-goguery. Moreover, most Anglo Democrats were still mired in the politics of the past. As early as the mid-1960s the Texas State Democratic Executive Committee found that Democratic vote totals were declining and that the party had only a tenuous hold on a majority of the electorate. Party leaders were aware of the resources and energy that Republicans were investing in the state but dedicated little effort to reenergizing their base (State Democratic Executive Committee 1964a). The party did not even engage in outreach efforts to minority voters when civil rights activism was reaching its peak (Texas Democratic Party 1964). Indeed the party leadership appeared content to ignore the long-term impact of current demographic and political changes. In 1966 the Texas State Democratic Executive Committee passed resolutions on traffic safety, outdoor recreation, and consumer credit. The same committee overwhelmingly voted down resolutions to raise teacher salaries and increase the farm labor minimum wage to $1.25 per hour (Democratic Committee on Platform and Resolutions 1966).

From Idar and Garcia's perspective, decoupling voting behavior from ethnic solidarity was a difficult but necessary political project. Conservatives had a secure lock on the state party, and even the most liberal Anglo leaders were reluctant to risk their political future by openly identifying with minority voters and their issues. Their disheartening task was to create alliances with liberals and then negotiate with conservative Democrats who did not take their issues seriously. Mexican Americans were the most disadvantaged group in Texas, but ethnically defined social movements would confine their influence to limited areas of the state and ultimately undermine the task of coalition building. Idar and Garcia further argued that ethnic claims in electoral politics could destroy the possibility of achieving descriptive or substantive representation. Given the high level of racial tension in Texas at the time, civil rights organizations were ineffective vehicles for furthering the interests of their community. Indeed any endorsement bestowed upon aspiring politicians by these groups or their leaders constituted a "kiss of death" for their candidacies (Idar 1960/1961).

Race, Partisanship, and the Decline of PASO

A negotiated partisan identity with all its compromises and limitations proved to be more enduring than racial solidarity for Mexican Americans. PASO's design as a social movement and party caucus was unworkable even at its most influential point. Its members agreed that Mexican American social and economic problems had reached a crisis point and that PASO had a mandate to find an appropriate solution ("P.A.S.O. Political Association" n.d.). But the group did not have a well-developed ideology or blueprint for political action. As a result PASO was unable to contain what one reporter called the "sloshing tides" of personality conflicts, personal ambition, and ideological differences ("Struggle for PASO" 1963). Albert Peña favored disruptive tactics and an adversarial position toward the Democratic Party in order to force concessions. Civil rights leaders argued that PASO's goal should be social and economic integration through participation in government. American GI forum president Hector Garcia endorsed that view and argued that good citizenship was "more important than candidates. They come and go every two years . . . we're Americans, first, and Americans, second. We are Texans too" (E. Johnson 1964). Finally, some argued that PASO should become a caucus within the Democratic Party and sponsor candidates for public office.

Those who believed that racism was receding called for a deeper engagement with the Democratic Party. Tony Bonilla argued that PASO should adopt the broadest definition of its goals and purposes. Adopting the party vernacular, he said that Texas liberals could be "conservative, moderate, or liberal-liberal." Bonilla condemned Albert Peña's organizing drives in Crystal City for their confrontational tactics and the opposition they generated from Mexican American business owners and professionals ("The Struggle for PASO" 1963). He argued that Peña and others involved in PASO's South Texas campaigns were "brainwashed" to believe that Anglos were their enemies (López 1963). In 1964 Albert Fuentes Jr. echoed this position when he ran for the Democratic Party's gubernatorial nomination. His platform was a laundry list of liberal policies: raising the minimum wage, greater unemployment compensation, and increased public works spending. Fuentes endorsed the expansion of civil rights protections but also claimed that racism was little more than a misunderstanding: "When an individual takes the time to visit with his neighbor, he'll find out, 'By golly, he's a human being, after all.' Racism is nothing but a failure to understand one's fellow man, that's all" ("Albert Fuentes" 1964).

Albert Peña, in contrast, saw new opportunities for political gains by tapping into Mexican American discontent with the Texas Democratic Party if PASO kept its militant stance and tactics (McCrory 1965). PASO was bent on disrupting any reconciliation with conservatives, beginning with a campaign to oust Governor John Connally from office ("Anti-Connally Move" 1967; McCrory 1967). At the 1967 PASO convention they charged the governor with defrauding the people of Texas. They were incensed by his use of the Texas Rangers violently to break agricultural strikes in South Texas and deny farmworkers freedom of assembly (Banks 1967a). In retaliation they vowed to damage the prospects of politicians like senatorial candidate Waggoner Carr, a Democrat on record opposing farmworker unions as well as all of the Johnson administration's civil rights initiatives (Associated Press 1966).

Albert Peña believed that membership in the Texas Democratic Party required too many unacceptable concessions. His intention was to advance the status of Mexican American politics, to lift "the cactus curtain. We are going to put an end to Jim Crow in a sombrero hat. We can do without the 'Tio Tomases,' we're through with the vendidos. We don't need a 'patron' and we don't need anyone to tell us how to vote" ("The Struggle for PASO" 1963). He said that the Mexican American voter would no longer fall into place behind a charismatic candidate "too simpatico for the 'Raza' to resist" and threatened to abandon the Democrats and begin working for "third and fourth parties" (Peña et al. 1969).

Over time Peña and his followers came to dominate PASO politics as more conservative members left the organization. In 1967 PASO passed resolutions calling for the abolition of the Texas Rangers and the defeat of Democratic governor John Connally, who refused to support a state minimum wage and farmworker rights to bargain collectively (Banks 1967a; "PASO Backing Kennedy" 1968). Speakers at PASO's 1968 convention called for equal civil rights, a higher minimum wage, better education, and an end to "Ranger brutality." The general membership also endorsed Robert F. Kennedy's bid for the Democratic presidential nomination ("PASO Backing Kennedy" 1968). During its 1970 convention, the group urged Mexican Americans to oppose Governor Preston Smith

Photo 3.1. Attorney General Robert Kennedy arrives at the airport in Chicago as guest speaker for the National American G.I. Forum Convention in 1964. Dr. Hector P. Garcia Papers, Special Collections and Archives, Texas A&M University–Corpus Christi, Mary and Jeff Bell Library. *Left to right*: Mr. Ramos, Mr. Duran, attorney general Robert Kennedy, James De Anda, Dr. Hector P. Garcia, and Mr. Ponce.

and senatorial candidate Lloyd Bentsen Jr. in the upcoming general election. They passed another resolution urging support of La Raza Unida Party in South Texas and came just short of endorsing GOP gubernatorial candidate Paul Eggers and senatorial candidate George Bush Sr. ("PASO Opposes Smith, Bentsen" 1970).

To demonstrate the depth of its discontent with the Democrats, PASO invited Republican officeholders to speak to its membership. In 1966 PASO refused to endorse Waggoner Carr, the Democrat running against Republican senator John Tower, and was proud of the working relationship that it established with Tower ("PASO Names Fuentes Successor"

1966). Some PASO leaders actively campaigned for Tower and promised to continue attacking "phony Democrats" (Ford 1967). Later they
boasted that they had played a major role in engineering Carr's defeat
in the senatorial race ("Abolish Rangers" 1967; "Connally Discontent"
1967; Conde 1968).

Under Albert Peña's leadership, PASO cast aside any pretense of partisan loyalty. PASO activists made appearances at Republican Party func-
tions, praised its growth, and called for a competitive two-party system
(McCrory 1966a; "PASO Firms Up Independence" 1966). Republicans
were happy to dislodge as many Mexican American votes from the Democratic column as they could. Paul Eggers, Republican candidate for governor, vigorously courted the Mexican American vote and argued that
"in 1966, many Mexicans helped advance the two-party state by supporting the reelection of Senator John Tower . . . As governor, my door will
always be open to you" ("PASO Backing Kennedy" 1968).

Albert Peña believed that the Democratic Party would change only if it
was threatened with defeat (Ignacio García 2000: 157). The group soon
went on the offensive against all major Democratic politicians. In 1970
the organization passed a resolution opposing the candidacy of Governor
Preston Smith and senatorial candidate Lloyd Bentsen. It condemned the
governor for firing his Mexican American aide and urged support of La
Raza Unida candidates in South Texas ("Group Votes" 1970; "Smith and
Bentsen" 1970). PASO criticized liberal senator Ralph Yarborough for
not having enough Mexican Americans on his staff (Yarborough 1969).
By the end of the decade all Democratic politicians were under attack
by Albert Peña, who declared: "I have made no commitments to campaign for anyone this November election except for La Raza Unida Party.
Where that party is running candidates—in Hidalgo, Dimmit, La Salle,
and Zavala counties—I shall do what I can to help them get elected. As
long as [the Democratic] party is the only viable party in this state it will
give us governors like Shivers, Connally, and Smith, and it will defeat
men like Ralph Yarborough with hacks like Bentsen" (Peña 1970b). Peña's
frustration was reflected in his increasingly strident rhetoric that called for
racial unity and recognized that Chicanos had a "unique past and a unique
destiny" (Peña 1970a).

Peña's threats and deep involvement with Chicano politics in South
Texas ramped up the anti–Democratic Party rhetoric but alienated PASO's
more conservative followers (Montejano 1987: 283–284). He argued
that the future of the Democratic Party in Texas lay in an electoral coalition of Mexican Americans, blacks, organized labor, and independent lib-

erals (McCrory 1963). However, few accepted the claim that organizing a Chicano third party in South Texas was consistent with the aims and purposes of the Democratic Party. Opponents also failed to see the logic in helping Republican party candidates or running for governor on the Republican ticket, as Albert Fuentes did in 1966 ("Fuentes on Call" 1966; "Fuentes Receptive" 1966; "GOP Boss" 1966). By the late 1960s PASO's membership and influence were in steep decline.

Texas Democrats and the Politics of Legitimation

Democratic Party leaders were slow to take the rise of the Republican Party seriously. The State Democratic Executive Committee (SDEC) concluded that the close margin of victory for the Kennedy-Johnson ticket in 1960 was a cause for deep concern. Moreover, the committee believed that the Republican Party did a better job of mobilizing its base and persuaded many conservative Democratic voters to defect (State Democratic Executive Committee 1964a). The party leadership was increasingly alarmed by the prospect of losing control of state government. In subsequent years the problem for Democrats only became worse. In a 1968 report the chair of the SDEC summed up the party's recent history:

> In 1952 . . . the Republican presidential candidate received a majority of the votes in Texas. In 1961, . . . a Republican was chosen in a special election by the slender margin of less than 11,000 votes. Last fall, in six special elections to fill vacancies in our Texas House of Representatives, the Republicans won three of them. Today, Texas has one Republican in the U.S. Senate, three Texas Congressmen, two Texas Senators and eight State representatives. These challenges may not be pleasant but I believe they should be faced-up to now before they become even more unpleasant or even fatal. (Baum 1968)

But the growing threat did not move the Democratic Party to reenergize its base by following the national party's lead. The state party's 1964 platform made no mention of civil rights or an expanded social welfare system. Rather, it vaguely endorsed the idea of equal opportunity in civil society "with respect for merit, worth . . . and reward based on intelligence, industry and initiative" ("Platform of the Democratic Party" 1964). In 1966 the SDEC refused to endorse increased funding for public education or a more generous worker's compensation program. Labor leaders asked the SDEC for a resolution supporting a minimum wage for farm labor, arguing that current wages for farmworkers were insufficient to provide the basic necessities of life and that "shameful" levels of poverty in South Texas needed to be eradicated. The SDEC voted the resolution down (State Democratic Executive Committee 1966). The only allusion to civil rights in the state party's Declaration of Principles was a condemnation of "irresponsible demagogues [who] disseminate doctrines of discord and disorder in the name of justice. Those who preach civil disobedience and the flouting of law and order undermine the very foundations of our freedom" (Texas Democratic Party 1966).

This was a standard response from the Texas Democratic Party. The SDEC chair who issued the report on Republican Party gains created recruitment committees for youth, the elderly, and women but none on discrimination or civil rights. At the same time the state Democratic Party could not ignore the aggressive organizing by activists like Albert Peña. It could diffuse charges of racism, however, by issuing symbolic pledges and incorporating carefully selected individuals into its ranks. Texas governor John Connally was the first to employ this strategy successfully on a large scale. Elected in 1962, he came from the same conservative tradition as his predecessors, aggressively defending oil and agricultural concerns while limiting the growth of state educational and social services. Like governors before him, Connally's civil rights agenda was little more than an acknowledgment of state and national currents. He promised equal treatment before the law and the same economic opportunities for all citizens. He added that economic mobility would come not through an expanded social welfare state but through increased industrialization. He argued for high-quality public education in order to promote equal opportunity and economic advancement based upon ability and capacity. Finally, he pledged to appoint a greater number of Mexican Americans to state boards and commissions (Connally ca. 1962).

Connally's vague commitment to racial equality was at odds with his behavior, especially his attacks against Texas farmworkers. In 1966 farmworkers from the impoverished Rio Grande Valley marched to Austin to protest poor working conditions, violence by the Texas Rangers, and the need for an agricultural minimum wage. Governor Connally and senatorial candidate Waggoner Carr confronted the marchers outside of the Capitol and told them to turn back. Connally refused to meet with them and resolved to oppose a minimum wage for farm labor, in defiance of public opinion on the issue (Byers 1972). He also struck at the most important symbol of the Mexican American civil rights movement: the struggle of farmworkers for a higher standard of living (Belden 1966). Connally would go on to become one of the most popular governors in postwar Texas according to public opinion polls, but not among Mexican Americans (Belden 1968b).

John Connally presided over a state party under attack by PASO, the Kennedy Administration's civil rights agenda, and an energized Republican Party (Banks 1963). Connally's senior political advisors thought that the time had arrived for the governor to bolster his standing among Mexican American voters. To counter the widely held view that his administration was biased, they urged him to appoint conservative Mexican Americans to positions in his administration. They said that he could safely ignore PASO's radicals but that he needed to reward Mexican Americans who had supported him during the primary and general election. State Democratic Executive Committee member John Peace put it bluntly: "we need very badly to appoint one of our Mexican supporters to some type of board or commission." He recommended people like Dr. E. T. Ximenes, who was considered particularly effective during Connally's campaign, especially "when certain of the Latin elements would become volatile and flighty." But Peace also warned against tokenism. He pointed out that Connally could choose from a large pool of individuals capable of ably serving his administration, thereby avoiding those who were unknown to his coalition members or who supported his opponents (Peace 1963).

John Connally proved to be an agile and astute politician when it came to engaging Mexican American discontent. He agreed to start integrating his administration and the Democratic Party and seized the initiative by reaching out to his Mexican American allies. Despite Connally's opposition to farmworker organizing and other issues of importance to Mexican Americans, he knew that PASO's militancy was just one manifestation of Mexican American discontent. He also knew that he could increase racial representation in his administration without altering his agenda. In other words, if Connally needed to integrate his administration, the change would take place on his terms.

The vetting process proceeded with care. Not surprisingly, the people that his aides recommended for appointments were not the firebrands of PASO but moderate voices, some of whom were unknown in civil rights circles. When the Democratic Executive Committee met in San Antonio after Connally's inauguration, conservatives like Lalo Solis and Humberto Quintanilla were asked to attend. The Bexar County Democratic chair invited all local "big wheels," but longtime activists like Albert Peña were "conspicuous by their absence" (Bomar 1963). Instead Connally built relationships and solicited opinions from old-guard civil rights organizations like LULAC (Connally 1964; T. Bonilla 1964; W. Bonilla 1964). He invited their leaders to the governor's mansion and solicited their recommendations for appointments (Connally 1964; T. Bonilla 1964; W. Bonilla 1964). When appointments were decided, Connally was careful to tap into a pool of moderate community activists with records of community service that his staff considered responsible and who would not embarrass the administration with disruptive behavior (Looney 1966). The governor also projected a conciliatory image by speaking before Mexican American Optimist Clubs, Chambers of Commerce, Rotary Clubs, Knights of Columbus, Kiwanis Clubs, and other groups not normally engaged in the electoral process (Connally 1963). Finally, he solicited the cooperation of Mexican American elected officials to boost the number of Mexican Americans applying for state jobs (Connally 1963).

A little more than a year after taking office, John Connally named twenty-five Mexican Americans to state regulatory commissions ("Latin American Appointees" 1964). The list grew to forty the following year. It included professionals, business owners, and attorneys with deep involvement in community affairs. Some held advanced degrees from schools like Harvard Medical School, the University of Southern California, the University of Texas, and Southern Methodist University ("Latin American Appointees" ca. 1965). In the spring of 1965 the governor appointed Carlos C. Cadena, a professor of law at St. Mary's University, as an associate justice of the Fourth Court of Civil Appeals. The appointment delighted Mexican Americans in South Texas, who saw it as a major sign of recognition and a response to heavy ethnic lobbying and negotiations ("Laredoans Pleased" 1965). South Texas attorneys, politicians, and Henry González lobbied the governor when the court of appeals vacancy first appeared. They touted Cadena's character, ability, and contribution to the community as a valuable asset to the state (H. González 1964; Kazen 1965; Raba 1965; "Victorious Party Leaders" ca. 1965). As the Democratic Executive Committee chair put it, such a decision would be a "good move" politically (Daniels 1965). The appointment earned Connally the gratitude of key Mexican American politicians. Upon Cadena's appointment, Philip Kazen thanked the governor and said that the appointment received "an extremely favorable reaction all up and down the river. We feel that it is not only a meritorious appointment, but one which is an extremely popular one among all Latin Americans of Texas" (Kazen 1965). John Connally capped his targeted appointments by selecting Roy

Barrera to fill out a vacancy as Texas secretary of state ("Mom's Counsel" 1968; "The New Secretary of State" 1968).

The long-term working relationship between Lyndon Johnson and John Connally was mutually advantageous for containing ethnic and racial insurgencies. Shortly after Johnson was elected president in 1964, he came under intense pressure to pay closer attention to the problems facing Mexican Americans. The president responded by creating the Inter-Agency Committee on Mexican American Affairs and promised to hold a White House conference (Inter-Agency Committee on Mexican American Affairs 1967). Johnson asked Governor Connally to help him navigate the treacherous waters of Mexican American politics by identifying individuals he could invite to the conference who would take their work seriously and not discredit the president with disruptive behavior (Looney 1966). The conference had potential advantages for both men. Johnson could avoid a further escalation of problems with Mexican Americans and solidify his ties with Mexican American elected officials (McPherson 1966). For his part, Governor Connally could build bridges to the most conservative Mexican American activists and reward them with an appointment to a prestigious national conference. To that end the governor solicited nominations from Optimist Clubs, Mexican Chambers of Commerce, Rotary Clubs, the Knights of Columbus, the Texas Good Neighbor Commission, and Kiwanis Clubs. He made sure to broadcast the message of inclusive politics and asked his political allies to forward names of individuals from all regions of the state (Drake 1966a).

The planned conference gave Mexican American activists a national platform for the first time. Once it began, all participants would be free of the president's control. Thus a heightened sense of concern among the president's advisors permeated the selection process. An effort was made to find people invested in their community and careers. Professionals, business owners, elected officials, attorneys, bankers, high school teachers, and doctors dominated the lists forwarded to the president for review (de la Garza 1963b; Garrett 1966). The safest choices were Connally's current political appointees, veteran Democratic Party activists, and leaders of friendly organizations like LULAC and the American GI Forum (Connally 1966; Robles 1966; "White House Conference" ca. 1966). Proven Democratic stalwarts like congressmen Henry B. González and Kika de la Garza were asked to nominate individuals that they believed would advance the Johnson administration's agenda (North 1966a). Names were circulated between the Texas governor's office and the White House, and

Photo 3.2. *Left to right*: Dr. Hector P. Garcia, President Lyndon B. Johnson, American G.I. Forum chair Augustín Flores, and Corky González from Colorado pose at the White House Lawn. Dr. Hector P. Garcia Papers, Special Collections and Archives, Texas A&M University–Corpus Christi, Mary and Jeff Bell Library.

background checks were conducted on all potential participants. Some were suspect from the onset because of their temperament and political ideology, but every person received careful scrutiny (Califano 1966a; E. P. Foley 1966; North 1966c). Ray Pearson of El Paso assured them that his list contained individuals who were active supporters of the governor or who would at least be neutral (R. Pearson 1966). The individuals on the list forwarded to the governor were described with terms like "straight thinking, conscientious individuals, men of the highest caliber," people who would give the president or governor "no cause for embarrassment" (Drake 1966b). Governor Connally's allies shared the president's worries and warned against inviting "militants" lest they build "a political Frankenstein which, at the slightest provocation, will turn against him" (Kazen 1966).

The White House staff members were very careful to identify enthusiastic supporters of the president (Ramos 1966). They wanted participants whose criticism of the administration was restrained, who could offer practical solutions, and who had credibility in the Mexican American community. Radical community activists threatened to boycott the conference and sponsor their own "Brown House" conference where attacks on the president would be severe and well publicized. Hence the president's staff went to great lengths to assemble a politically safe group of participants but was also careful not to list only token representatives. For presidential aide John Macy this was a recurring problem: "I have been searching for individuals who are respected in both the Mexican and Anglo communities, and who are neither so well assimilated that they can be accused of bein [*sic*] an Uncle Tom, nor so militant and vitriolic that they cannot bring to the Commission a rational attitude" (Macy 1966). Macy sought individuals like LULAC national president Alfred J. Hernández, a well-respected leader who was also a "100% Johnson man" (Macy 1968).

Governor Connally helped the president find individuals like Hernández by giving him an extensive list of his own appointees, elected officials, professionals, civil rights leaders, and Democratic Party officials (Connally 1966). By carefully engaging Mexican American critics of his administration in Texas, Connally also aided the president's measured response to an increasingly "restless Spanish-surname community" (Califano 1966a). Their concessions were carefully calibrated and sometimes cynically administered in order to maximize Mexican American support for the Democratic Party. For example, the person recruited to head the administration's civil rights work in the Southwest had to be well known and "carry a resounding title" (North 1966b). Two Texans, GI Forum activist Vicente Ximenes and former LULAC national president Oscar Laurel, were particularly attractive because of their willingness to moderate their group's criticism of the administration. Regardless of the administration's motives, Mexican American Democrats jumped at the opportunity. Lobbying by civil rights organizations on Laurel's behalf was so intense that one presidential aide proposed that he and a colleague "form a club. This club could be called the 'Let's Show Administration Appreciation of the Loyal Mexican-American Groups by giving Oscar Laurel a Presidential Appointment'!" (Nobles 1967). Laurel was later appointed to the National Transportation Safety Board (Wirtz et al. 1967).

These appointments went to mainstream Democrats who were happy to do the party's political work. In the 1960s the Democratic Party could choose from a growing list of experienced leaders like John J. Herrera of Houston, William Bonilla of Corpus Christi, and Oscar Laurel of Laredo, all of whom were party loyalists and former LULAC presidents (Martin 1965). They understood Democratic Party liberalism to be virtually synonymous with civil rights activism. The case of Herrera is instructive in this regard. When inquiring about a position in the Johnson administration, Herrera touted his long history of activism with the Democratic Party. In 1948 he had participated in the senatorial campaigns of James V. Allred and Lyndon B. Johnson. From 1954 to 1958 he was a candidate for the state legislature. He was a member of the ¡Viva Kennedy! clubs in 1960 and led the ¡Viva Johnson! clubs in Harris County. Herrera also held membership in the American GI Forum, the Knights of Columbus, and the Sons of the Republic of Texas and was a scoutmaster in the Boy Scouts of America. In his words, "I have been active in all local, state and national elections since I was twenty (20) years of age. I have taken great pride in my activities on behalf of the community, the state and nation—both for Latin-Americans and Anglo Americans" (Herrera 1966).

These exchanges did not go unnoticed, and some liberals characterized Governor Connally's appointments and recommendations to the Johnson administration as ethnic patronage (Ford 1968). Maury Maverick argued that the governor was not increasing minority representation at all. Instead he was stifling black and Mexican American interests by choosing the most conservative members of the minority community to serve in government (Maverick ca. 1968a). Maverick was correct in arguing that liberals lost ground when the governor played on ideological divisions among Mexican Americans; but, like other politicians, Connally was rewarding his supporters and quashing his ethnic critics. The governor even created some new allies in the process. For example, PASO's loud rejection of John Connally and senatorial candidate Waggoner Carr drew a quick defense of the governor by state representative Tony Bonilla. Bonilla lashed out against PASO's strategy of disruption and its support for Republican candidates. He asserted that if those who operated outside of the statehouse had the opportunity to see how government actually operated they would find that "Governor Connally's programs would indicate and reflect that he has been the most progressive Governor that we have had in the history of our state." Bonilla called Waggoner Carr "a man with fresh ideas, young and vigorous. Voting for a United States Senatorial candidate should not be put on the basis of who can do more for the Americans of Mexican descent, the labor unions, big or small business, but the issue is who can do more for the people of the state of Texas" (T. Bonilla 1966). Two former LULAC presidents urged full support for the Democrat Carr, a remarkable request given his lack of concern for the problems of the poor, his segregationist history, and his hostility toward farmworkers ("Demos for Tower Group" 1966; "Lulac Past President" 1966).

Tony Bonilla's spirited defense of John Connally sprang from a combination of party loyalty and personal philosophy. He was also up for reelection. The first-term state representative faced a strong challenge in the Democratic primary from Al González, a community activist who did not believe that racial interests and party identity were so easily conflated. González was backed by the American GI Forum, and the primary campaign was an acrimonious struggle between visions of race and representation. In his campaign literature Bonilla said that he was a representative of all people and never used his "Spanish name to secure a block vote" (Tony Bonilla Campaign 1966). Bonilla called González the candidate of old-style ethnic politics and a puppet of American GI Forum founder Hector Garcia. He further charged the two men with spreading hate and dissension by framing Texas politics as a struggle between rich and poor (S. Pearson 1966a). Bonilla's campaign literature touted a record of representing all people fairly and impartially (Tony Bonilla Campaign 1966). In turn, González accused Bonilla of "siding with our enemies" (S. Pearson ca. 1966). Al González proudly accepted the support of the old-guard civil rights organization and said that Bonilla's accusations harmed the unity and harmony of the community (H. Garcia et al. 1966; Pearson 1966b). The personal attacks continued on Spanish-language radio stations, where the candidates' political ads disparaged each other's ethnic loyalty, business ethics, and personal integrity (B. Duncan 1966). At one point Bonilla challenged González to "repudiate the smears, hate and falsehoods" of his campaign (S. Pearson 1966a; J. Wood ca. 1966).

Bonilla later characterized the contest as a conflict of personalities, which it was. But the dispute was also about the representation of racial and political interests in government. Mexican American politicians were increasingly free to construct hybrid political identities and were far less accountable to civil rights organizations. The decoupling of electoral politics and social movement organizing gave politicians more freedom to define their racial identity and affiliate with political factions of their own choosing. However, these identities were not just a by-product of social and economic assimilation. Mexican Americans who ran for public office or were appointed to a position in state government and the Democratic Party were building new alliances and support networks. The variation of

Mexican American ethnic identity in state politics was made possible by an expanding network of supporting individuals and groups, all of whom had an interest in shaping the way ethnic identities were articulated.

This dynamic was not a theoretical exercise but an active conflict over values and policy. For example, state senator Joe Bernal, an elected official closely allied with insurgent movements of the 1960s, knew exactly what politicians like John Connally were doing when courting conservative groups and individuals. At one point he was so frustrated with Connally that he called the governor's attitude toward Mexican Americans "insulting" (Bernal 1968). Still, Bernal believed that American society was constantly evolving, embracing new groups and expanding the scope of freedom (Bernal 1970b). He thought that political integration might provoke a backlash in the short run but was far more worried that the suppression of social protest would create a political vacuum readily filled by extremists (Bernal 1969; Bernal ca. 1970). His reputation for angry ethnic confrontation was belied by his support for racial reconciliation. He argued that all Texans had a common multiracial past with "great Texas patriots" like Sam Houston, Francisco Ruiz, Stephen F. Austin, José Antonio Navarro, Lorenzo de Zavala, and others (Bernal 1970a).

As Mexican Americans integrated into the Democratic Party it became clear that associating with social movement organizations like the United Farm Workers Union, PASO, or La Raza Unida would hamper their political careers. Albert Peña refused to compromise with party conservatives. In 1966 he called the choice between Republican John Tower and Democrat Waggoner Carr in their U.S. Senate race a choice between tumors and cancer (McCrory 1966b). When Peña spoke at the 1968 National Democratic Convention, he warned that Mexican Americans were Roosevelt and Kennedy liberals who were frustrated with the southern conservatives in control of the state party. He predicted violence in the street and defeat for the Democrats at the national level, telling the delegates that John Connally was so unpopular that he was booed off the stage at his last appearance before a large Mexican American audience (McCrory 1968; Peña 1968). Peña and PASO activists condemned both parties and the short-term politically convenient relationships that they developed with Mexican American elected officials and voters ("Smith and Bentsen Opposed" 1970). Political representation in the two major parties consisted of hand-picked "house Mexicans" (Peña et al. 1969).

This type of ethnic agitation yielded diminishing returns for Peña in a rapidly changing political landscape. Leaders like congressman Henry González derided Peña for working outside the party structure and supporting Republican candidates for public office. He pointed out the folly of trying to create change by supporting Republican politicians who opposed civil rights legislation and labor protection. González scoffed at the idea that support for Republicans who opposed integration and voted against every measure from minimum wage to antipoverty programs would somehow result in gains for the poor and racial minorities (H. González 1967c). Peña's reasoning made no sense at all to González: "If there are those who believe that voting and working for a reactionary will bring progress, and there seem to be a few, I can only feel sorry for them. As for me, I prefer to stand by the party that has helped, and not just offered empty promises" (González 1966b).

While Albert Peña and others were deriding Waggoner Carr, González, Kika de la Garza, and the rest of the Texas Democratic congressional delegation joined President Johnson and all other major Democratic elected officials in endorsing Carr's candidacy (W. Davis 1966; K. de la Garza et al. 1966). In exchange for their support, Henry González wanted two things from Carr. First, he wanted an assurance that Carr would support basic Democratic Party policies such as the minimum wage, aid to cities, environmental protection, and housing (H. González 1966c). Second, González wanted Carr's assurance that he would support the Democratic Party and its leaders. Carr promised to do both of those things and put this in writing (W. Carr 1966; Sinkin 1966). Albert Peña was correct that politicians like Connally and Carr alienated the Mexican American voter. An independent poll of 4,700 Mexican American voters in 1967 found overwhelming Mexican American support (91 percent) for the farmworker cause. Citing the governor's refusal to raise the minimum wage, his hostility to farmworkers, and the use of the Texas Rangers to break up farmworker strikes, 62 percent thought that Connally was anti-Mexican. They also rejected Waggoner Carr for the same reason during his 1966 campaign for the Senate (Cen-Tex Advertising 1967). Henry González knew where Connally and Carr stood on these issues but argued that they still merited support from other Democrats because they strengthened the alliance and made public officials like himself better able to represent Mexican American interests.

Incorporation splintered racial and ethnic politics in Texas. Ethnic identity alone generated few if any practical strategies for activists to pursue and often resulted in alliances that stood the logic of group loyalty on its head. For example, during its 1967 convention, the League of United Latin American Citizens honored Governor Connally and asked him to deliver the keynote address. Outside of the convention hall, five hundred farmworkers booed and picketed the event. Demonstrators wanted an increase in the state minimum wage and the removal of the Texas Rangers from Starr County, where strikes were underway (Garces 1967). While United Farm Worker union leader Cesar Chavez spoke to the crowd and asked for the organization's support, LULAC members kept demonstrators out of the hall, ostensibly for not purchasing tickets or being improperly dressed (Garces ca. 1967; Gray ca. 1967).

The Last Revolt: La Raza Unida Party

The time between John Connally's departure from public office in 1969 and the election of the first Republican governor of Texas in 1978 was a period of transition in Texas race relations. Two conservative Democratic governors, Preston Smith (1969–1973) and Dolph Briscoe (1973–1979), served when Chicano Movement radicalism reached its peak in Texas. Smith spent his two terms fending off attacks by Chicano movement groups before he was voted out of office under a cloud because of his involvement in a stock fraud scandal. He was succeeded by Briscoe, who was narrowly reelected in 1972 when La Raza Unida Party won 6 percent of the popular vote, almost tilting the election in favor of the Republican Party. It was one of the most turbulent periods in modern Texas history, as racial incorporation continued at a steady pace.

Preston Smith began his first term by offering to work with the Mexican American legislative delegation and soliciting their help in crafting legislation (P. Smith 1970). The gesture came from a man who had no history of outreach to minority representatives and was apparently unaware of the racial upheavals that had preceded his election. Smith was genuinely surprised when he came under heavy attack by Chicano Movement radicals and by the numbers of protesters at his public appearances. Unlike John Connally, Smith did not understand the civil rights movement and blundered from one disastrous episode to another (Aguirre 1970; "Smith's Ex-Aide Backs Foe" 1970). Instead of building bridges to conservative Mexican Americans, the governor went on the offensive against demonstrators and threatened to cut off funding for social service programs that they favored (L. Cárdenas 1969). The governor ordered the Texas Department of Public Safety to monitor the activities of Chicano Movement organizations that he deemed subversive, including PASO, the United Farm Workers, and the Colorado Migrant Council ("DPS Officer Reports" 1970). Student protests, farmworker organizing, and activities of the civil rights establishment were also carefully watched. His office was especially interested in the activities of La Raza Unida Party (Carl n.d.).

Preston Smith possessed few of his predecessor's skills and had difficulty conducting business with the most moderate community activists. Early in his administration, Mexican American civic leaders asked the new governor to meet with them in San Antonio to discuss the slow pace of economic change. The gathering quickly spun out of control when the governor arrived late: some audience members demanded an apology and others called him a racist (McCrory 1970a). Smith's ineptitude worried Mexican American politicians like state senator Joe Bernal, who wanted a good working relationship with the new governor. Bernal organized an effort to mend fences between Mexican American leaders and Smith by arranging for him to speak with community activists at a public forum (McCrory 1970c; P. Thompson 1970). Bernal scheduled another meeting with the most sympathetic audience of community leaders and activists that he could assemble, but to no avail. The well-publicized event quickly deteriorated when the governor revealed that he had little knowledge of the most basic problems facing the community, which antagonized attendees. Even those with high hopes of working with the new governor were dismayed by his ignorance. When asked how he would deal with the problems facing Mexican Americans, Smith said that he had recently visited with some members of the Mexican American community: if they were unhappy, "they don't seem that way to me" (Ford 1970a).

Despite Smith's clumsiness, his supporters tried to keep the lines of communication open. A day after the highly publicized confrontation with Chicano Movement radicals, thirteen of those present sent the governor a letter disassociating themselves from the demonstrators. The doctors, lawyers, and business owners who signed the document apologized for the disrespect shown to the governor (Benavides et al. 1970; Office of Governor Preston Smith 1970). In spite of this goodwill, Mexican American activists in the Democratic Party bore a heavy burden when their governor behaved badly. Chicano radicals ridiculed them for "apologizing, kneeling down and begging." Party activist Gene Rodriguez expressed "utter disbelief" at the governor's fumbling but rationalized that Preston Smith's "long years of dedicated public service" probably kept him uninformed of the problems facing Mexican Americans. He recommended the governor take a crash course to learn about Mexican Americans and African Americans in Texas ("Governor Urged" 1970). Joe Bernal urged the governor to announce some new employment and civil rights initiatives. Others recommended that he strengthen lines of communication with a special community liaison. Instead the governor further humiliated Bernal and other Mexican American Democrats by rejecting the recommendation, arguing that he would not "fragment" his office with a special assistant for Mexican American affairs. He denied that there was any discrimination against Mexican Americans in employment and education (Ford 1970; "Touchy Meet" 1970). He compounded his problems during a school boycott in Houston led by state representative Lauro Cruz and other Mexican American leaders. Instead of offering to help, the governor maintained that he could do nothing about their problems ("Chicano Leaders" 1970).

Mexican American Democrats were joined to the governor by party affiliation, a relationship that put them at odds with the Mexican American voter. A poll commissioned by Smith's reelection campaign in Corpus Christi in 1969 found that only 18 percent of all Mexican Americans said that the governor demonstrated a willingness to help them, while 61 percent said that he did not make an honest effort to communicate with them (J. Morales 1968c). His indifference toward the ethnic vote had played itself out in the previous year's election campaign. Smith formed a "Viva Smith" outreach organization that he claimed emerged because of "Mexican American interest in my campaign" (Office of Lt. Governor Preston Smith 1968). During the campaign, however, the most that Smith could muster in his outreach to Mexican Americans was to say that "my door has always been open. I sincerely ask your support. I care about all of our people" (Elect Preston Smith 1968). The best argument that Smith had for his candidacy was that he represented a governing coalition superior to that of the Republican Party (McCrory 1970b). Interactions with the governor left Mexican American Democrats shaking their heads in disbelief: "he's hard to talk to. I've met him, but he just says 'how are you' and I say 'how are you' and that's it" ("Texas Latin Vote" 1968).

During the 1968 gubernatorial campaign, Smith hired Johnny Morales, a political operative from San Antonio, to coordinate outreach to Mexican American voters. Morales was alarmed by the lack of grassroots support for Smith's candidacy. He insisted that Smith pay attention to this growing electorate or lose it to his more aggressive opponents. The traditional Democratic tactic of working with a select few white-collar professionals, who seldom associated with the poor or lived in their neighborhoods, would no longer work in the highly contentious civil rights era (J. Morales 1968a). Morales visited a number of rallies, including some in the Valley, where he found that "there wasn't a single person, other than myself, that showed up to represent Preston Smith." His opponents were either present or had a team of workers handing out leaflets and campaigning on their behalf (J. Morales 1968a). Polling numbers revealed that 61 percent of Mexican Americans felt that Preston Smith cared little for them. He was faulted for a lack of concern for the poor, his support of big business, and his ties to Governor Connally (Cen-Tex Advertising 1968). One of Smith's advisors reported another problem: "I went to the meeting in Rio Grande and it was just like an organizational meeting for Republicans. LULACs, G.I. Forums, PASO were there in full force. F. R. Garcia, leader of Amigos for Eggers, spoke and told how for the first time the Mexicano was heading for progress and only Eggers could give it to them—about 800 attended" (J. Morales ca. 1968).

Morales told Smith that he was vulnerable to a revolt by Mexican American political activists so repulsed by the Democratic Party that they were prepared to support Republican candidates. Believing that they had little to lose under a Republican administration, they formed support groups like "Amigos for Eggers" and "Mexican Americans for Better Government" to promote their candidates. Morales further warned that many Mexican Americans had supported Senator John Tower in 1966 and vowed to continue until conservative Democrats were ousted from the party (J. Morales 1968d). Preston Smith had so little goodwill among Mexican Americans that some leaders were openly calling for his defeat. Bob Sánchez, a veteran Democratic activist and civil rights attorney, cited a series of instances during Smith's time in the legislature where he opposed labor and civil rights legislation. He called Smith a "two faced hypocrite" and vowed to derail his candidacy ("Smith's Interest" 1968; "'Viva Smith' Base" 1968). He and his colleagues vilified the party's nominees for statewide office, calling Preston Smith and senatorial candidate Lloyd Bentsen reactionaries who held a callous disregard for their people (Democratic Rebuilding Committee 1970a). Bob Sánchez believed that a Republican governor could be no worse than a Democrat. A Republican governor might even dismantle the South Texas political machines that thrived under the Democrats, as one of Sánchez's colleagues reasoned: "No Republican Governor is going to sit idly by while border bosses deliver votes in outrageous numbers to the opposing party. The border bosses of South Texas have managed to survive only because they functioned within a one party system and because no governor or attorney general of the opposing party ever controlled state government" (Shapiro 1970).

During Smith's 1968 campaign, Johnny Morales, who was serving as one of his field organizers, reported that the lieutenant governor was facing a hostile reception from minority voters, combined with an aggressive outreach by the Republican Party. Smith had a major problem on his hands. Some observed that the Republican challenger was making a serious effort to win Mexican American support and might succeed in capturing a significant percentage of their votes (Don Politico 1968). In a series of reports and observations, Morales reported to Smith that in South Texas groups like LULAC, the American GI Forum, and PASO either were not participating or were actively supporting Republican candidate Paul Eggers (J. Morales 1968a, 1968b, 1968c, 1968d, ca. 1968). Smith's weak support in South Texas and the unexpectedly strong challenge from the Republican Party prompted Smith to step up his own campaign outreach, a move that his challenger ridiculed as "a sudden interest in the Mexican Americans after ignoring them for 18 years" (Morehead ca. 1968). The Republican Party was publishing ads in South Texas newspapers attacking Smith's legislative record on labor and civil rights. Their ads linked his politics to those of his predecessor and asserted that he would "follow in the footsteps of the Connally tradition and keep the Mexicano in bondage" (Ortiz ca. 1968). Eggers pointed out that the lack of Mexican American progress in education, employment, and civil rights took place under Democratic governors. The Eggers campaign even aired a corrido, which said in part ("Radio Jingles" ca. 1968):

Eggers quiere para nosotros,
Todo de lo mejor
Lo que merese el Mejicano
Que es sincero y trabajador

Eggers, tu pueblo te pide
El Mexicano te quiere,
Tu eres nuestra Esperanza
De tu pueblo Mexicano

Eggers wants for us
Only the best
The Mexican people deserve it,
Who are honest working people

Eggers, your people need you
The Mexican American wants you,
You are our only Hope
For your Mexican Community

Despite the criticism leveled against Preston Smith and the persistent charges of racial bias, he did little to try to broaden the party's coalition after his election in 1968. He would go on to lose in the 1972 Democratic Party primary to Dolph Briscoe, who eventually won a narrow victory in the general election. As governor Briscoe largely resembled his predecessors in terms of their relations with racial and ethnic minorities. He campaigned on a platform of tougher sentences for drug dealers and violent criminals, institution of the death penalty, and a pledge not to raise taxes. He also opposed the disarming or disbanding of the Texas Rangers (Briscoe 1972). Governor Briscoe's policy platform contained a vague promise to support higher education in Texas and an equally vague commitment to promote bilingual education "where needed" (Briscoe 1973b).

Briscoe's candidacy faced unique challenges because he ran for governor the year that La Raza Unida Party ran its own candidate. Frustrated with Anglo dominance in the state's electoral system and a lack of social progress, several South Texas communities elected local officials under the banner of La Raza Unida (Shockley 1979). In 1972 La Raza Unida fielded candidates for statewide office. Its gubernatorial candidate rocked the Democratic Party by garnering 214,149 votes—an amount that almost cost Dolph Briscoe the election. Although the number of votes that the party's candidate received was small in comparison to the 1,631,724 votes tallied by Briscoe and the 1,534,460 by his Republican challenger, Henry Grover, the depth of discontent that the election revealed was significant. Over 50 percent of all Mexican American voters in twenty-two Texas counties cast their vote for the party's candidate, Ramsey Muñiz. Muñiz's supporters tended to live in less populated areas of Texas and were more likely to be poor, first-time voters, less attached to the Democratic Party, and subject to the political domination of an arrogant Anglo minority. In rural counties, the Mexican American vote for La Raza Unida was as high as 90 percent. La Raza Unida tapped the frustration that many Mexican Americans felt at the slow pace of social and economic reform. Even in cities La Raza Unida's appeal took large numbers of Mexican American votes away from the Democratic Party, higher than previously estimated. For example, in Bexar (San Antonio) and Harris (Houston) Counties Mexican Americans gave almost a third of their votes to Ramsey Muñiz, 32 percent and 31 percent, respectively (Márquez and Espino 2010).

Prior to the election, liberals warned the Democratic Party leadership of the growing dissatisfaction with its traditional conservatism and the negative consequences that this could have for the party. La Raza Unida Party's insurgent campaign demonstrated the weak hold that the Democratic Party had on Mexican Americans. La Raza Unida was a party with almost no money and an inexperienced leadership team and had begun its statewide campaign less than a year before the election, but it still made deep inroads into a Democratic voting bloc. Moreover, the Democratic nominee for the presidency, George McGovern, was making overtures to minorities in Texas by utilizing them in his campaign and to formulate health, education, employment, and civil rights policies (McGovern 1972). American GI Forum president Hector Garcia warned Briscoe that La Raza Unida constituted a real threat in the upcoming election and could greatly harm the Democrats if he vacillated on civil rights issues (S. Pearson 1972). State senator Joe Bernal, state representative Bob Vale, and House candidate Matt García personally urged Dolph Briscoe to stop catering to the dwindling number of conservatives in their party and cast his lot in with minorities, the poor, and other liberal voting groups. They asked him to commit to increasing minority representation and to declare the party's support for the United Farm Workers union's lettuce boycott ("Everything You Ever Wanted" 1972). Hence the 1972 election was a critical point for Democratic Party leaders. Dolph Briscoe could have acted decisively to realign his party in the face of new challenges and accelerate the incorporation of minorities into the fold. Instead he did just the opposite.

During the national Democratic Party convention in July, Briscoe chaired the Texas state delegation and cast his delegate vote for segregationist Alabama governor George Wallace, infuriating minorities and liberals ("The Longest Shot" 1972). His support for an icon of American racism was characterized as ineptitude and a gratuitous insult to minority voters (Byers 1972; Ford 1972a). Briscoe called the segregationist Wallace a "constructive force" in the Democratic Party. He argued that Wallace supporters participated "in good faith at every level of Democratic party procedures" and that their voices should be heard (Ford 1972b). A more concise explanation is that Briscoe was a wealthy banker and rancher largely detached from the needs of minority voters. The outpouring of anger from minority delegates at the national convention caught him by surprise: when confronted on the floor of the convention "Briscoe turned red in the face, began sweating profusely and managed only to sputter in protest against his critics" (Wiese 1972).

A Changing Democratic Party

In Texas and other parts of the country, disruptive activities by African American and Chicano radicals prompted concessions to the more moderate elements of the movement (Piven and Cloward 1979; McAdam 1982; Haney-López 2003). Soon after the 1972 election, Democratic Party officials tried to diffuse the revolt by reaching out to Mexican American activists. Calvin Guest, chair of the Texas Democratic Party, convened a meeting with South Texas Raza Unida members, promising increased representation and power if they participated in party affairs. Guest, a close ally of Governor Briscoe, was a symbol of the Anglo-dominated party that Chicano radicals resented. But he came with the message that he and the rest of the Democratic Party were happy and eager to have them become party members. He pledged to do everything in his power to include all Democrats in every aspect of the party's deliberations (Texas Democratic Party 1974c). His project was called the Democratic "rebuilding" and was designed to solidify the party's coalition, which included regaining the goodwill of Mexican American voters. Guest declared that the Democratic Party would accept La Raza Unida activists without bias and urged them all to join the party ("Texas Demo Goal" 1973). For some, this was a real turning point in Democratic Party politics. Blandina Cardenas said that the combined force of ethnic mobilization and a changing calculus on the part of high Democratic Party officials constituted a political turning point for the state: "Since the late 1960s there have been Texas power politicians [who] at key moments stopped resisting. Lyndon Johnson is a classic example in the fight for civil rights. Calvin Guest did the right thing. That moment was for Calvin Guest" (B. Cardenas 2004).

The governor's change of heart coincided with the national Democratic Party's new rules designed to ensure state loyalty to the national party's platform. Those rules instructed state parties to restrict participation to Democratic voters, to publicize and conduct open meetings, to adopt more representative formulas for selecting delegates, and to adopt an aggressive program of minority recruitment and antidiscrimination practices at every level of its activities (Democratic National Committee 1973). The changes were welcomed by liberal activists. Billie Carr said that it was time for Texas Democrats "who have formed the backbone of our party—those who were concerned in 1972, McGovern supporters, Muskie supporters, Humphrey supporters, Blacks, Chicanos, organized labor members, women, young people—to join together in our common goal of preserving the gains of reform and participation that permanent party rules can achieve" (B. Carr 1974). Mexican Americans had begun making inroads to the Democratic Party in cities like El Paso, Corpus Christi, and San Antonio and wanted to consolidate their gains now that the Texas Democratic Party was under pressure from the national party to increase minority representation at the state and national conventions and on its key committees (Barragan 1972; O'Brien 1972).

In 1974 the national Democratic Party held a mid-election convention to instruct its activists on the new principles of delegate selection that ensured the participation of women and minorities (Quintanilla ca. 1974). Calvin Guest observed that the plan mandated representation by women and minorities, a goal that he said "would become a model for the entire nation" (Texas Affirmative Action Committee 1974). Guest reminded all Democratic party officials that delegates chosen for the upcoming presidential election were subject to grounds for challenge and possible denial of seating if they did not follow the new affirmative action guidelines (Guest ca. 1974). The Democratic Party's Affirmative Action Committee sent letters of inquiry to activists in South Texas, San Antonio, and El Paso and soon began flooding the airwaves with ads encouraging Mexican Americans to participate in their precinct conventions (Quintanilla 1974). On a 30-second public service television announcement, country western star Johnny Rodriguez sang:

> Hello, I'm Johnny Rodriguez
> God gave me a voice to sing with
> and I'm grateful.
>
> You have a voice too
> Your nation gave it to you
> You can use it when you go to vote
> on election day
>
> Oh, and don't forget
> to go to your precinct convention
> on election night.
> (TEXAS DEMOCRATIC PARTY AFFIRMATIVE ACTION COMMITTEE 1974)

Anglo liberals welcomed the rule changes that eliminated practices like excluding blacks, Mexican Americans, and women (B. Carr 1976). The affirmative action campaign was aimed at "traditionally underrepresented" groups, and the party's liberals now wanted the program to succeed (Hickie 1974). They knew that conservatives had not given up hope of preserving their control of the party. In 1974 supporters of George Wallace ignored the new guidelines and excluded minority participants from their caucuses (Calhoun 1974a; Democratic Committee for Responsible Government 1974). The national guidelines were already securing change in Texas, however, and some SDEC members protested loudly against any remaining resistance (Pangburn 1974). The party reached a point where the governor and chair of the state Democratic Party could no longer make arbitrary decisions. At the 1974 Nominations Committee meeting in Austin, Governor Briscoe submitted his handpicked slate of at-large and alternate delegates for the next Democratic Party national convention. Under the chairmanship of Calvin Guest, the nominations were accepted by a voice vote and challenges from the floor were not recognized (Noblet 1974). When Guest reneged on his promise of a more open party, this time dissenters possessed legal tools that they could use to uphold the principle of equal access. Utilizing the new party rules, Mexican American activists responded with a suit filed by the Mexican American Legal Defense and Education Fund challenging the delegate selection process of the Democratic National Committee (Strauss 1974). The institutional keys to racial incorporation were now in place.

Conclusion

During the early 1970s fissures in the Democratic Party coalition were temporarily repaired. On the campaign trail Governor Briscoe demonstrated that he could engage his liberal critics. When confronted by Chicano radicals who pressed him to appoint four Mexican Americans to top administrative positions, he replied, "'I am very much interested in opening up state government positions to members of the minorities . . . but I see no reason to stop at four.' It brought the house down" ("Baa, Baa, Baa" 1972). Soon after narrowly winning election, he created an office of equal employment opportunities to guarantee that "all qualified persons, regardless of race, culture or sex, are guaranteed equal and fair opportunities for employment, for placement, and for advancement in Texas State Government" (Briscoe 1973b). The conservative governor had found a winning formula. Nine months after taking office, he had one of the highest approval ratings in Texas history (Belden 1973).

Despite Briscoe's popularity among his conservative base, Democrats understood that their party was changing. Racial minorities and liberals were well organized and were gaining more leverage while conservatives were losing control. By 1978 they had organized their own Moderate Conservative Democratic caucus (Mod-Con) to "restore" the Democratic Party's platform and message. The caucus leaders charged that the State Democratic Executive Committee had become so radical that it had invited "Caesar Chaves" (Cesar Chavez) to address the SDEC at its next meeting (Moderate Conservative Democratic Caucus ca. 1978). The balance of power had shifted to the liberals, and conservatives found themselves organizing a caucus and instructing their followers on the precinct, county, and state convention process ("How to Be a Mod Con Delegate" 1978; Lacy and Permetti 1978). Anglo liberals had long endorsed the idea of a more inclusive party, but they were also afraid that it would endanger the party's prospects in a racially conscious state. Maury Maverick, who had lost a bitterly contested Democratic primary to Henry González in 1961, applauded the progress that minorities made in removing barriers to electoral participation. At the same time he believed that those reforms would polarize the electorate:

> The white Anglo liberal in the South is going to more and more become a gadfly and he is going to have to understand that about himself. That's important. That's all right. I'm a gadfly and I understand that role, but now that the Supreme Court has said that you run in smaller legislative districts instead of countywide, the blacks are going to elect blacks for another hundred years and the browns are going to elect browns. Where in the hell is a white liberal going to get elected in the smaller races in Texas? There is nowhere in Bexar County that I can run. I don't have a constituency anymore. That wiped out, I think, the white liberals in the smaller races in Texas. (Maverick 1975: 28)

Maverick argued that integration came at the expense of the Democratic Party's ability to win elections. He was correct that Anglo voters would start deserting the party and the Democrats would lose control of state government, but this was only in part because of a perceived racial threat. In the early 1960s Ronnie Dugger, a liberal journalist and Democratic Party activist, was hopeful for a new era of democratization. Dugger believed that racial reform was long overdue but shared some of Maverick's concerns, given the unrest that he witnessed in Texas along with pent-up anger and continuing discrimination. The worst-case scenario was that Mexican Americans would reject Anglo liberals' belated outreach. "It is natural that members of an oppressed and exploited minority group are more impatient for power and recognition than Anglo liberals who have not had to suffer the life long handicaps of racial prejudice" (Dugger 1962). He was afraid this conflict would destroy the Democratic Party but soon found a decided lack of enthusiasm for strident ethnic politics among many Mexican American leaders and activists. Even in the earliest phases, most of those attracted to the Democratic Party tended to be moderate reformers. Albert Peña steered PASO in an angry, nationalist direction, but his influence was limited. Dugger wrote that "PASO has not found the going easy even among the *Mexicanos*, some of whom prefer to take their politics with condiments blander than PASO's *jalapenos* (hot peppers)" (Dugger 1963: 114).

Texas electoral politics did undergo an ethnic revolt, but most of it took place outside of the Democratic Party. La Raza Unida Party delivered an unequivocal message of discontent with the political and social status quo. Its uncompromising politics and impressive accomplishments attracted attention in the media and academia, but La Raza Unida soon succumbed to problems that have hobbled third parties in the past: a lack of funds, difficulty placing its candidates on the ballot, and the adoption of its issues by one of the major parties. In the case of Raza Unida, however, the dramatic rise and rapid fall of this insurgent party was weakly related to the steady emergence of a Mexican American leadership cadre in the Democratic Party. These activists made gains through networks and organizations in place long before the ethnic nationalism of the 1960s. They were the ones who began working in the Democratic Party at a time of racial exclusion while bearing the condemnation of their colleagues and the uncertainties of party loyalty. They believed that their work was essential for social progress but saw the choice between undesirable alternatives as a condition that they hoped to change (H. Garcia 1957b). Leaders like Hector Garcia understood that Democratic politicians often did not faithfully represent the community, but the party coalition offered the best hope for the future even as Mexican Americans continued to be "poor . . . abused, insulted, and humiliated" (H. Garcia 1956; my translation). Activists like Hector Garcia were deeply committed to the Democratic Party and understood that the reform process was slow but was occurring. None of them endorsed the idea of a racially based party or thought that Raza Unida aided their cause. When PASO opposed the reactionary Waggoner Carr in his 1966 bid for the U.S Senate, those Democratic activists were angered. They acknowledged Carr's shortcomings but argued that opposition to the Democratic Party nominee was folly because Republicans did not care about Mexican Americans at all. As one activist put it,

Carr's defeat meant that Texas did "not have a vote in the United States Senate. Republican Tower kills the vote of Democrat Yarborough. Had Carr been elected, he would have voted with Ralph Yarborough more than the Republican. Carr and Yarborough would have voted together more often than Tower and Yarborough" (Dickens 1969: 238).

CHAPTER 4

The Quiet Revolution

Albert Peña, who helped organize PASO and La Raza Unida, thought that the Democratic Party would only change with sustained outside pressure. He threatened party leaders with fragmentation, third-party revolts, and losses at the polls if they did not take the Democrats "to the people" (Peña 1972b). Peña never wavered in this belief, but when the Democratic Party began incorporating more Mexican Americans into its governance structure PASO and La Raza Unida were effectively neutralized. Moreover, Governor Briscoe only began reaching out to liberals and minorities when subjected to intense internal pressure and the threat of legal action for violating national party rules. From this perspective, Albert Peña was a more effective agent of change as a Democratic Party activist than as the leader of an ethnic insurgency. In 1968 he was part of a group that challenged the Texas State Credentials Committee at the national party convention for its lack of adequate racial representation. Peña was also part of a national movement that eliminated the winner-take-all method of delegate selection, which had the effect of virtually eliminating minority representation in Democratic Party conventions (Maverick ca. 1968b). In 1971 he headed a group that used the national party mandate for greater racial and gender representation to file formal complaints against the State Democratic Party (Peña 1971). Peña charged that the state party was in contempt of these mandates "under the guise of vague, undefined, and arbitrary party rules" (Peña 1972b).

Mexican Americans now possessed more effective tools to leverage influence in their party. The national rules effectively bound the party to increase the number of women and minorities at all levels of administration. It was a sharp departure from the time when Anglo politicians quickly forgot their political debts to Mexican Americans after an election or re-

sponded cynically to grassroots pressure with symbolic administrative appointments. The challenge to the party's method of selecting its delegates
prompted a detailed fifteen-page response from the Texas party's legal
council and a speech by the party chair to the State Democratic Party
Executive Committee (Texas Democratic Party 1974a; J. White 1974).
Chandler Davidson found that the new rules "blew open the clogged access routes to Democratic Party power both nationally and in Texas. In
Texas, the 'flexible quota' provision provided a battering ram for the rank-
and-file participants—women, minorities, and Anglo liberals—who for
so long had been knocking futilely on the door of the party's inner sanc-
tum" (Davidson 1990: 172). Mexican American Democrats now had the
resources to challenge racial exclusion, which Albert Peña swiftly did after
the new rules were adopted (Mexican American Democrats 1974). One
immediate result was a more representative party: in 1972 twenty-seven
Mexican Americans attended the national Democratic convention as delegates and alternates (Office of the Spanish Speaking 1972).

Longtime Democratic Party activist Sylvia Rodriguez saw firsthand
how changes in party rules created new opportunities for minorities. She
argued that the nationally mandated changes forced accountability upon
conservative party leaders. Talking about appointments to the party's governing structure, she asked: "[C]an you imagine Governor Connally pick-
ing a young, Mexican American activist from South Texas? Or Governor Preston Smith naming a flamboyant Black state representative from
Houston? Of course not!" (S. Rodriguez ca. 1978: 2). When the Democratic Party's system for selecting officials and representatives changed,
new voices were heard (Schneider 2008). Activist Blandina Cardenas
concurred with Rodriguez's assessment and called the change a breakthrough: "suddenly you had *Mexicanas* coming from areas of the country
where they had always been in the background . . . and they began to ap-
pear in many different roles" (B. Cardenas 2004).

Liberals and minorities were now at the center of a movement with
real prospects to change everything from delegate selection to party conventions, racial representation, and the governing structure of their party
(B. Carr ca. 1976). The new openness was celebrated by Anglo activists
like Billie Carr: "in 1972, Texas had written rules for the first time in the
history of the Democratic Party of Texas. We had rules written in a book
for everyone to read. What a miracle!" Another first was the more equitable working relationship between Anglo and minority liberals. As Carr
observed, "that is the way it should be between blacks, Chicanos, labor
and Anglo liberals. When they divide us is when they conquer us" (B. Carr
n.d.). By 1978, after only six years, liberals had a working majority on the

State Democratic Executive Committee. Billie Carr was so pleased that she submitted a resolution at that year's state convention commending the SDEC for its work (Cogburn and Carr 1978).

The multiracial alliance strengthened the liberal cause, but Mexican Americans knew that race was still relevant in Texas politics. By the early 1970s Mexican Americans were better organized than ever, and in 1972 they declared their arrival by creating their own party caucus, the Mexican American Democrats of Texas (MAD). A new caucus representing all liberals, the Texas Democrats, was created to serve as an umbrella organization that would coordinate the work of new or existing clubs and caucuses (Texas Democrats Organizational Report n.d.).

Liberals were further aided by some important legislative and legal victories. In *White v. Regester* (1972), the Supreme Court affirmed previous federal court decisions and declared that at-large election systems in Dallas and Bexar Counties diluted the minority vote and prevented the election of minority representatives. In *Graves v. Barnes* (1974), the court found that all the state's remaining multimember legislative districts also illegally diluted minority voting strength. As a result of subsequent litigation, single-member districts were created in the Texas counties with heavy concentrations of Mexican American voters: Bexar, Dallas, El Paso, Travis, Nueces (Corpus Christi), Jefferson (Beaumont), McLennan (Waco), and Galveston. In most of these areas, newly formed districts allowed for the election of minority representatives for the first time (Brischetto et al. 1994: 244–245).

The 1975 application of the Voting Rights Act to the Southwest extended new federal protection to the minority vote in Texas. It eliminated voter dilution schemes and provided for bilingual election materials, preclearance, and extended federal observer protections to any jurisdiction where more than 5 percent of the voting-age citizens were members of a language minority and where less than half of the voting-age population registered or voted in the 1972 elections. The 1975 amendments to the act made permanent the ban on literacy tests in voter registration and empowered individuals to bring suit, a role previously reserved for the Justice Department (de la Garza and DeSipio 1993: 1479–1482). Extending the Voting Rights Act's protection to Mexican Americans gave political organizations like the Southwest Voter Registration Education Project (SVREP) and the Mexican American Legal Defense and Education Fund (MALDEF) the legal leverage that they needed to dismantle discriminatory voting systems throughout the state and register new voters. The extension of the Voting Rights Act in conjunction with Supreme Court precedent resulted in a significant expansion of the Mexican American electorate and changes to electoral systems throughout the state that had depressed minority representation for generations:

> When the [SVREP] began its work in 1976, 488,000 Mexican Americans were registered in Texas. Ten years later, approximately 1 million were, even though their registration rates remained much lower than those of blacks or Anglos. But in addition to its registration drives, SVREP's legal staff also became involved in voting litigation. Between 1974 and 1984 SVREP and MALDEF filed eighty-eight suits in widely scattered Texas jurisdictions. (Brischetto et al. 1994: 242)

The institutional barriers to greater minority representation were falling. Over 58 percent of all objections raised under the Voting Rights Act challenged the method of election; another 33 percent involved redistricting and reapportionment (Cotrell and Polinard 1986: 71–72).

In his analysis of the Voting Rights Acts and Latino representation, John Garcia (1986: 51) found that its greatest impact was at the local level. Modest increases in representation were registered everywhere after its implementation, but the increase was greater in Texas than in other southwestern states. In 1983–1984 there were twenty-four Mexican American legislators, four in the State Senate (12.9 percent) and twenty in the House (11.3 percent), with most of the gains occurring after the 1975 extension of the act. Although the numbers were small, the percentage increase was dramatic across the Southwest with the exception of Colorado. Again, Texas was notable for a big increase in the number of mayors, city council representatives, and school board members:

> A 44 percent increase in Hispanic councilpersons occurred in Texas between 1973 and 1980, though again, there have been sub-regional variations, with more gains occurring in south, west, and central Texas. For Hispanic mayors, gains have been made in [Texas and New Mexico], with more dramatic ones occurring in Texas (an 88 percent increase between 1973 and 1980). The recent reelection of Henry Cisneros as mayor of San Antonio further enhances the political visibility of Hispanic officeholders. The pattern of gains is more strongly demonstrated for Hispanics serving on local school boards, where their numbers almost doubled from 1968 to 1978 in Texas. The possible effect of the VRA [Voting Rights Act] on gains in the number of Hispanic local officeholders is clearly more visible in Texas than in any other southwestern state. (J. Garcia 1986: 61)

Table 4.1. Number of State Hispanic Elected Officials in Southwestern States, 1973–1984

States and Offices	1973	1975–1976	1977–1978	1979–1980	1990–1981	1982	1984
Arizona							
Governor/Lt. Governor	0	1	1	0	0	0	0
Other State Executive	1	0	0	0	0	0	0
State Legislature	11	10	10	10	11	12	11
Judges/District Attorney	1	1	1	5	—	—	26
California							
Governor/Lt. Governor	0	0	0	0	0	0	0
Other State Executive	0	0	0	0	0	0	0
State Legislature	5	7	8	8	9	7	7
Judges/District Attorney	13	8	9	9	—	—	12
Colorado							
Governor/Lt. Governor	0	0	0	0	0	0	0
Other State Executive	0	0	0	0	0	0	0
State Legislature	4	6	7	8	9	9	6
Judges/District Attorney	1	1	1	1	—	—	6
New Mexico							
Governor/Lt. Governor	1	1	1	1	1	1	1
Other State Executive	1	2	2	0	3	3	5
State Legislature	33	29	32	30	32	31	32
Judges/District Attorney	11	15	18	17	—	5	—
Texas							
Governor/Lt. Governor	0	0	0	0	0	0	0
Other State Executive	0	0	2	0	0	0	0
State Legislature	14	15	19	21	22	21	25
Judges/District Attorney	3	12	16	24	—	—	—

Source: J. Garcia 1986: 63.

The New Democrats

This new generation of Mexican American Democrats saw little utility in pursuing the community-based pressure tactics of PASO and La Raza Unida. Indeed some went on the offensive against Chicano Movement leaders and organizations. The center of the storm was in San Antonio, where congressman Henry B. González led a crusade against the Mexican American Youth Organization (MAYO). Leaders of MAYO, created in 1967 by the founders of La Raza Unida Party, were vocal critics of the civil rights establishment and elected leaders, accusing them of selling out their people (Ignacio García 1989: ch. 1). MAYO members were committed ethnic radicals who cared little for racial reconciliation. As one spokesperson famously said, "To hell with the gabacho—if he doesn't move over, we'll run over him" (Mexican American Youth Organization ca. 1968). MAYO's tactics alarmed Henry González because he believed that they would lead to a level of civil conflict that might take generations to remedy ("HBG May Request Grand Jury Probe" 1969).

Henry González used his political power and prominence to investigate the group's activities and discredit its leaders. He threatened the Ford Foundation with a loss of its tax-exempt status for funding MAYO projects, charging the group with circulating hate literature and fomenting "civil disorder" ("Details Are Sought" 1969; "González to Report" 1969). González also attacked the newly formed Southwest Council of La Raza for funding the Mexican American Unity Council, a group that was using the funds to organize nationalist politics in San Antonio. He charged that political activists "consumed by prejudices" staffed both organizations. He questioned their maturity and judgment and called for greater scrutiny of both groups and their funder, the Ford Foundation (González 1969b). González ramped up his attack against the Ford Foundation, charging that the Mexican American Unity Council was both dangerous and irresponsible and that its bureaucracy was corrupted by cronyism, questionable political activities, lax administration, vague goals, and a lack of tangible achievements (González 1969c). For González, Chicano Movement activists were the "new racists," morally equivalent to white supremacists (Lee 1969). He placed his opposition to cultural nationalism within the context of his own record of civil rights work:

> Fifteen years ago as a member of the City Council of the city of San Antonio, Texas, I asked my fellow Council members to strike down ordinances and regulations that segregated the public facilities of the city, so as to end an evil that ought never to have existed to begin with. That Council complied, because it agreed with me that it was time for reason to, at long last, have its day. Eleven years ago I stood almost alone in the Senate of the State of Texas to ask my colleagues to vote against a series of bills that were designed to perpetuate segregation, contrary to the law of the land. I saw the beginnings then of a powerful reaction to

racist politics, and I begged my colleagues to remember: "If we fear long enough, we hate. And if we hate long enough, we fight. I stand for justice, and I stand for classless, raceless politics. I stand for action, and I stand for freedom. I stand against violence, racism and anyone or anything that threatens our ability in this land to govern ourselves as free people" (H. González 1968).

When González fought with Chicano Movement radicals, he was policing the boundaries of the Democratic Party at the same time. He targeted elected officials and political organizations with any ties to the movement. He charged Albert Peña with holding contradictory political loyalties. In his mind, the Bexar County commissioner should do one of two things: disavow all ties to the radicals or leave the Democratic Party ("González Says MAYO" 1969). González said that the fight with MAYO was the latest chapter in an old struggle with extremism: "I've had to fight the radical right—the John Birch Society—and now I guess I'll have to fight the Castro-Communist sympathizers" (Don Politico 1969). Texas Democrats closed ranks with González, Democratic congressmen Eligio (Kika) de la Garza, O. C. Fisher, J. J. (Jake) Pickle, and Abraham Kazen and issued their own condemnations of the MAYO militants ("Militant Latins" 1969). De la Garza charged that MAYO militants threatened other Mexican Americans who disagreed with them and that "their wrath and hate is bent on their own people" (Culhane 1969). González's South Texas colleagues in the state legislature signaled their support for his forceful and sustained attack on Chicano Movement radicals by introducing a resolution praising him for his fair manner, honesty, and integrity in "the cause of the large Mexican American minority" ("Resolution Would Praise" 1969).

González even attacked the civil rights establishment for viewing the world in stark racial terms. When San Antonio LULAC members censured González for not promoting the employment of Mexican Americans through the Equal Employment Opportunity Commission, he lashed out at their presumption and logic (Valdez 1967). "Let it be clear to you that I am not a professional Mexican," he said. "Only merit and equal opportunity should count when considering individuals for government employment." He added that "it is incomprehensible to me that anyone could insist on discriminatory hiring of a man whose duty is to be nondiscriminatory" (H. González 1967e). He roundly criticized targeted social programs for Mexican Americans and noted that the social service programs of the New Deal and the Great Society were created to solve social problems but not to give preferential treatment to any ethnic group (H. González 1967b; G. Sánchez 1967).

Albert Peña labeled González a renegade, detached from the community and unqualified to speak for the poor ("Peña Questions González' Credentials" 1968). Criticizing Henry González as an ethnic token gained little traction, however, given the congressman's long record of civil rights work. González had opposed extension of draft laws since 1963 and had even published two surveys of Vietnam War casualties that demonstrated that poor and uneducated Mexican Americans were more likely to be drafted and (once in the military) more likely to serve and be killed in combat, which he attributed to Anglo-dominated draft boards (H. González 1969a). González was a strong supporter of antipoverty legislation and critic of the Bracero Program and maintained a bilingual staff in his San Antonio office (E. Rodriguez 1976: ch. 5). Finally, González was outspoken on the issue of land stolen from Mexicans after the U.S.-Mexico War, an important rallying point for Chicano Movement radicals. In 1969 he called for a congressional inquiry that would establish the legitimacy of claims, redress injustices, and eliminate opportunities for unscrupulous individuals to exploit the issue ("Spanish Land Grants" 1969).

González asked that critics of the Democratic Party familiarize themselves with the War on Poverty to see the ways in which the party produced concrete benefits for Mexican Americans. These social welfare services materialized through partisan alliances, not through ethnic agitation. He pointed to his party's record of accomplishments: billions of dollars allocated for public education, small businesses, farm loans, veterans' benefits, and public works, all while steering the country through six consecutive years of economic expansion (H. González 1966a). González argued that U.S. society was undergoing a profound change: "American political parties have been very effective in implementing Democracy in our country because they have stimulated the electorate on many occasions to sit up and take notice of the various candidates and of the issues at stake" (H. González 1967d). He spoke in lofty terms, predicting that Mexican Americans would some day rise up and build a new world for everyone (H. González 1967a). Reflecting on his own long career, González said: "[I]n the beginning the fight seems lonely. But once a voice is raised and that voice is inherently right, it's not long before you have allies and get support—and you win the day. You can't keep down a right position for long in a freely elected democracy" (Michelle Garcia 1999).

González celebrated the incorporation of Mexican Americans into politics and government, but he spoke less about the attendant political empowerment and how that bolstered his career and his ability to prevail over his political enemies in MAYO and La Raza Unida. González and other Mexican Americans entering party politics were simultaneously harbingers of change and agents of the political establishment. In contrast, PASO and La Raza Unida Party remained outside the Democratic Party governing structure, its funding sources, and its network of elected officials. La Raza Unida's surprising performance in the 1972 election prompted an invitation from the Democrats to join its ranks but little more. The organization's narrow ethnic vision and extrainstitutional mode of operation rendered it unable to sustain its modest electoral gains in South Texas or to penetrate the Democratic Party's decision-making structure.

Even at the height of its influence, La Raza Unida failed to attract experienced politicians to run under its banner. American GI Forum president Hector Garcia and Democratic state senator Joe Bernal both refused invitations to run as the party's gubernatorial candidate in 1972. Willie Velásquez, one of La Raza Unida's founders, concluded that ethnically based social political parties were doomed to failure (Sepúlveda 2003: xxiii). He left La Raza Unida in 1968 to form the Southwest Voter Registration Education Project to focus on voter registration and redistricting lawsuits (Sepúlveda 2003: 72). Velásquez believed that the party's ideological rigidity dampened its potential to influence politics in an arena that required negotiation and concession (J. Rodriguez 1987). La Raza Unida's fate was sealed when its first gubernatorial candidate, Ramsey Muñiz, was convicted on federal drug trafficking charges, leaving the Chicano party without a visible leader. Although the party continued to field candidates for state office every election cycle, each campaign garnered fewer and fewer votes until the final statewide campaign in 1978, the year the party lost state funding for primaries (Ignacio García 1989).

After La Raza Unida's demise, some Mexican American Democrats credited it with accelerating party reform, but by that point even casual talk about ethnic solidarity was uncommon in the caucus ("After the Revolution" 1982; R. Bonilla 2003; T. Bonilla 2003; A. Chapa 2005). Little in the historical record suggests that Mexican American Democrats were interested in leveraging influence through third-party politics. In fact the opposite was true. The first real opportunity for liberals and minorities to exercise influence in the Democratic Party sparked an exodus from La Raza Unida. Entire Raza Unida chapters defected to the Democratic Party in some areas (Pycior 1997: 240); the numbers were so large and the movement so quick that they were dubbed the "born again Democrats" (Ignacio García 1989: 202). La Raza Unida's leader, José Ángel Gutiérrez, warned the new converts that Democratic Party reforms were a sham and a trap, but to no avail ("Raza Unida Campaigns" 1978).

The reason that few Mexican American Democrats worried about the demise of La Raza Unida was that their incorporation into the Democratic Party was parallel but often unrelated to the volatile politics of the Chicano Movement. Mexican American Democrats did not owe their successes to La Raza Unida; nor could the insurgent party sanction anyone outside of its besieged stronghold in Crystal City. Mexican American Democratic activists credited their success more to years of party reform and coalition building than to the disruptive tactics of La Raza Unida. They also understood that major legislation like the Voting Rights Act had a far more profound impact on voter registration and further political leverage within the Democratic Party. As Juan Maldonado, an early chair of MAD, said: "It encouraged people to work at improving the system. It gave us a feeling of security . . . it put some federal teeth into registration" (Bain and Travis 1984: 50).

Another reason that ethnic nationalism in party politics rapidly declined after 1972 was because Democrats did everything they could to destroy La Raza Unida. In 1977 then secretary of state Mark White initiated actions that blocked state financing of Raza Unida primaries and raised the minimum number of votes needed for funding to 20 percent of the total vote count. These changes were dropped only after an intervention by the U.S. Justice Department, which said that the action was a violation of the Voting Rights Act (R. Vara 1977). Governor Briscoe was a constant critic of La Raza Unida's activities in South Texas. He referred to Crystal City as "little Cuba" and called for a federal investigation of its government. The governor blocked federal grants designated for Zavala County, an act that culminated in the humiliating termination of gas service to Crystal City due to an unpaid $800,000 debt ("Briscoe Raps Grant" 1976; Hannan 1976; Box 1977; G. Thompson 1978). Under siege, La Raza Unida's leaders fought to prevent the collapse of strongholds in South Texas. José Ángel Gutiérrez called Governor Briscoe and attorney general Mark White racists who were using their position to shore up a repressive system. He told MAD members that a radical Chicano alternative on the ballot gave them leverage within the Democratic Party (J. Á. Gutiérrez 1999: 268). In the interests of group progress, he said, Mexican American politicians needed to come to La Raza Unida's aid ("Gutierrez' Unbending Stance" 1977).

Photo 4.1. Vice presidential candidate Sargent Shriver, Dr. Hector P. Garcia, Texas state representative Carlos Truan, and commissioner Albert Peña of San Antonio (*back foreground*). 1972. Dr. Hector P. Garcia Papers, Special Collections and Archives, Texas A&M University–Corpus Christi, Mary and Jeff Bell Library.

Help was not forthcoming. Mexican American Democrats declined even to lend rhetorical aid to the beleaguered party and instead supported Briscoe and White's attack on La Raza Unida. For Raza Unida activists, the lack of ethnic solidarity was disturbing. Martha Cotera argued that Mexican American Democrats "should have kissed the ground we walked on because we made it possible for them to be empowered, [but] once Raza Unida was removed as a threat, we got thrown in the trash bin" (Cotera 2004).

Mexican American Democrats were in no mood to thank La Raza Unida. Instead a chorus of denunciations rang out against the renegade party. They were especially angered by its practice of running candidates against Mexican American Democratic candidates in tight primary or general elections (Castro 1974; Dugger 1980b). Politicians like state representatives Ben Reyes and Gonzalo Barrientos called the practice a dirty trick and refused to forgive the party or its activists (Ivins and Franz 1974; E. Smith 1974). Ben Reyes called La Raza Unida's campaigns "illogical" and declared that the Democratic Party was more effective in dealing with the issues most important to Mexican Americans (Castro 1974). By then civil rights activists had washed their hands of ethnic political parties. American GI Forum founder Hector Garcia charged that La Raza Unida caused confusion and division by running candidates against Mexican American Democratic incumbents. He was also dismayed by the negative impact that third-party politics could have on ethnic representation at the state and national conventions (H. Garcia 1974). LULAC president Ruben Bonilla declared that he was happy to see La Raza Unida "in the political cemetery where it belongs" (Ignacio García 1989: 219).

Mexican American Democrats worked almost as hard as the Anglo leadership to do away with remnants of ethnic nationalism in Texas. State senator Tati Santiesteban of El Paso called on Mexican Americans to accept the responsibility and hard work that came with party membership and compete head-to-head with Anglo activists and politicians (Henderson 1974). The son of immigrant parents, Santiesteban believed that his election to public office in the Texas House in 1967 and then the Senate in 1973 was an example of what could be accomplished by working through the political system. He wanted young Mexican Americans to enter politics but to follow his example rather than what he considered the dead end of "the militant, angry, Chicano power advocate" (Fish 1973).

Still others argued that the renegade party was mired in the politics of the past and failed to keep up with changes in the larger society ("Area Solon" 1970; Luna 1991: 27–28; M. Martínez 1998). New leaders like Leonel Castillo, Houston city comptroller, pronounced ethnonationalism dead, adding that there were new opportunities for "the bright young Chicano politician, the young lawyer, the young doctor" who aspired to public office (Smyser 1977). In other words, a fresh generation of activists began to emerge, whose prospects would suffer in a political atmosphere clouded by ethnic and racial tension. Castillo broke from PASO years earlier to concentrate on registering new voters and strengthening the Democratic Party in places like Houston, where Mexican Americans were making gains (Untermeyer 1974).

Congressman Henry B. González and his allies launched a campaign to stamp out any remaining support for La Raza Unida. During the 1978 midterm elections, he and other members of the Mexican American Legislative Caucus actively campaigned for the Democratic ticket. All fourteen members conducted a seven-city tour in South Texas to support the Democratic Party's candidates and warn Mexican American voters of the "trickery and deceit" practiced by the Republican Party and Raza Unida (J. Montoya 1978; Bridges 2003: 183). Leonel Castillo observed that Mexican Americans had become a force within the Democratic Party and that their influence continued to grow (Howell 1975). But integrating the party's ranks was not enough; Mexican Americans needed to consolidate their gains and expand and energize the Democratic Party base. Conservative Anglo voters were leaving the party. The real danger to Mexican American interests, he believed, was not in fringe politics but in the growing partisan divide (Crossley 1972). Castillo warned that Texas politics was ripe for a minority takeover, but that minority was a "group of people known as Republicans" (Moody 1975).

The Mexican American Democrats

La joven bien conocida
Su nombre es Irma Rangel
Viene ha pedieles su apoyo
Para servirles muy fiel.
LICHA ZAPATA, "CORRIDO DE IRMA RANGEL"

With the creation of MAD, Mexican American activists finally had a vehicle through which they could negotiate with Anglo Democrats (Bernal 1977b). Among the five hundred Mexican American delegates to the 1974 State Democratic Convention were many veteran activists and elected officials: Joe Bernal, Leonel Castillo, Paul Moreno, Alicia Chacon, Gonzalo Barrientos, Sylvia Rodriguez, and Carlos Truan (Moya et al. 1974). By the late 1970s MAD had forty-seven chapters across the state and over six thousand members. By September 1976 nine MAD members were serving on the state Democratic Executive Committee (Orozco n.d.).

Given their members' biting critique of Chicano Movement politics, the ideology of the new caucus was surprisingly vague. The Mexican American Democrats' archival records contain little material that defines their goals and tactics. Their newsletters, correspondence, and internal documents consist of accounting records, caucus minutes, fund-raising documentation, and announcements, but no elaboration of a guiding worldview or appeals for racial unity. Bilingual education, the state minimum wage, and civil rights enforcement emerged as points of importance during campaigns and legislative debates, but there was no attempt to frame these issues within a larger policy agenda.

MAD did not have an ideological center because it was not an interest group or a social movement organization, unlike other Mexican American groups. Instead it was a network, a resource for its members to utilize as they jockeyed for leadership in the Democratic Party and pursued their political careers. Of course, MAD members committed themselves to the Democratic Party and the idea of bridging the racial, national, religious, and gender divides. Beyond the goal of uniting their party, MAD members were independent of the group, its leaders, and each other. They tended to be more liberal than Anglo Democrats, but not because the caucus held to a set of political principles serving as a litmus test for membership (Bernal 1977a). Sylvia Rodriguez, one of MAD's founders, believed that she had no practical way to prioritize issues or resolve differences of opinion among its members. Her only option was to "vote my conscience and to support or oppose issues based on my decisions" (S. Rodriguez ca. 1978: 18). When speaking for its members, MAD's responsibility was to "come across as the VOICES OF REASON [emphasis in the original]." If party officials ignored its interests, the caucus made it clear that it represented "a *vital part* of the Democratic Party in Texas—the Mexican American Democrats" (Mexican American Democrats ca. 1974; emphasis in the original).

MAD had no central organizing theme or party line because its most powerful members were elected officials who did not answer to the caucus. They were a new breed of ethnic politicians adept at assembling their own multiracial coalitions and believed that they owed their careers to the coalition of voters that put them in office.

The best known was congressman Henry B. González, who became an icon of ethnic politics in Texas and the most successful Mexican American politician of the post–World War II era. Other, less celebrated politicians were elected to public office with little racial discord. Their experiences point to the incorporation of an ethnic leadership class and changing attitudes in Texas.

El Paso County was one of the first to elect Mexican American representatives to the state legislature. State senator Tati Santiesteban and state representative Paul Moreno were elected in 1966 and 1967, respectively. At a time when race relations were tense and conservatives dominated the party machinery, both candidates ran successfully in at-large elections and scored impressive victories. Neither man had run for public office before, and neither encountered racial resistance during the course of the campaigns. Notably, Paul Moreno ran for public office because he was angry about widespread discrimination. He was an outspoken liberal who opposed the Vietnam War, supported La Raza Unida Party, and served in office for forty-one years, becoming known as the "conscience" of the House. When looking back on his first election, however, Moreno saw it as a harbinger of new opportunities for Mexican Americans. Social and legislative reforms after World War II enabled individuals like himself to achieve unprecedented socioeconomic mobility. For example, he called the GI Bill "the most important bill that has ever been passed in my life-time. Ever. Because that got us thinking of college. That got us thinking about law school, about medical school, about professional school. Had it not been for the GI Bill I suppose none of us would have done it. It was a door opener for all minorities" (Moreno 2004).

After attending the University of Texas Law School, Moreno returned to El Paso in 1963 and two years later ran for the city council but lost. In 1966 he decided to run for an open seat in the state legislature, claiming a victory backed by a coalition of liberal Anglo voters and big support from Mexican American voters. He believed that the social incorpora-tion, in the form of citizenship and tightly knit political communities, that had taken place in prior decades was decisive in his electoral victory. Citizenship was especially important, he argued, because it broadened and diversified the electorate: "in the barrio, for example, where I grew up, I didn't have one friend that was an immigrant. We were all born in this country, all of us. When I ran we were so closely knit because all of us could vote. All of us were citizens. The only detriment was the so-called poll tax" (Moreno 2004).

In a similar vein Tati Santiesteban saw no reason why he could not win a free and open election in the mid-1960s. He had a simple cam-paign slogan: "[I am] the most qualified candidate in the race" ("Three Seek Post" 1966). He also vowed to serve El Paso County and the needs of all people; his platform did not even mention civil rights when he ran for the Texas Senate. He pledged to hold the line on sales and property taxes, oppose a state income tax, increase vigilance over state agencies and their expenditures, and take a tough stance on law and order if elected (Tati [Santiesteban] to Texas Senate 1972). Born in 1934, Santiesteban claimed that he never experienced racial discrimination while growing up in El Paso. When asked why he decided to run for public office he said: "Why not? People like me, why not? I wasn't supposed to win and all of that but I did and it was not difficult. Everything was easy. I was popular and smart and I made good speeches. I was easy to like. I had an attractive

Photo 4.2. State senator Tati Santiesteban at his gubernatorial swearing-in ceremony, 1975. University of Texas at El Paso Library Special Collections Department.

wife. I could speak Spanish and English. I didn't have a chip on my shoulder. I was never discriminated upon, not that I can think of. You asked me what I hoped to accomplish? I was going to run for Pope!" (Santiesteban 2003).

When it came to racial bias, Santiesteban believed that prejudice against Mexican Americans was based on anti-immigrant bias and their low economic status. He knew that race and class overlapped but believed that little was gained by framing public policy issues divisively by appealing to specific racial groups. For example, he was a vigorous supporter of a state minimum wage law, which he privately called the "Mexican Right to Eat Law" (Santiesteban 2003). He pointed to his legislative successes as another indicator of the potential to move the body politic in a more inclusive direction. He also cited two symbolic achievements as evidence of a more nuanced state politics. In 1975 Santiesteban, in his role as Senate president pro tempore, served as governor when the governor and lieutenant governor were both out of the state. Serving as "Governor-for-a-Day" was a traditional honor, but it made him the first Mexican governor of Texas since 1835 ("Santiesteban Replaces Briscoe" 1975;

"Santiesteban's Day" 1975). Lieutenant governor William Hobby announced his appointment in Spanish ("President Pro Tempore" 1975).

Other Mexican Americans were elected to office with little racial controversy. In some cases their opponents would resort to race baiting, only to see the tactic backfire or fall flat. In his first bid for the Texas House of Representatives in 1975, a group calling itself Alarmed Citizens of Travis County tried to brand Gonzalo Barrientos as an ethnic radical. The group accused him of being "an Anglo hating, bomb-throwing, brown revolutionist" for his support of South Texas farmworkers and student protesters at the University of Texas (Dugger and Philpott 1974). The claim was a clear distortion of Barrientos's long history of public service. During his college years, Barrientos was a student activist and worked with Volunteers in Service to America (VISTA). He called for protection of the environment and more funding for public education, in addition to his support for issues like a stringent code of ethics for elected officials and a new state constitution ("Barrientos Will Run" 1972). The centrist Democrat believed that the anger and race baiting stemmed from his

Photo 4.3. State senator Tati Santiesteban walks under the governor's honor guard at his swearing-in ceremony, 1975. University of Texas at El Paso Library Special Collections Department.

support for a corporate income tax and a revision of the state's system of school financing (Shipp 1974; "Barrientos Expresses No Worry" ca. 1974). In his words,

> I was the candidate who happened to be Mexican American. I ran on issues, progressive issues, hopefully representing the majority of the people in my district. In fact I won the second time I ran for office. Of course here in the district that I represent, the Mexican American percentage is something like 14%. So that I ran on issues and representing what people want to see accomplished. (Wheat 1978)

Carlos Truan also experienced race baiting during his 1976 bid to unseat a conservative South Texas Democrat from his state senatorial seat. Ads published by the Concerned Citizens of South Texas tried to link the moderate Truan to La Raza Unida's anti-Anglo rhetoric (Concerned Citizens of South Texas ca. 1976; Parks 1976a, 1976b). Truan was also condemned for having served as director of the Southwest Council of La Raza, a nonprofit organization dedicated to voter registration, bilingual education, and business development projects (Parks 1976c). The racially charged accusations were condemned by the local press, and Truan won easily in both the primary and general election ("Belief That Truan Best" 1976; Carpenter 1976; Hubbard 1976; G. Jones 1976). Post-election analysis found little evidence of racially driven voting. In fact the ugly charges motivated few voters; Truan won his seat with a record low turnout ("4 Incumbents Defeated" 1976; "McKinnon Carries Refugio County" 1976). The *Corpus Christi Caller-Times* held up Truan's victory as proof that innuendo and fear would not sway the electorate and that South Texas candidates could be judged by their politics, not race ("Process Itself Biggest Winner" 1976).

Even in rural South Texas politics was breaking away from the domination of the political machine system, where wealthy Anglo farmers and ranchers engineered the election of local representatives (Cruz 1998). Irma Rangel was born in Kingsville, where she successfully pursued careers as a schoolteacher, a school principal, an attorney, and a politician (Giovanola 2005). Rangel made political history by becoming the first woman to serve as Kleberg County Democratic chair in 1974. Two years later she became the first Mexican American woman to be elected to the Texas House of Representatives. The ease with which she disposed of an incumbent supported by the powerful South Texas King Ranch surprised many local observers ("Rangel, Truan and Dreyer" 1976; Newton 1977;

Crawford and Ragsdale 1982: 334). Rangel's success was all the more noteworthy given her strong support for farmworker labor organizing and her tendency to say that the political system was "monopolized by the gringos" (Vela 1978: 35).

Finally, Lauro Cruz became the first Mexican American from Houston to serve in the Texas House after the legislature redrew Harris County into three multimember districts in 1966 (Cruz 1998: 15). Redistricting gave the Harris County liberals an opportunity to capture one of those seats. In the next election cycle, the AFL-CIO, PASO, Harris County Democrats, the Teamsters, and local black organizations were at work organizing the Democratic base (J. Castillo 1998: 23–24). Cruz, like others, arrived on the scene with a desire to participate in Democratic Party politics when he decided to run for state office (G. Martínez 1997: 50). Cruz recalled his surprise at the incongruity between the era's racial strife and the conventional politics of the Mexican American caucus in the state legislature. This tendency to accommodate and blend into the background of the legislative process caught him off guard: "Nobody in the legislature would rally the Raza . . . They were not cause oriented . . . Shoot! . . . For years I didn't even know that Henry Sanchez could speak Spanish. And he was from [South Texas] Cameron County!" (Cruz 1998: 20).

Crashing the Party

Mexican American activists hoped that a growing Mexican American electorate and a growing number of Mexican American elected officials would move the Democratic Party to the left because it could no longer win elections or pass legislation without their help (Chacon 2003). Still, they began with little experience in the legislative process and had to struggle for every concession. Leonel Castillo recalled that only in the mid-1970s did they begin to understand the internal workings of the Democratic Party machinery. What he meant was that they had gained access to basic facts previously denied to anyone outside a small circle of powerful politicians. The State Democratic Party conventions were no longer an opaque process. They now knew the agenda, where deals were negotiated in committee, and, for the first time, the convention floor plan (J. Castillo 1998: 38–40).

One of the first things that MAD attempted to do was to replace the incumbent Democratic Party chair, Calvin Guest. Guest had served as Governor Briscoe's campaign manager in 1972 and then as Democratic Party chair. MAD members distrusted him and passed a resolution condemning Guest for negative and insensitive actions toward Mexican Americans (McCrory ca. 1976). Leonel Castillo ran against Calvin Guest in 1974 and again in 1976 for the chair of the State Democratic Executive Committee ("Elect Leonel Castillo" 1974). His first run prompted Governor Briscoe to offer Castillo the newly created position of vice chairman for minority affairs, a proposal that he flatly refused ("Castillo Calls Race" 1974). Castillo tried again in 1976, an opportune time to test the Democratic Party's commitment to openness. The MAD membership also knew that Guest was vulnerable. Several other factions within the party were unhappy with his leadership, and a search had begun for a compromise candidate to replace him (Welch 1976; Montgomery 1976). Furthermore, Leonel Castillo had all the qualifications for the position. He had impeccable centrist credentials, having spent four years in the Peace Corps and directed federal job training programs in Houston (Waldrep 1971). In 1971 Castillo was elected Houston's first Mexican American controller, defeating the white incumbent who had held the office since 1945 ("Castillo Beats Oakes" 1971). As a candidate, Castillo offered years of experience, integrity, and a lifelong commitment to the Democratic Party ("Who Is Leonel Castillo?" ca. 1974).

From MAD's perspective Calvin Guest was also vulnerable because of his inability to reconcile the ideological extremes in his party. Despite clear progress, liberals were still frustrated over the slow increase of gender and racial representation in the state party and continued resistance from the SDEC ("Women, Liberal Coalition Defeated" 1974). Vocal right-wingers, who included supporters of Alabama governor George Wallace, also raised their own demands for representation at state and national conventions (Bonavita 1974). Castillo, hoping to become one of the most powerful figures in state politics, found that some of his presumed allies were openly hostile to his candidacy. At the 1974 state convention, he recalled labor representatives who "were calling me a Spic, asking me if I spoke English, telling me to go back to Mexico, refusing to shake my extended hand, booing me before I spoke, and who displayed more hostility toward me and my supporters than I thought still existed in Texas" (L. Castillo 1974b).

The racist harassment of Leonel Castillo was disturbing, but it was not the wall of exclusion that Mexican Americans faced in the 1950s. When Castillo filed a complaint with Texas labor leaders, he drew a quick reply from Texas AFL-CIO president Harry Hubbard. Hubbard assured Castillo that those actions did not take place under instructions from labor's leadership, "especially mine." He acknowledged the bigotry displayed by union members during the convention and committed the labor movement to work for greater inclusion in Democratic politics (Hubbard 1974). For his part, Governor Briscoe avoided confrontations with the newly empowered liberal faction. In June of 1973 Briscoe signed into law Texas's first state-supported bilingual education program. State representative Carlos Truan of Corpus Christi sponsored the measure and credited the governor, the lieutenant governor, and the Speaker of the House with the support necessary to pass the legislation ("Bilingual Education Program" 1973). Governor Briscoe continued appointing blacks and Mexican Americans to state commissions, declared a personal commitment to affirmative action, and scheduled regular meetings with civil rights organizations (Parish ca. 1974; Tiede 1974; "Governor Dolph Briscoe's Mexican-American Appointments" ca. 1979).

Although Castillo failed to dislodge Calvin Guest from his post, Mexican American activism produced further concessions from the governor and greater cooperation from their Anglo peers. Governor Briscoe appointed his friend Rodolfo Flores as his special assistant for Mexican American affairs. Flores, a senior vice president at Briscoe's First State Bank of Uvalde, became the governor's reelection campaign coordinator ("The Rodolfo Flores Family" n.d.; "Organizing Committee" ca. 1972). Two MAD members, Joe Bernal and Alicia Chacon, were official delegates to the Democratic national convention in 1976 ("The Convention" 1976). That year Leonel Castillo was elected Democratic Party treasurer ("Democrats Approach Harmony" 1976).

Mexican American activists wanted power and had new legal tools that they could use when political persuasion failed. After Castillo's mistreatment at the state convention, MAD charged the Texas Democratic Party with racial and ethnic discrimination, a violation of party rules (Texas Democratic Party 1974a). They were determined to force Governor Briscoe to make the hard decision of choosing between his rural conservative base and the growing minority vote (McCrory 1976b). Their complaint said that 5.2 percent (four) of the seventy-six delegates to the National Democratic Convention were Mexican American yet 18 percent of the state population was Spanish surnamed. They added that Mexican Americans traditionally supported Democratic candidates with margins exceeding 85 percent of their total votes cast (Bernal and Castillo 1974; Bernal 1974b). State senator Joe Bernal argued that an integrated Democratic Party was a fact of life and that it was time for the party to reorganize and consolidate its expanding base. He believed that the Democrats could

change their politics and still win elections if they protected and cultivated the Mexican American vote. The Mexican American voter was not
a "sleeping giant" but the victim of a rigged electoral system. Instead of
sleeping, the giant "was drugged—with heavy doses of the poll tax, annual voter registration, gerrymandering, at-large elections, and winner-
take-all conventions" (Bernal 1977a).

Despite the race baiting surrounding Leonel Castillo's bid to unseat
Calvin Guest, the Texas Democratic Party was actually changing in significant ways. Four years after liberal, female, and minority activists sued
the State Democratic Executive Committee over the lack of diversity, the
SDEC had a liberal majority and a black woman serving as its vice chair.
The SDEC went on to pass resolutions praising the United Farm Workers
and farmworker organizing (Guarino 1978). Governor Briscoe appointed
enough Mexican Americans to positions in his administration for MAD
to declare that he had made more appointments of Mexican Americans
than any other governor—six state judges, a district attorney, seven university regents, and sixty-seven members of state boards and advisory
commissions ("Appointments of Governor Dolph Briscoe" 1977; "The
History of M.A.D." 1977). Three MAD members were appointed to the
State Democratic Executive Committee in 1974, and Joe Bernal was the
first Mexican American elected to the Democratic National Committee.
The number of MAD members in the SDEC rose to five in 1974 and
nine in 1976 (Bernal 1977c; "Chronological History" 1977). In order to
realize the goal of greater diversity, the SDEC required Calvin Guest to
submit a detailed affirmative action plan to expand the representation of
young people, Mexican Americans, and blacks (Guest 1978). MAD even
claimed that it received more cooperation from state chair Guest than
from any previous chair ("The History of M.A.D." 1980). As one leader
put it, "we don't dislike Calvin Guest as much as we used to" (G. Jones
1978).

Prominent Anglo Democrats like Bob Bullock began to reconcile
themselves to the new reality. When Bullock ran for comptroller in 1974,
his Republican opponent charged that he was a racist turned opportun-
ist for championing equal opportunity. The accusation was based on Bullock's vote for the 1957 school segregation bills when he was a member
of the Texas House of Representatives. Bullock repudiated his votes and
claimed that they were based on ignorance and a belief that no minority
activists were denouncing the legislation at the time (K. Miller ca. 1974).
He elaborated: "I don't know of anyone who is proud of those votes.
I'm not proud of them, but I'm man enough to admit they were wrong"

(S. Watkins 1974). Bullock vowed, if elected, to launch an aggressive minority hiring campaign, a sentiment echoed by his Republican challenger (Calhoun 1974a).

The new face of Texas Democratic politics was more youthful, ethnic, and female. Politicians like Bob Bullock cast their political fate with an increasingly liberal party, but conservatives were rethinking their affiliations and loyalties. As a veteran activist observed, "[T]he reason I can see the change is because my family has been part of the structure. Before it was cut and dried . . . [Now] they don't go along with the governor just because he says so" (Barta ca. 1976). The new turn of events surprised some conservatives trying to counter the new liberal and racial insurgency. As one activist put it, "[W]e never had to be organized before" (Barta 1976).

The Increasing Significance of Ideology

The late 1970s was a period of partisan transition in which Mexican American influence on the state two-party system was unmistakable. Economic modernization, demographic change, voting rights legislation, and mandates from the national party opened the Texas Democratic Party to change and power sharing. In response to this rapidly changing political terrain, both major parties recast their appeal to Mexican American voters. Republicans were more innovative in this respect, arguing that they offered the most reliable path to social equality. The Republican Party had little to lose and much to gain by draining votes away from an increasingly liberal Democratic Party. For Anglo Democrats, power sharing was a new concept; the transition to a diverse party was hard fought and drawn out. As one Republican operative recalled, the Democrats were slow to change because prior to the 1970s high Democratic Party officials did not care about anything except holding office. "They didn't have to care so they didn't" (Knaggs 2005).

An energized Republican Party was quickly turning the decades-old conflict between conservatives and loyalists, previously fought within the Democratic camp, into a competitive two-party system. Conservative Democrats continued to hold power in Texas, but ethnic representation was normalized as overt racism was rare: politics more closely reflected constituent ideology and local economic interests. The 1972 Ralph Nader Congress Project offers a window into the partisan realignment in Texas. In a series of field reports on Texas congressional representatives the project gathered detailed information on their constituents and the political context in which they were elected. The report on Texas found that congressional representatives tended to be more conservative in rural districts and in cities where minorities were a small percentage of the population. In urban areas where minorities were a larger part of the population, congressional representatives were more liberal and responsive to their issues.

The most conservative representatives tended to come from the east, west-central, and panhandle areas, many of which were rural districts with few minority constituents. For example, O. C. Fisher was a congressional representative from the west-central twenty-first district. His district's economy was based on farming and ranching, and 87 percent of the population was Anglo. Fisher went out of his way to thwart programs assisting Mexican Americans, opposing an increase in the minimum wage for farmworkers, extra unemployment compensation, the Civil Rights Act of 1964, and the Voting Rights Act of 1965. The conservative Americans for Constitutional Action gave his voting record an 89 percent rating, while the liberal Americans for Democratic Action gave him a score of 0 (Taylor and Brown 1972: 13). George Mahon, chair of the House Appropriations Committee from the west panhandle nineteenth congressional district, was vehemently opposed to the 1964 Civil Rights Act and the Voting Rights Act of 1965. He also opposed school busing and voted to weaken the Equal Opportunity Commission. Like Fisher, he received high ratings from conservative organizations (Pullen 1972). W. R. Poage of the Texas eleventh district rose to become chair of the House Agriculture Committee. He worked in 1951 to expand the Bracero Program that brought hundreds of thousands of guest workers to the United States. He called the program the "best kind of foreign aid" for Mexican families who might otherwise starve. He also denounced the minimum wage as "illegal, impractical and immoral" (Millet 1972: 12). Conservatives like Olin Teague in the eastern sixth district represented Mexican Americans in districts where they constituted a small minority. When asked why he received such a high percentage of minority votes despite his opposition to civil rights legislation, he gloated, "[W]ell, hell, who else are they going to vote for? There's no one else to vote for!" (Glazer 1972b: 4).

In congressional districts where Mexican Americans were a significant portion of the population the Ralph Nader Congress Project found more liberal political representation. Congressman Henry González of San Antonio built his political career on equal opportunity and fairness. He was rated by the liberal Americans for Democratic Action as one of the most liberal representatives in Congress—barring his hawkish position on the Vietnam War and defense appropriations. In all other respects he was "a classic liberal Democrat in the New Deal tradition, voting for more federal spending in housing, education, and health care" (Reno and Zill 1972: 10). He was not the only liberal with a large Mexican American constituency. Abraham Kazen, representing the South Texas twenty-third district, joined Henry González in 1957 for a record-breaking 36-hour filibuster aimed at blocking passage of Price Daniel's segregation bills. Like González, Kazen focused his energy on education, employment, and poverty (Townsend 1972: 2). He told the project interviewers: "I'd be the happiest man on earth if I could just find jobs for my people" (Townsend 1972: 1). In other parts of the state congressional representatives moderated their politics as the minority electorate grew. In Corpus Christi, labor leader Manuel O. Narvaez said that his congressman, John Young, "used to be 100 percent against us, but now he voted only twice against us. He is friendly and does little favors for individuals." In 1972 the American GI Forum gave the congressman its highest rating, noting that he had adopted the group's positions on housing, food stamps, and equal employment (Glazer 1972a: 7–8).

In some congressional districts, growing political influence resulted in the election of Mexican Americans who could be as conservative as the Anglos they replaced. In 1964 Eligio "Kika" de la Garza was elected after an Anglo incumbent chose not to run for reelection. De la Garza defeated a PASO-endorsed Mexican American candidate in the Democratic primary before going on to win the general election for the South Texas fifteenth district. De la Garza was a strong defender of ranching and farming interests in his rural South Texas district. The Nader Congressional Project author found that "his Conservative stance was also an implied guarantee that social change would not come galloping into the fifteenth district to alter the status quo and existent power structure. The 'complexion' of the fifteenth district's congressional representative changed, but political power remained the same" (Gomes 1972: 17).

Congressman Richard C. White had represented the far-west sixteenth district in El Paso County since 1965. White actively courted the Mexican American vote and entered his legislative accomplishments benefiting Mexican Americans in the Congressional Record. He sponsored legislation promoting bilingual education, higher education loans, vocational training, local parks, and health services. White worked to "increase the opportunities for American citizens of Latin American heritage to share more of the benefits living in a land dedicated to principles of equal opportunity for all" (Taylor 1972: 9). The Ralph Nader Congress Project found that White's ability to appease conservative Anglos and reformers earned him grudging respect from Mexican American activists (Taylor 1972: 2). The ethnic composition of El Paso's voting-age population favored the Democrats. Over 40 percent of the district was Mexican American. They typically delivered overwhelming majorities to liberal candidates, making it almost inevitable that one would challenge the incumbent. That challenge came in 1970 when Raymond Telles, the first Mexican American mayor of the border city, ran against Richard White in the Democratic primary. Telles portrayed himself as a strong ethnic candidate but lost the primary election two to one, failing to garner enough Mexican American votes to log a respectable showing ("Texans Support All U.S. House Vets" 1970; Taylor 1972: 13). A page had been turned in West Texas race relations. Mexican Americans in El Paso were not as "hungry" for descriptive representation as they had been in the 1950s when Raymond Telles was first elected (Mario García 1998: 143). Richard White's progressive voting record on civil rights and social welfare legislation made him difficult to assail in his working-class district. One activist said that White was always "very responsive, very receptive to the Mexican American population" (Mario García 1982). The Anglo congressman was so popular that the local Mexican American Political Association endorsed him over Telles during the 1970 primary (Mario García 1998: 145–146).

Conclusion

After sixteen years of service, Albert Peña lost his election bid to the Commissioners Court in Bexar County in 1972, the year Ramsey Muñiz headed La Raza Unida's ticket. His defeat came at the hands of Albert Bustamante, an aide to congressman Henry B. González. One of Bustamante's critiques of Peña was that he was more concerned with supporting radical causes than with representing his constituents (Peña 1996). That year Joe Bernal lost his state senate seat to a conservative Republican. It was a close race in which he lost votes to a La Raza Unida candidate, but Bernal also lost the support of his Democratic colleagues. He was censured by Democrats in the State Senate for participating in PASO and marching with farmworkers in South Texas. State representative Guy Floyd from San Antonio attacked Bernal for participating in demonstrations, charging that Bernal was in the streets arousing statewide resentment when "responsible" people were working for major infrastructure projects and "better housing and better jobs for underprivileged minorities" (Ford 1969).

Congressman González agreed that it was appropriate for the Democratic Party to discipline its members and felt that neither man should have been surprised that more Democrats did not come to his aid. The greatest irony of the 1972 election, he said, was that La Raza Unida helped defeat two of its most vocal Democratic supporters, state senator Joe Bernal and county commissioner Albert Peña. He further noted that Bernal was defeated in a district that Bernal had drawn himself and that Peña had lost to "a complete political rookie" (McCrory 1974). Bernal believed that he was punished by the Democratic Party for his commitment to social justice but conceded that La Raza Unida Party doomed his candidacy:

> I lost by a hundred and seventeen votes, and when I look at the count, the Raza Unida had drawn 3,500 votes out of my district for Raza Unida, and they couldn't vote in the second primary. They wanted to, but they couldn't vote in the second primary because they had registered as a third party. So, if I'd have had those 3,500 I would have won by 3,500. And I'd still be a senator! (Bernal 2009)

As the Democratic Party changed, the link between Mexican American party participation and ethnic advocacy weakened. The dual strategy of combining community organizing with party activism that characterized PASO and La Raza Unida was undermined by a competitive two-party system. The most talented social movement leaders gravitated toward the Democratic Party and then worked to consolidate their gains and build a more progressive party coalition. Independent organizations like PASO and La Raza Unida were a threat to that project. In areas of the state where Mexican Americans were a large part of the population, incorporation into Democratic Party politics evolved without the intraethnic conflicts taking place in San Antonio and South Texas. According to Alicia Chacon, ethnic nationalism did little to move the process forward in El Paso County: "I mean, we were controlling the party by then . . . We had just taken over by our sheer numbers" (Chacon 1996: 85). What worried her more was the cooptation process. She argued that the Mexican American Democrats became a vehicle for assimilating individual politicians into the Democratic Party, integrating them into the mainstream of the party rather than holding it accountable to the community (Chacon 1996: 163–164). State representative Paul Moreno also believed that MAD was not controlled by community groups or leaders but conceded that it was an important vehicle for ethnic self-defense and networking in the Democratic Party. Most MAD members were liberal Democrats, and the organization helped them secure leadership positions in the party and the legislature (Moreno 2004).

State senator Carlos Truan shared Moreno's stance. Prior to his election to public office, Truan had a long record of activism in the League of United Latin American Citizens. He continued to work with community-based organizations but firmly believed that the changes in race relations that took place during the 1970s were irreversible and that ethnic unity in electoral politics yielded few benefits. In his mind, the greatest danger to Mexican American interests was a Republican takeover of state politics. During his tenure in office, when his party controlled the legislature, he "authored the bilingual education law, the adult education law, the food stamp program, and the Civil Rights Commission bill. I did those things with the help of my fellow Democrats" (Truan 1998b: 34).

State senator Gonzalo Barrientos agreed with Carlos Truan that MAD's objective was to help their party build "a large, welcoming tent" (Barrientos 2009). But other forces would undermine the goal of building a working majority for the Democratic Party. In 1978, just as Mexican Americans had begun exercising more influence in the Democratic Party, a Republican was elected governor for the first time since Reconstruction. Mexican Americans voted overwhelmingly for the Democratic candidate John Hill, who still lost to Republican Bill Clements. Hill received 75 percent of all Mexican American votes, the highest percentage of all groups, with Mexican American voters in Corpus Christi, San Antonio, and Houston delivering over 80 percent of their vote for him. La Raza Unida's meager 3 percent of the vote that year was dwarfed by the 19 percent of the Mexican American vote that Republican Clements received (Meza 1978). The rise of the Republican Party to power in state government threatened programs supported by Mexican American Democrats (Viamonte 1979). Conservative Democrats who had historically blocked progressive social legislation now emerged in a resurgent and unified Republican Party (Barrientos 1978; Vaughan 1979). As their numbers shrank, Democratic representatives began resorting to procedural delays or even to leaving the legislature when it was in session in order to deny the Senate the two-thirds quorum that it needed to conduct business (Bonavita 1979; Heard 1981). Mexican Americans had arrived in state party politics, but once again their hands were tied.

CHAPTER 5

A Two-Party State

In 1978 we were fat, dumb and lazy and happy. We presumed the Republicans couldn't win. We said some harsh things in the primary. They were too harsh and the scars didn't heal.

BOB SLAGEL, TEXAS DEMOCRATIC CHAIR, ADDRESSING THE 1982 MAD ANNUAL CONVENTION (STOLER 1982)

By 1978 Texas had a functioning two-party system, Republicans were winning elections, and the state Democratic Party finally began to resemble the national party in its ideology and governing structure (B. Carr ca. 1979a, ca. 1979c). Texas liberals increased their numbers and influence to the point that one activist characterized the 1978 Democratic state convention as a "real love-in." The festivities were cut short, however, when Bill Clements stunned the Democrats by becoming the first Texas Republican governor since Reconstruction later that year (B. Carr ca. 1979b). The historic defeat gave greater traction to the argument that Democrats could no longer win elections without mobilizing blacks and Mexican Americans (Dugger 1979). The Democrats of Texas (DOT), the party's liberal caucus, formulated a new narrative for the party caucus, asserting that Texas liberals "have always been committed to broadening our state party structure to include women, blacks, Chicanos and young people" (Texas Democrats ca. 1976). Anglo liberals began to speak more about the "natural" alliance of voting blocs with overlapping interests, though some recognized long-standing schisms among these groups. Labor lawyer and liberal activist Chris Dixie believed that it was time for Anglo liberals to acknowledge their errors: "In humility, we remember, also, our mistakes. We failed to endorse Henry González for governor. And we have put more than a few in public office whose political ethics proved to be fragile" (Dixie ca. 1977).

A Democratic Party under siege was more receptive to appeals for inclusion than ever before, especially for a rapidly growing bloc of Mexican American voters. In 1978 Texas had 591,950 Mexican Americans who were registered to vote: 58 percent, compared to 60 percent for blacks and 64 percent for Anglos (Southwest Voter Registration Education Project 1978: 21). After a Republican captured the governor's office in 1978, party officials spoke more about incorporating more "special interest organizations" like Mexican American and black Democrats. The Democratic Party committed itself to charter new caucuses in order to promote and sustain the party's diversification (Texas Democratic Party 1978). By the early 1980s a working alliance was in place within the liberal wing of the Texas Democratic Party. The Mexican American Democrats, Coalition of Black Democrats, and Labor Caucus scheduled their own meetings during state conventions and coordinated their work with white progressives (B. Carr 1982). The State Democratic Executive Committee, once a bastion of conservatism, was passing resolutions calling for aggressive civil rights enforcement and support for affirmative action (State Democratic Executive Committee 1983).

This turn in Democratic Party policies was part of a larger realignment in Texas that culminated with a Republican takeover of the state (Dyer et al. 1998). The modernization of the Texas economy that boosted the prospects for greater minority representation also increased the number of upper-income and white-collar professionals, who tended to vote Republican (Dyer et al. 1988). Minority advances at the national level and gradual empowerment of racial minorities in Texas politics cemented the Democratic Party's image as the voice of liberal American politics. The Republican Party grew as disaffected conservatives abandoned the Democrats, and by 2004 Texas was once again a one-party state (Lamare et al. 2007: 286–287). One of the few bright spots for the Democratic Party in the twentieth century came in 1982 when it captured the governor's mansion, sweeping statewide offices and maintaining majorities in both houses of the legislature. But the state's politics were moving steadily in the Republican Party's favor:

> in the 1984 elections, Ronald Reagan easily carried Texas, Phil Gramm became the second Republican from Texas elected to the U.S. Senate, and, perhaps more important, Republicans gained seats in both the state Senate and State House. Republicans also made significant inroads in

county elections, winning twice as many seats as they had held prior to the election. In 1996 Republicans swept every statewide election and for the first time in 125 years won a majority in the state Senate. Two years later, the Republicans captured control of both houses of the state legislature for the first time since Reconstruction and cemented that control in 2004. (Lamare et al. 2007: 290–291)

The Republican Party's takeover of Texas state politics hastened the end of racial group advocacy in the electoral realm. Mexican American voters were an increasingly influential voting bloc. But, more importantly, the Democratic Party was quickly losing its ability to elect its nominees to public office, especially at the state level. Although the party celebrated the diversity of its base, political solidarity across its various constituencies was more important than ever. As late as 1970, eight years before Bill Clements was elected governor, Albert Peña and others were still arguing that support for Republican candidates would help create a responsive two-party system (Byers and McNutt 1970; Democratic Rebuilding Committee 1970b). As Bob Sánchez put it, the strategy was to force change on the Democratic Party by undermining its candidates: "[Y]ou will recall that the first time we did this it was when Tower beat Blakely. On that occasion we simply went fishing. On the next occasion, when Tower beat Carr we went a step further and actually came out and voted for the Republican Tower" (R. Sánchez 1970).

Even at that time activists in both parties understood that threatening to aid the Republican Party lacked credibility. Republican strategists knew that leaders like Albert Peña and Bob Sánchez were just frustrated with the Democratic Party and were not potential converts to the Republican cause (Wiese 1970; M. Smith 1972; Untermeyer ca. 1972). They also knew that a small but significant number of Mexican American voters identified as Republicans. Republican-sponsored polls revealed that as many as 20 percent of all Mexican American voters identified with or leaned toward the Republican Party, even during the La Raza Unida's 1972 revolt (Armendariz 1972). Republican strategists believed that it was possible to secure the Mexican American middle-class and social-conservative vote, thereby cutting into the Democrats' share of the ethnic vote by 30 or even 35 percent (Knaggs 2005).

The Republican Party conducted its outreach efforts in ways reminiscent of the Democratic Party's 1960 ¡Viva Kennedy! campaign. Senator John Tower set the Republican Party formula in the early 1970s with his "Tejanos por Tower" campaign ("10 Chicanos Form Group" 1972).

Table 5.1. Party Identification among Texans by Socioeconomic Factors, 2005

	Republican 39%	Democrat 25%	Independent 23%	Other 10%
Age				
18–29	41	25	22	7
30–39	43	23	19	13
40–49	43	21	18	15
50–59	39	24	26	9
60 and older	36	30	26	7
Race/Ethnicity				
Hispanic	26	34	29	8
Anglo	47	21	22	9
Black	8	58	17	12
Gender				
Male	40	20	27	10
Female	29	30	18	10
Region				
East	39	23	26	9
West	43	25	27	5
South	34	31	22	11
North	42	24	22	9
Gulf	47	28	18	7
Central	33	27	30	8
Income				
Less than $10,000	27	42	22	7
$10,001–20,000	27	38	19	12
$20,001–30,000	33	34	26	7
$30,001–40,000	33	27	25	14
$40,001–50,000	40	22	23	11
$50,001–60,000	41	32	16	9
$60,001 and above	52	16	21	9
Education				
Some high school	29	40	20	8
High school grad	34	30	22	9
Some college	43	25	16	14
College grad	45	18	29	7
Graduate school	40	22	26	11

Table 5.2. Total Offices Held by Republicans by Year, 1974 to 2004

Year	U.S. Senate	Other Statewide	U.S. House	Texas Senate	Texas House	County Office	State Board of Education*
1974	1	0	2	3	16	53	
1976	1	0	2	3	19	67	
1978	1	1	4	4	22	87	
1980	1	1	5	7	35	166	
1982	1	0	5	5	36	270	
1984	1	0	10	6	52	377	
1986	1	1	10	6	56	504	
1988	1	5	8	8	57	608	5
1990	1	6	8	8	57	717	5
1992	1	7	9	13	58	814	5
1994	2	13	11	14	61	900	8
1996	2	13	11	17	68	950	8
1998	2	18	11	16	71	973	9
2000	2	18	11	16	71	1,231	9
2002	2	27	15	19	88	1,327†	10
2004	2	27	22	19	87	1,390	10

Source: Halter 2006: 85.
* The State Board of Education was not elected until 1988.
† County offices are estimates by Halter 2006.

Tower's outreach was premised on the assumption that Mexican Americans' cultural values resonated more strongly with the policies and platform of the Republican Party. On the campaign trail, Tower reminded Mexican American audiences that both Anglos and Mexicans fought against Antonio López de Santa Ana at the Alamo, took part in the Texas declaration of independence, and prevailed in the battle of San Jacinto (Knaggs 1986: 67). It was an argument that Mexican Americans had made in the past to counter the racist contention that they were foreigners and to emphasize that many could trace their ancestry to the first settlers in Texas and the fight for Texas Independence ("Albert Fuentes" 1964; Márquez 1993). The Republican Party would take the state's complex history to support the narrative that Mexicans and Anglos were united by a common conservative legacy. Instead of interpreting Texas independence as an Anglo victory over Mexico, the war was cast as a struggle for freedom, as a bridge over the racial chasm.

The Republican Party could correctly point out that the Democratic Party ignored Mexican American leaders and issues (McCrory 1969; Bonavita 1970). As one party operative put it, "all the problems Mexican Americans are suffering from, such as unemployment, civil rights violations, and menial jobs, have occurred under Democrats" ("When Choosing a Party" 1978). While Anglo and Mexican American Democrats wrangled over representation, the Republican leadership had a free hand to shape its electoral message. In his 1978 reelection campaign, John Tower honed his strategy for minority outreach. Calling the project "Estamos de Acuerdo" (We Have an Understanding), the senator spent $13 million in a media blitz (Sosa 2009: 117). The goal was to cast doubt on Democratic sincerity and ward off any accusations of racism that might be lodged against him ("Media Strategy" ca. 1978; Wiese 1978). To that end, Tower hired David Martinez of San Antonio and Celso Moreno of Corpus Christi to devise his outreach strategy ("Tower Aide Promoted" 1978). The two spent the bulk of their time in cities like San Antonio and El Paso. Their appeal to the Mexican American voter centered on employment and Republican claims for better stewardship of the economy. As one of Tower's biographers recalled,

> it was decided an outreach program must be launched to the M-As [*sic*] in several urban areas of Texas with whom Tower could relate better since his Armed Services Committee Assignment. In San Antonio, El Paso and Corpus Christi, their high M-A populations contained many civilians who worked in white and blue collar jobs on military installations. Their concerns might be more focused on adequate funding for those installations, or in smaller communities, keeping the installations open, rather than on some of LBJ's welfare schemes. (Knaggs 1986: 65)

Tower's Spanish-language ads promised a quality education for everyone and preservation of the family. He pledged to promote policies that would help "to get everyone into the free enterprise system. To help everyone who wants to be an owner" (R. Garrett 1978). Tower happily pointed out that his Democratic opponent, congressman Bob Krueger, did not have "one Hispanic American above clerical level on his Washington staff, nor has he ever had one" (McCrory 1978). Tower even aired his own corrido. "El Corrido de John Tower," a nine-verse ballad, praised Tower as the champion of the Mexican American people (Sosa 2009: 118).

Bill Clements worked closely with Tower during his own 1978 campaign for governor (Knaggs 1986). The two coordinated their public appearances and get-out-the-vote campaigns. Clements hired veteran strategists and organizers from Tower's previous campaigns to manage media, polling, and phone banks (Bridges 2003: 140–141). Like Tower, Clements understood that any Republican Party candidate would receive few Mexican American votes. Polling data confirmed that Mexican American voters favored liberal Democratic candidates by a two-to-one margin (Hernández 1978: 3). But Clements was not trying to win the majority of their votes. As one campaign aide put it, "[I]f we get any percentage above 18%, Bill Clements will be your next governor" (Bridges 2003: 157). Based in part on this strategy, Republican Clements served two nonconsecutive terms as governor of Texas, from 1979 to 1983 and from 1987 to 1991.

Clements staffers organized support groups called "Mexican American Democrats and Independents for Clements." The campaign created a "Hispanic Regional Headquarters" for South Texas and placed one in all major urban areas in the state (L. Vara 1978a, 1978b; Vera 1978a). Each had a chair responsible for the Hispanic outreach ("Hispanic Chairman" ca. 1978). Clements operatives vowed to take his campaign "to the heart of the Barrio" (J. Chapa 1978). Candidate Clements advocated traditional Republican issues like minimal state government, fiscal restraint, and local control but took a clear stand against discrimination, declaring that Mexican Americans were tax-paying citizens deserving of equal treatment. His outreach was vigorous: Clements made contact with political and religious leaders in every city he visited (Vera 1978b). Clements criticized his predecessor for the growth of government during his term and vowed to uphold equal opportunity in the business world, an important issue to Mexican American business owners (Márquez 2003: ch. 5). Clements also offered Mexican Americans equal access to his office—an appealing prospect to conservatives who often found themselves thrown together with liberals in civil rights organizations like LULAC and the GI Forum.

Clements's aggressive radio and television campaign centered on the themes of hard work, individual initiative, family ties, and, most importantly, questioning loyalty to the Democratic Party (Ed Yardang and Associates ca. 1978). Clements senior advisor G. G. Garcia argued that Mexican Americans might be liberal in their political outlook but it was untrue that "they want something for nothing—that's what the Democrats peddle and the Republicans have come to believe. We are an extremely self-reliant, suspicious, and parochial people with a strong conservative philosophy borne [sic] of inherent traits. For example, the people in this area traveled hundreds and even thousands of miles in search of a livelihood, back-breaking stoop labor. Does this sound like a people who has a strong manifestation of liberal political philosophy?" (G. G. Garcia ca. 1978). To drive this point home, the Clements campaign purchased airtime on forty-eight Spanish-language radio stations in Texas. One used the voice of Ben Fernandez, who was conducting his own campaign for the Republican Party's presidential nomination (R. Garrett 1978). His bilingual ads said:

> When you think about it, Mexican American families, like you and I really have the same basic philosophies of the Republican Party. A philosophy that says that work is honor—that nothing is free. That the family is the strength behind true happiness in the home. That we have the same opportunities as has any other citizen. This is Bill Clements's philosophy too. (Ed Yardang and Associates 1978)

The Republican outreach of 1978 also played on partisan divisions among civil rights leaders. Former LULAC National presidents William Bonilla and Manuel González enthusiastically supported the candidacies of both Bill Clements and John Tower. The two argued that Republican opposition to the social welfare programs of the 1960s was fully consistent with an antidiscrimination civil rights agenda. In their words, the Democratic Party created "give-away" programs that harmed Mexican Americans by taking away their pride and ambition ("Tower Endorsed" 1978). Clements's campaign message was cast in upbeat and culturally informed terms, but the candidate's blunt manner offered little comfort to civil rights leaders like Bonilla and González who were making the argument that Mexican American interests were best served by a Republican administration. During the 1978 campaign, Clements stopped at a historic mission outside Goliad. He praised the Spanish settlers of Texas for the civilization that they brought to the New World. He said that the Spanish had taken the local Aranama Indians and "domesticated them—kind of like you tame a wild animal. Is this area of Texas more productive, more fulfilling of God's purpose . . . than when there were let's just say 5,000 Indians here eatin' insects? These questions sort of answer themselves." When pressed to clarify his position on issues of importance to Mexican Americans, he blurted: "I'm not running for governor of Mexico, you know" ("Meanwhile Back at the Alamo" 1978).

After his election, Clements worked to remedy his public relations missteps by promising to fill the void left by the Democratic Party's decades of neglect. To highlight his point the governor circulated a legislative "furniture" list—the names of Democratic representatives with large Mexican American constituencies that he considered particularly inept and ineffective. He ridiculed the Democratic Party's history of creating special committees or assigning individuals to deal with minority problems and concerns but little else. Clements said that as governor he would end the practice of tokenism and would name Mexican Americans to high positions on his staff as integral parts of his administration (G. G. Garcia ca. 1978).

Under the Clements administration the Republican Party fully engaged Mexican American voters. In late 1979 the governor convened the first Hispanic Leadership Institute, his vehicle to explore common political ground with business groups and civil rights organizations like LULAC and the American GI Forum. The groups welcomed the opportunity to meet with the governor and during the meetings identified areas where they agreed with his positions or were ready to cooperate with his administration ("Minutes of the Hispanic Leadership Meeting" 1979). Clements tapped the business community as a sounding board for political proposals that would have an impact on the Mexican American community. He formed a committee called the Hispanic Leaders of Texas to advise him on issues like the implementation of his policy agenda or the most efficient use of federal monies. Participants raised questions about the details of the governor's immigration proposals, civil rights enforcement, state employment, and bilingual education ("Hispanic Leaders of Texas" 1980b; "Governor Clements and the Hispanic Leaders" 1981; "Hispanic Leaders of Texas" 1981; R. Montoya 1981b). When Clements ran for reelection two years later, Richard Montoya, the governor's special assistant for Mexican American affairs, argued that Clements had a better record than all previous governors on civil rights protection, having made over fifty Hispanic appointments to state posts early in his first term. In Montoya's words, "estamos de acuerdo, sí se puede [we are in agreement, yes we can]." The governor was ready to help Mexican Americans, but political, economic, and educational equality would be realized only with "the famous ingredient called 'individual effort'" (R. Montoya 1980).

Bill Clements took special care to nurture an important group of ethnic conservatives, his fellow business owners (Clements 1979). He concentrated on economic development—especially infrastructure development—and trade with Mexico (Flynn 1979; Aurispa 1982d). In order to keep the lines of communication open, Karl Rove, the governor's special assistant for administration, met with Hispanic civil rights and business leaders on a quarterly basis (R. Montoya 1981a). He proposed the creation of a small-business investment bank and a minority small-business investment corporation, ideas targeted toward Mexican American business owners (Aurispa 1981a). The Clements administration built strong communication links with the Texas Association of Mexican American Chambers of Commerce (TAMACC), an emerging conservative voice and friend of the Republican Party (Villalpando 1981). In order to keep lines of communication open Governor Clements met with Mexican American business owners on a monthly basis (Aurispa 1981a). At the governor's request the organization campaigned for Ronald Reagan during his 1980 presidential campaign (Aurispa 1981a). The Texas Republican Party chair observed that TAMACC was the only Hispanic group in the nation to endorse the Republican presidential ticket and President Reagan's economic policies. Realizing that it was an opportunity for Republicans, he urged the state and national party to engage minority business organizations (Upham 1981a, 1981c). The Republican Party chair reminded business leaders that their support of President Reagan and Governor Clements meant that Republicans in turn would support them (Upham 1981b; "Texas GOP Pays Tribute" 1982).

One of Clements's first acts as governor was to address the Rio Grande Valley Mexican American Chamber of Commerce, where cheers and applause interrupted his speech twenty-seven times ("Governor's Comments" 1979). The governor took his public relations campaign to South Texas, meeting with business owners and sitting for interviews with the Spanish-language media (G. G. Garcia 1980a). Clements appointed TAMACC members to the Texas State Industrial Commission and kept close contact with the organization, a gesture that elated its leaders. He later issued a declaration that the second week of September would be "The Week of the Latin Industrialists and Businessmen" (Clements ca. 1982). Because of his support for Mexican American business, the governor was honored by TAMACC at its annual convention and awards banquets (H. Gutierrez 1982a, 1982b; Woodward 1982). Speaking to the organization of business owners, he said that Texas would not levy any new personal or corporate income taxes. He promised that as long as he was governor Texas "will not have either tax!" (Clements 1982a).

Governor Clements reiterated his commitments to fighting crime, job creation, and international trade. He promised more Mexican American representation on state boards, commissions, courts, and task forces (Clements 1982b). The governor's advisors felt that this openness would foster closer ties with civil rights organizations, especially their most conservative members (Aurispa 1981b). In his meetings with Mexican

American leaders Clements reiterated his long-held support for the Voting Rights Act, a popular piece of legislation once opposed by prominent Democratic Party politicians. He supported a temporary guest worker program but promised strict safeguards against the abuse of foreign labor. He also spoke out in support of limited bilingual education reforms, though he carefully avoided any detailed discussion of his proposals (Aurispa 1981a; Montoya 1982).

The governor soon mastered the symbolism of civil rights rhetoric: the full rights of citizenship, loyalty to the United States, sacrifices in the nation's military conflicts, and descent from the state's earliest settlers (Aurispa 1981c). He called Cinco de Mayo, the most important patriotic holiday in Mexico, a day worthy of celebration "wherever freedom loving people live" (Clements 1981b). Like John Tower, Clements said that the history of Texas was defined by "people like Juan Seguin, a captain in the Texas Army at the battle of San Jacinto, and Lorenzo de Zavala, Vice President of the Republic of Texas" (Clements 1981a). When Ronald Reagan visited during midterm elections, Clements joined the president in paying special tribute to American GI Forum leader Hector Garcia. He called Garcia a great civil rights leader who improved the lives of all Texans ("Reagan, Clements" 1982).

Though Bill Clements was adept at invoking the icons of Mexican American ethnic identity for his own uses, he was always clear about his policy goals. When civil rights activists first met with the governor they identified bilingual education, farmworker protection, and police brutality as their most pressing priorities (M. Montemayor 1979; Salinas 1979). Governor Clements wanted to keep cordial relations with civil rights groups but reminded them that he campaigned on a pledge to cut government costs by reducing services. He also promised to promote agriculture and ranching, a potentially explosive issue because of the sector's heavy reliance on low-wage manual labor. The governor carefully navigated this treacherous landscape by creating an office of migrant affairs and sponsoring a two-day conference on farmworker health, community development, and employment training early in his first term (Piña 1979). These initiatives did not mean that Clements wanted to reform the state's agricultural labor policies. Indeed, the governor's economic development policy included a guest worker program, a proposal that drew scorn from Mexican American legislators and grassroots groups (Davis 1979). Clements did not retreat, asserting that a guest worker program would promote economic growth while still protecting agricultural workers. When pressed about the potential for the kinds of abuses endemic to the Bracero Program, Richard Montoya, the governor's director of regional development, assured the governor's critics that the state would provide a verifiable identification and protection system for all, regardless of race or color (R. Montoya 1982).

The governor knew that he could not finesse the issue of low-wage agricultural labor and did not try. Early in his first term the Texas Farm Workers Union was lobbying for legislation that would grant collective bargaining rights to agricultural workers. The union was conducting a well-publicized strike policed by officers from the Department of Public Safety and the Parks and Wildlife Department. Union and community leaders alike complained that law enforcement agencies violated the civil rights of striking farmworkers and their children (G. G. Garcia 1979b; Ruben Garcia 1979). Although assisting farmworkers would be enormously popular among Mexican Americans, it certainly would have alienated Clements's powerful backers in farming and ranching (G. G. Garcia 1979d). Because it was impossible for him to find common ground with the union leaders, he was counseled against meetings with them at all (G. G. Garcia 1979e, 1979f). The governor's staff concluded that he had nothing to gain by supporting farmworker issues. The most that could be done in a conflict between farm owners and labor was to express a vague willingness to meet the governor's critics "at the halfway mark" (G. G. Garcia 1979c).

Clements Republicans

Bill Clements was elected governor with few Mexican American votes. He did, however, name a large number of minorities to positions in his administration. In a process reminiscent of the one initiated by Democratic governor John Connally in the mid-1960s, the Clements staff scrutinized all candidates for loyalty to conservative causes and track records of participating in Republican Party activities (Vera 1978a). All individuals were carefully screened to assure that they had worked for the governor's electoral campaign, contributed money, or demonstrated a strong desire to support the governor's agenda (Beltram 1982; G. G. Garcia 1979a, 1979h, 1980b).

Like former governor Connally, Clements solicited lists of potential appointees from his conservative Mexican American supporters, who in turn warned him against applicants who were Democrats in disguise, unreliable, or in some cases just "whacko" (S. Garcia ca. 1982). The governor's advisors reminded him that driving a wedge between ethnic and political representation was a delicate task. Ignoring the ethnic vote would undermine Republican outreach at a time when the Democrats still controlled most state offices. Likewise, appointing obscure individuals with few connections to their community would discredit the Republican cause in the eyes of a group that still had strong community bonds. The partisan logic was almost exactly the same one utilized by Democratic governor Connally two decades earlier. Appointing ethnic tokens *"will not significantly increase our support in the minority community*. In fact, more often than not, it will have the obverse effect. To appoint a black or brown on the recommendation of others without our input may unnecessarily expose you to the charges leveled at past Governors of appointing *coyotes* and Uncle Toms"* (G. G. Garcia 1979g; emphasis in the original).

Mexican American activists were divided over the new governor's appointments and exchanged ugly recriminations, but conservatives welcomed the debate (Abrams 1982; "LULAC Lauds Clements" 1982; Trejo 1982). A new partisan narrative emerged. Tony Bonilla and Sylvia Hernandez Mattox complained that the Democratic Party had become a paternalistic party supporting an ever-expanding welfare state with few ideas to ensure long-term prosperity (Blalock 1984). Former LULAC president William Bonilla and Louis P. Terrazas of the Republican National Hispanic Assembly accused the Democrats of fiscal irresponsibility. Under a Republican administration, they reasoned, Mexican Americans would be able to participate more fully in the economy if the government took action to lower interest rates and keep inflation under control (Republican National Hispanic Assembly 1982). The newly formed Mexican American Republicans of Texas (MART) added its voice to the dialogue by arguing that the Republican Party offered a break with the past and an alternative solution to community problems (Mexican American Republicans of Texas 1981: 5–6). Roy Barrera Jr., whom Clements appointed as a state district judge, contended that group-based organizing was an artifact of the past. He said that the time had finally arrived when a person's skin color, religion, and heritage were no longer deciding factors in Texas politics ("Candidate Hits Record" 1986; "San Antonio Judge" 1986).

Governor Clements nurtured this cadre of ethnic conservatives. He hired a special assistant to serve as a liaison between his office and conservative civil rights activists and elected officials. One of this assistant's responsibilities was to help Clements nominate Mexican Americans to his administration and elevate the status of Mexican Americans working for a Republican governor (Arnold 1981). Clements established a task force on equal opportunities for women and minorities with the charge to examine all state practices and laws, identify barriers to equal opportunity, and identify corrective action that could be taken by state government (Office of the Governor 1981). In his first term Clements appointed 11 Mexican Americans to judicial posts, more, he claimed, than any Texas governor since World War II (Governor Bill Clements Campaign ca. 1983). Clements also named 143 Mexican Americans to different boards and posts, 13.6 percent of all appointed positions in state government ("Clements' Hispanic Appointments" ca. 1983).

Throughout the nomination process the narrative of race and representation aligned along partisan lines. When Clements appointed conservatives Raul González to the 13th Court of Appeals and Roy Barrera Jr. to Bexar County's 114th Criminal Justice Court, liberals charged him with tokenism. The uproar puzzled the governor's aides, one of whom wondered why liberals complained and explained that all gubernatorial appointments were political by nature. All job seekers, he said, "better pay [their] dues in the Republican Party to win an appointment in this administration" (Malone and Arnold 1981). These appointments validated the worldview of conservatives like LULAC president Oscar Moran and Ed Bernaldez, state director of the American GI Forum. Both declared that under a Republican administration more opportunities were available than ever before. Mexican Americans, they said, came to the United States with a dream and "the dream was coming true." Going on the offensive, the LULAC president scolded his liberal detractors: "You cannot deny the Hispanic appointments. You cannot deny the open door policy. The governor . . . is a governor for all Texans" (Hutcheson 1982; Tiede 1982).

Bill Clements was the governor for all conservative Texans. He disarmed the ethnic critics of his administration and party in a manner reminiscent of debates that civil rights activists had in the 1960s and 1970s. This time, instead of Henry B. González and the Mexican American Democrats demanding partisan loyalty, it was a Republican governor and his ethnic allies policing partisan boundaries. When running for a second term, Clements campaigned on this theme, disparaging the Democratic Party for undervaluing Mexican American voters and their policy preferences. He argued that it was not the Republican Party but liberal activists who were out of step with Mexican Americans and that their exclusion from state government had taken place under a Democratic watch (Henry 1982). Clements pointed to his support of the Voting Rights Act, increased educational opportunities, and an end to workplace raids by the Immigration and Naturalization Service (INS). As governor he increased

Table 5.3. Comparison of Hispanic Voter Registration and Turnout in the United States and the Five Southwestern States

	1976	1980	Increase	Percent
Registration				
United States	2,646,090	3,426,990	780,810	30
Arizona	92,500	105,200	12,700	14
California	715,600	988,131	272,531	38
Colorado	81,000	114,201	33,201	41
New Mexico	135,000	170,900	35,900	27
Texas	488,000	798,563	310,563	64
Turnout				
United States	1,820,580	2,172,711	352,131	19
Arizona	58,300	72,588	14,288	25
California	522,400	643,285	120,885	23
Colorado	60,000	83,366	23,366	39
New Mexico	97,300	116,212	18,912	19
Texas	278,200	415,253	137,053	49

Source: Southwest Voter Registration Education Project 1983.

the number of highway contracts awarded to minorities and created an office of regional business development and an office of minority business development. In order to make sure that his message was not lost, he kept in close contact with the leaders of established groups like LULAC, the American GI Forum, and the Texas Association of Mexican American Chambers of Commerce (Governor Bill Clements Campaign 1983).

The governor and the Republican Party were adjusting to a newly empowered voting bloc just as the Democrats were. When Clements narrowly defeated Democrat John L. Hill in 1978, Mexican American voter registration and turnout were increasing significantly. From 1976 to 1980 Mexican American voter registration was up 30 percent in the Southwest, with registration in Texas increasing 64 percent. Turnout was up 19 percent overall, with Texas Mexican Americans increasing their turnout by 49 percent. Although their turnout rate still lagged behind that of Anglos, the number of Mexican Americans voting in gubernatorial elections doubled from 1978 to 1982. In four years the number registered to vote increased by 41 percent: an estimated 318,742 voted in the governor's race, a dramatic 86 percent increase (Brischetto 1982: 1).

Bill Clements did not make significant inroads into the growing ethnic vote but targeted those most likely to support the Republican Party's candidates and its philosophy. The governor knew that Mexican Americans were a liberal voting bloc but were less attached to the Democratic Party than were African Americans. Mexican Americans voted two to one for Democratic candidates, but strong identification with the Democratic Party only stood at 56 percent. Moreover, those with high income, education, and occupational status were more likely to consider themselves independent voters (Brischetto 1985: 19–20). As a voting bloc Mexican Americans were less cohesive than African Americans, but big majorities identified problems like unemployment and lack of social services as their most important issues, favoring increased government spending on domestic social programs (Brischetto 1983: 3–4). Mexican Americans were not moving to the Republican Party in large numbers, but Robert Brischetto and Rodolfo de la Garza (1985) observed that

> the Democratic Party should not assume that it may continue to count on unquestioned support from future generations of politically active Mexican Americans. However, in their policy orientations, they articulate "liberal" preferences on all issues examined except abortion. Republicans . . . would do well to focus their energy on recruiting and mobilizing younger, better educated Mexican Americans. (Brischetto and de la Garza 1985: 33)

Reweaving the Democratic Party Coalition

Mexican American activists became an integral part of the Democratic Party's coalition in the 1970s, even as the party's candidates for statewide office continued to be conservative Anglos. They were individuals who over long careers established themselves in a party previously unaccountable to liberals and minorities. The result was an increasingly liberal and integrated party base with an old guard Anglo elite. This tension once again put Mexican American Democrats in the difficult position of negotiating with and supporting deeply flawed Anglo leaders in the name of party solidarity.

The best example of the unresolved racial conflicts within the Democratic Party came in 1982 when attorney general Mark White became the Democratic Party's gubernatorial nominee and went on to unseat Republican Bill Clements. White had served as Texas secretary of state under Dolph Briscoe and was later elected state attorney general. In 1975

White infuriated Texas minorities by lobbying against extending the Voting Rights Act to Texas. At a time when the Mexican American Democrats were suing the party over its biased rules and procedures, White testified before the U.S. Congress that the old barriers to full voting participation in Texas were gone. He conceded that people of color were failing to exercise their voting rights at the same rate as Anglos but argued that the gap was rooted in socioeconomic disparities—a contention vehemently disputed by black and Mexican American elected officials (Jordan 1975; Wiese 1975). Mark White opposed federal oversight of state voting practices, further asserting that minority voters experienced few problems and that Texas demonstrated good faith in addressing those that remained. In his testimony White added that the state "finds itself in the apparently contradictory position of wholeheartedly supporting the goals of those who wish to extend the Voting Rights Act of 1965 to Texas and opposing certain of those amendments which do so as being unnecessary and counterproductive" (McGrath 1975b). White argued that Texas was prepared to accept the "solemn responsibility" of protecting minority voting rights (White 1975). In effect, Attorney General White opposed the extension of federal protection to an important bloc that would help elect him to office seven years later.

White's opposition to an extension of the Voting Rights Act incensed the Mexican American Democrats. MAD leaders, having sued the Democratic party leadership for racial discrimination only a year earlier, were incredulous that a Democratic attorney general would argue before Congress that racism in Texas politics was a thing of the past (Bernal 1974a, 1974b; Castillo 1974c; "State Officials Sued" 1975). Leonel Castillo testified before Congress as well and offered a diametrically opposed interpretation of the facts, urging passage of the Voting Rights Act's extension to Mexican Americans because of continued racism and discrimination. He supported his testimony with a detailed, 29-page report documenting numerous cases of harassment and intimidation of Mexican American voters in Texas. Castillo's list of grievances included denial of registration certificates; denial of assistance to non-English speakers, illiterates, and disabled voters; biased use of residential requirements; inaccessible voting places; and difficulty in obtaining registration materials (L. Castillo 1975).

Mark White's opposition to an extension of the Voting Rights Act dogged him during his bid to unseat Governor Clements. His Mexican American critics were loud and angry. State representative Hugo Berlanga called the former attorney general "totally unacceptable." He said that White "could do more damage to the Hispanic community than anyone

Photo 5.1. Irma Rangel with Texas governor Mark White. Irma Rangel Collection, South Texas Archives, Texas A&M University–Kingsville, Box 230, Folder 6, Item 955.

since John Connally" ("Mexican American Democrats Divided" 1982). Former LULAC president Ruben Bonilla accused White of cowardice and racial demagoguery (McLemore 1982; Garza 1986: 5). Bonilla sponsored a motion at the Mexican American Democrats' yearly convention condemning White for his failure to support an extension of the Voting Rights Act (Palomo ca. 1982). When MAD members voted to endorse a candidate in the Democratic primary, White came in last ("Mexican American Democrats Divided" 1982).

Republicans fueled the attack against White. They characterized him as the prime example of a complacent Democratic Party official indifferent to the needs of minorities and the poor. Republican Party press releases reminded the minority electorate that Governor Clements supported an extension of the Voting Rights Act while his Democratic opponent testified against it as Texas attorney general (Republican Party of Texas ca. 1982). In one of the most publicized events of the 1982 campaign Clements delivered a blistering attack against White on September 16, Mexican Independence day. He also dedicated a monument honoring Hispanics in Texas (Balz 1982).

Mark White went on to win the 1982 Texas gubernatorial election, a feat credited in part to the aid of Mexican American elected officials and their subsequent get-out-the-vote campaign (Mark White for Governor 1982b; "Democratic Effort" ca. 1982). Energetic get-out-the-vote drives were essential because Mexican Americans were less than enthusiastic about White. In the Democratic primary White was the least-favored candidate, receiving only 36 percent of their vote. He was the only winning Democrat in the general election who did not receive majority Mexican American support in the Democratic primary (Hernández 1982). Tepid backing by minority voters was a concern for White because Anglo support for the Democratic Party was dropping precipitously. During the 1980s Anglo voting for Democratic gubernatorial candidates dipped below 50 percent, but Mexican American support for Democratic candidates held steady in the mid-80s (Brischetto and Avina 1986). On average 88 percent of rural and 86 percent of urban Mexican Americans cast their votes for White—almost twice the Democratic voting rate of Anglo voters (Brischetto 1982: 3, 25).

Mexican Americans were part of the Democratic governing structure and a reliable voting bloc, but the party was losing its majority status. When White won the Democratic Party's gubernatorial nomination in 1982, the Mexican American Democrats could no longer skewer him without endangering their own party. MAD quickly reversed itself and vigorously endorsed his candidacy. Ruben Bonilla, previously one of White's harshest critics, publicly supported his candidacy in warm, personal terms. Bonilla conceded that the two disagreed at times but said that he wanted to emphasize that "Mark White and the Bonilla family have been friends for many, many years" ("Bonillas" 1982). He later joined a group of Mexican American mayors from South Texas in a campaign to unite all Democrats in support of White (Bonilla 1982; "Hispanic Groups" 1982). MAD's newfound enthusiasm for candidate White was virtually guaranteed from the onset because, as one member put it, the group was obligated to stand "100% behind our party's candidates" (A. González ca. 1982). Indeed the MAD rules and bylaws required everyone fully to support all of the Democratic Party's nominees as a condition of caucus membership (Mexican American Democrats n.d.). For his part, White promised a new era of cooperation between Texas Hispanics and the governor's office (M. White 1982). He said: "[A]s Governor I will have an open door to all Mexican American groups such as MAD, LULAC and the G.I. Forum. I will expect MAD to be instrumental in the appointment process of my administration and will rely on MAD for recommendations to key positions in state government" ("Mexican American Democrats Candidate Questionnaire" ca. 1982).

Mark White won a narrow victory over Bill Clements with the strong backing of low-income, working-class, and minority voters—the long elusive "natural" coalition of liberals. White captured 71 percent of lower-income whites, 16 percent of upper-income whites, virtually 100 percent of the black vote, and 86 percent of the Mexican American vote (Davidson 1990: 177). He owed his success to an alliance of interests in which Mexican Americans were an increasingly influential part. Mexican Americans not only delivered an overwhelming majority of their votes to White but were participating in the Democratic primary at a higher rate than the general voting public—they were 18 percent of the registered voters but 27 percent of those who went to the polls (Diehl 1982a). Only seven years after he opposed an extension of the Voting Rights Act to Texas, Governor White said that "the government I create will be formed in coalition with the leaders of the Mexican American community. That it will be a government committed to raise the economic levels of Mexican Americans across the state" (White ca. 1982a). He added: "[I]f you call Austin, you better be able to speak Spanish" (Attlesey 1982).

For the first time the Democratic Party nominee and later governor openly embraced a multicultural Democratic Party: "[W]e're the party of the many and the poor and the dispossessed[, which] includes not just dispossessed, it includes people who need help, and that's really what the Democratic Party stands for in my judgment" (White 1987). White claimed a record of defending minorities against discrimination, protection of historically black colleges, criminal prosecutions against violent white supremacy groups, and a revision of voter registration laws (Mark White Committee 1982a, ca. 1982b). He supported college work-study, guaranteed student loans, backed denial of tax-exempt status for colleges that discriminate on racial grounds, and increased state aid to state universities (Mark White for Governor 1982a). White made promises to teachers, blacks, Mexican Americans, and labor unions, saying that he would enforce and expand civil rights protection, increase Mexican American appointments at all levels, raise funding for bilingual education, increase teachers' salaries, protect collective bargaining rights for farmworkers, and fund new social service programs. Finally, he promised to do all of these things without raising taxes (Dugger 1982; Mexican American Democrats 1982; "Mexican American Democrats Candidate Questionnaire" ca. 1982).

After the election MAD activists pressed the governor to fulfill his campaign promises. In response White appointed five Mexican Americans to state boards and commissions, including one to the University of Texas Board of Regents ("White Keeps Promise" 1983). Gilbert Peña headed the administration's Criminal Justice Division, Rafael Quintanilla Jr. headed the Texas Department of Community Affairs, and Lupe Zamarripa was hired as White's special assistant (Henry 1983; Machado 1983; Pinkerton 1983). White later was instrumental in passing an indigent health care bill, a salary increase for state teachers, and a bill that narrowed the funding gap between the richest and poorest school districts. He led the Texas Senate and House to appropriate additional funds for unemployment benefits, worker's compensation for farmworkers, and preschool programs. In order to pay for the new programs, however, White broke his promise not to raise taxes (Reinhold 1985; McCall 2009: 73, 75).

Mark White could not refuse his base, but conservatives were outraged over tax increases. Businesses employed increasingly sophisticated methods to protect their assets from taxation. Oil and gas interests were especially active, as increased taxes on oil and gas production were long believed to be the only alternative to income taxes (Rips 1985). Some MAD leaders like state representative Gonzalo Barrientos, however, argued that the governor did not go far enough. Barrientos noted that White once called a special session of the legislature to discuss brucellosis (a bacterial disease affecting cattle), the Texas Employment Commission, and special appropriations for Texas Southern University while two of the Mexican American Legislative Caucus's highest priorities, a Human Rights Commission and worker's compensation for farmworkers, were ignored (Barrientos et al. 1983). The new governor faced the impossible task of appeasing his party loyalists while retaining the votes of ticket-splitting Anglo Democrats. By the end of his first term the dilemma had buffeted his administration from one direction to another, making him vulnerable to a Republican challenge. As one journalist observed, "[F]or four years Mark White has been unable to make up his mind. He has advocated one side, then the other, both, and neither" (Burka 1986b).

In 1986 the Republican Party mounted a political offensive against White, with former governor Bill Clements campaigning hard to regain the governor's seat. That year the Mexican American Democrats executive committee endorsed White and the entire Democratic slate for election to statewide office, though he would go on to lose his reelection bid (R. Bonilla 1986). MAD cemented a strong working relationship with a state governor and vowed to do all that it could to ensure his reelection, but the Democratic Party found it increasingly difficult to assemble a winning coalition. In order to elect Democrats to statewide office, it needed to field moderate candidates capable of attracting working-class and low-income Anglo voters as well as ensure a high turnout among minority voters, all in the face of a racially and ideologically unified Republican Party.

Fissures among Mexican American voters further complicated this diverse and unwieldy coalition. Poor and working-class voters were increasingly aware of the role that they played in Democratic politics but not convinced that they were rewarded for their loyalty. A report commissioned by Mark White's campaign warned that the party's traditional stronghold south of the "Mexican-Dixon" line (from San Antonio to El Paso) was becoming increasingly unreliable. Although it was unlikely that they would abandon the Democrats, turnout among low-income voters was likely to decline in this Democratic stronghold (Muñoz and Associates 1982). At the same time a growing number of assimilated voters were finding the Democratic Party's platform less appealing. Gene Rodriguez, MAD co-founder and member of the Democratic National Committee, worried that the party's ethnic base was eroding. Mexican American voters were reliably Democratic, but enough of them voted for Republican candidates to demonstrate that the utility of ethnic identity as an organizing tool was on the decline. The economic and demographic changes that strengthened ethnic organizing after World War II were now undermining the foundations of group solidarity in the Democratic Party. In Rodriguez's words, MAD needed to keep low-income Mexican Americans' loyalty to the party and "regain the confidence of emerging middle-class Hispanics in the midst of the dual assault from 1) fellow Democrats reacting to the 'special interest pawn' charge against the Party and 2) from Republicans targeting emerging middle class business and professional Hispanics" (G. Rodriguez 1985).

Mark White frustrated his liberal base with his promise not to increase taxes, but an economic recession forced Democrats to scale back their expectations. Halfway through his term, the governor told the legislature that expenditures would exceed income by $791 million in the next biennium if state spending continued unabated (Machado 1982; K. Thompson 1982; McCall 2009: 71). Texas faced a fiscal crisis. Mark White convinced the legislature that it was necessary to raise taxes, thereby alienating liberal and conservative voters just two months before the 1986 election. Even with the new revenues the state's budget shortfall negated any further expansion of its social welfare net. As White phrased it during what would become an unsuccessful reelection campaign, "[W]e can tighten our belts and bring our spending levels down to our income levels. And that is exactly what we are going to do" (McCall 2009: 76).

The End of Ethnic Confrontation

Despite their party's changing fortunes the mood was upbeat among Mexican American Democrats during the late 1980s and 1990s. The record reflects a pride in improved minority participation that had taken place since the group's creation and a sense that Mexican Americans were no longer engaged in a subaltern struggle over culture and civil rights. Rather they were players in shaping the course of the state's economic development, employment, and educational reform ("Simply MAD" 1986). They were part of a liberal coalition, full-fledged members of an integrated party system. In 1995 Carlos Truan was the most senior member of the Senate and the first Mexican American "dean" by virtue of his seniority. After thirty years in the Senate he had compiled an impressive legislative record by chairing major Senate committees and authoring legislation relating to bilingual education, childcare, adult education, and public housing. His accomplishments included the merger of South Texas colleges with the Texas A&M and University of Texas systems, a dramatic expansion of health-care services for South Texas, and the creation of a childhood lead poisoning and birth defects registry ("Carlos F. Truan" ca. 1995). For Truan, the long-term problems of poverty and lack of state services still plagued Mexican Americans, but the future was bright:

> [T]he Hispanic community has sought to gain entry into the mainstream of American life through the same kind of political empowerment used by every other ethnic group that has come to these shores. We have suffered for the classic reason—lack of political power, lack of representation in the halls of government where the decisions are made. The strides that have been made . . . have all resulted from the historic one person-one vote rule which crushed the at-large system, and the Voting Rights Act, and the subsequent election of Hispanics to the Legislature and to our successes in the Federal and State courts. (Truan 1990)

In contrast to the 1950s, candidates running for statewide office no longer patronized Mexican American leaders with symbolic gestures. Mexican American caucuses in the Senate and House used their numbers and partisan ties to advance their legislative priorities and investigate cases of racial and gender discrimination in state government (Galvan 1994; Lucio 1995; Senate Hispanic Caucus 1995). MAD regularly conducted screening and endorsements of candidates for state office at its annual conventions (Alonzo 1992b), and MAD members were active participants in national politics. MAD endorsed Jimmy Carter for president in 1976 and in 1980. Both times the group joined with other Latinos at the national level to help formulate the Democratic Party's national platform (Cherow-O'Leary 1980; McCrory 1980a, 1980b, 1980d). In 1992 Bill Clinton sought and won MAD's endorsement. As the *Economist* reported, Clinton worked to get the endorsement of the Mexican American Democrats and "did so early, attending the MAD convention in mid-January when everyone else was in New Hampshire" ("And Lest We Forget" 1992). MAD commanded the greatest direct influence at the state level. In 1990 former governor Mark White addressed the Mexican American Democrats convention and asked for their endorsement. Reminding his audience that when he was governor

> "the Hispanic community was a full partner in the development of our state's public policy," he added that he ". . . appointed Hispanics—many from MAD's ranks—to important state boards and commissions that run our state agencies. We also appointed a MAD member as the first Hispanic female district judge and a MAD member as Texas' first Hispanic Supreme Court Justice," White added. "I could go on and on listing the number of MAD members who were named to important positions, but the point is that we worked together—for the betterment of this state." ("White Asks MAD to Help" 1990)

Mark White lost in the primary election to Ann Richards, who would go on to win the governor's seat for the Democrats on a populist agenda. Richards energized the Democratic liberal base by campaigning for a "New Texas," a state that was diverse, "where opportunity knows no race or color or gender" (Sheeler 2000: 119, 120). She appointed so many women and minorities to state agencies that observers called her record "precedent setting" (Sheeler 2000: 83). MAD chair Roberto Alonzo noted the change and reminded his members that the organization had secured firm commitments from all candidates for statewide contests through a careful vetting process. In a letter to MAD members he said that it was because of their work for the Democratic Party that "we have Ann Richards for Governor." When MAD asked for appointments in her

Photo 5.2. State representative Irma Rangel with Texas governor Ann Richards during the 72nd Session in 1991. Irma Rangel Collection, South Texas Archives, Texas A&M University–Kingsville, Box 228, Folder 1, Item 16.

administration, "we got them" (Alonzo 1992a). He was correct about her appointments. A study conducted by the *Dallas Morning News* found that 45 percent of the nearly 2,700 appointments made by Governor Richards were women, compared with eighteen percent appointed by Bill Clements and twenty-three percent by Mark White. She also named twice as many minorities as either of her two predecessors. Alonzo praised the governor but reminded MAD members that they had to work in all phases of the electoral process: "You have to be at the table in order for this kind of thing to happen" (Slater 1994).

The growing number of minority elected officials and party activists in Texas was part of the long-awaited minority ascendency in state politics. Michael Rosenfeld (1998) found that by the early 1970s Mexican Americans had achieved descriptive parity in Texas and the Southwest. That is, the number of Spanish-surnamed elected officials was roughly proportional to their numbers in the general population. The gradual increase in the number of Mexican American representatives at all levels of government went hand in hand with socioeconomic progress. Mexican Americans and blacks gained unprecedented representation in the Texas legislature. They were part of a liberal ascendancy in Texas, but one that quickly reached its limits in a conservative state. Minority Democratic representatives like Mickey Leland and Henry B. González were some of the most liberal representatives in Congress. But Anglo Democrats from Texas were far more conservative than the typical Democratic House member and generally more conservative than the average southern Democrat (A. Watkins 1982: 5, 23).

Political trends did not portend well for Mexican American Democrats. But their political caucus in the legislature became one of the most effective groups in Austin before the complete reversal of the Democratic Party's fortunes. The Senate Hispanic Caucus named its priorities as public school aid, higher education initiatives in South Texas, Human Services, colonias, juvenile crime, emissions testing, and redistricting ("74th Legislative Priorities" 1995). Fourteen Mexican American state representatives traveled to Mexico to meet with Mexican officials to understand the impact of the North American Free Trade Agreement (NAFTA) (Cavazos 1991). They hoped to devise a plan to help impoverished areas of Texas in order to reap the benefits of the inevitable internationalization of trade (Truan 1992, 1998a). Now it was possible for them to have a significant impact on the policy-making process. As one observer put it,

> The 32 members—who include Hispanics plus non-Hispanic lawmakers who represent predominantly Hispanic districts—do not have the sheer power of numbers to impose their will in the Capitol, but their influence is formidable, and can in many instances determine whether a given piece of legislation will receive a favorable hearing or be consigned to the round file. ("Berlanga's Selection" 1995)

During a time when Mexican Americans were arguably at the highest point of their influence in the state capitol, the Democratic Party's power was ebbing. Ann Richards would only serve one term. Although public opinion polls revealed general satisfaction with her job performance and that she was well liked, Richards was politically vulnerable. Her conservative opponents attacked her outspoken defense of women's rights and association with liberal causes (Sheeler 2000: 108–109). Richards's appointments, which she declared would make government more open, drew partisan and sometimes racist criticism (Fikac 1993; Ray ca. 1993; Scott and Fuentes 1993; Stutz 1993). Officials in her administration were also worried. In an internal document circulated prior to her reelection campaign, the governor's staff concluded that her prospects were not good. She had failed to deliver on promised education reforms, which her critics attributed to a lack of substantive plans for the state. Like former governor Mark White, she alienated both her liberal base and fiscal conservatives by raising corporate and property taxes while simultaneously cutting social services. Finally, the report said that the large number of gay and lesbian appointments to her administration angered social conservatives and was "sure to be a GOP target" ("AWR News Articles" ca. 1993).

Ann Richards's political career ended when she lost her bid for reelection to Republican George W. Bush in 1994. The Democratic Party resumed its decline with her defeat, but Mexican Americans remained firmly incorporated into state politics even without an accompanying empowerment. Mexican American Democratic elected official Gonzalo Barrientos pointed to his twenty years in the Texas State Senate with pride. He and his colleagues had successfully passed legislation dealing with discrimination and civil rights. Barrientos was instrumental in passing the Top Ten Percent Plan, which increased minority enrollment in higher education by giving the top 10 percent of any high school graduating class automatic acceptance into any public Texas college. He was also gratified that he could represent a racially diverse central Texas district where policy mattered more than race or gender (Hunter 1998). Because of the growing number of conservatives in public life, however, politicians like Barrientos were forced to moderate their tone and compromise (Elizondo 1997). Not long after he won a seat in the Texas House of Representatives, Barrientos was much less sanguine about achieving the scale of change that he first thought was possible. He was struck by the difficulty of resolving social problems through the legislature, especially "complicated, Chicano-related issues." His own legislative priorities like bilingual education, minority access to the University of Texas system, and protection for migrant farmworkers proved far more difficult to achieve than he had imagined (Case 1976). He felt that in some cases practical solutions to these problems were virtually impossible to devise (Hendricks 1974). When first elected, Barrientos was very angry about racial and economic injustice in Texas but soon learned some hard lessons: "[W]hen you're a novice you try to do everything in the world. You cannot. You cannot try to resolve fifty different issues, you have to learn to take one, two, three at a time, but no more than that if possible" (Barrientos 2009).

South Texas representative Irma Rangel took a darker view of the legislative process. She agreed that social problems were deeply rooted in class inequalities and resistant to change and often found it impossible to serve her impoverished constituents adequately. In Rangel's mind the single most important thing that they needed was a higher standard of living. But in order to fund programs that would alleviate their suffering, she would have to convince a majority of Texans and the state's most powerful corporations to make painful financial sacrifices. Instead government was a place where interest groups fought against one another for limited state resources while the poor and working people got "trampled" (Rangel ca. 1982).

Politicians like Barrientos and Rangel were now part of a governing system with a structural bias against racial minorities and the poor. Moreover, as Mexican Americans made greater strides in government, they were less and less portrayed by the media (or saw themselves) as racial or ethnic agents. For example, Hugo Berlanga was elected to the State Senate in 1982 and rose to powerful leadership positions, including chair of the Senate Finance committee ("Berlanga Used Politics" 1991; Treviño 1991). In 1987 Berlanga became Speaker pro tem of the state legislature, an event that one journalist commented "was hardly noticed by the state's media." It was an accomplishment that transpired without the "First Hispanic Syndrome," the "near beatification of those Hispanics who make landmark breakthroughs in their field" (Hight 1991). South Texas mayor Arcenio García agreed that Texas politics had fundamentally changed. His said goal of improving the lives of the South Texas poor remained but would only find its solution through governing, a slow and complex process. Elected as mayor of Cotulla in 1972 and 1974, García said that the biggest problem facing Mexican Americans in public life was not racial representation but the practical, day-to-day work of government:

> There are some people who say we are still in the '60s. Those people have no vision. Our [Raza Unida] original goal was for representation and we've gotten that. We are on the Commissioner's Court, School Boards, Mayors . . . the original goal of acquiring barrio representation has been and is being met . . . [Now] they must deal with budgets, law enforcement, court systems, indigent services, how departments spend money. (Arcenio García 2003)

Dan Morales was the first Mexican American Texas state attorney general but had a sparse record of activism in community politics, civil rights organizations, and the Mexican American Democrats. Morales not only felt uneasy being identified as an ethnic public official but was one of the most conservative Democrats in the state. He was the first Mexican American elected to head a state agency in Texas history, a distinction

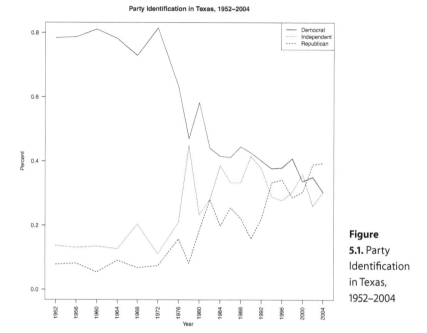

Party Identification in Texas, 1952–2004

Figure 5.1. Party Identification in Texas, 1952–2004

he wore uncomfortably. Morales was a new breed of Mexican American politician, assimilated to the point that his racial background had little bearing on his attitudes and actions. As state attorney general he issued a ruling in *Hopwood v. Texas* (1996) that prohibited racial preferences in the state's universities and colleges. He argued that formal equality gave minorities the best route to upward mobility and personally found racially conscious admission policies "pernicious and cynical" (D. Morales 1997). Morales distanced himself from the state's ethnic politics to such an extent that one journalist found him lacking in "the inspiration of [Henry] Cisneros [or] the ideological passion of Congressman Henry B. González" (R. Draper 1996: 168).

Morales did not identify with the partisan debates over ethnic interests and representation, preferring to stand apart from that discussion. As much as he tried, however, the ambitious Morales could not escape the political currents of a racially stratified state. The normalization of Mexican American participation in government and politics did not erase the power of racism to stigmatize. As seen in the next chapter, Morales would soon be ensnarled in an explosive mixture of racial and partisan politics that would have a profound impact on his career and on the Democratic Party.

Table 5.4. Voting in the 1978 Texas General Election/Governor's Race

| | Overall Votes | | | |
	Total	Hill	Clements	Others
Number	2,353,453	1,159,787	1,174,720	18,946
Percent		49.2	49.9	0.8

| | Mexican American Votes (27.2% of total votes) | | | |
	Total	Hill	Clements	Others
Number	161,010	121,241	31,236	5,796
Percent		75.3	19.4	3.6

Conclusion

Shifting demographics, a modern economy, and nonstop mobilization changed the complexion of Texas politics in the 1990s. In Texas and other southwestern states, the number of minority elected officials was proportional to their numbers in the general population or very close. Vast economic inequalities among the races remained. But in the process of gaining proportional representation the historical connection between race and political advocacy blurred during this period. The idea of racial advocacy receded into the background and the race-neutral, partisan vision of Henry B. González prevailed. The ethnic insurgency of La Raza Unida Party was soundly rejected as morally unacceptable and politically impractical. Few Mexican Americans entering party politics by the end of the twentieth century did so as ethnic advocates, and anyone tempted to do so was restricted by ideological counterarguments, party rules, and the need to cobble together an alliance with Anglo liberals. The elasticity of ethnic identity was demonstrated in this period when Mexican American Republicans formulated their own arguments about the proper role of race in politics and what constituted a logical or fair solution to racial inequality. Refusing to cede the racial high ground to the Democratic Party, Republicans made their case for minority progress via lower taxes, limited government, and formal equality. It was a strategy carefully planned and systematically articulated by Texas senator John Tower and Governor

Table 5.4. Continued

Mexican American Voting in Ten Metropolitan Areas

County	City-Urban Areas	Turnout *(Percent of all voters)*	*Percent for Hill*	*Percent for Clements*	*Percent for Others*
Bexar	San Antonio	30.1	83.7	11.8	4.5
Hidalgo	Pharr-Edinburg, McAllen	26.4	77.4	22.5	—
El Paso	El Paso	28.2	76.7	16.8	6.4
Cameron	Harlingen, Brownsville	27.0	78.7	19.3	1.9
Harris	Houston	19.1	82.5	17.4	—
Nueces	Corpus Christi	28.0	84.2	10.6	5.0
Webb	Laredo	26.3	62.6	35.0	2.3
Dallas	Dallas	26.7	59.2	38.3	2.4
Travis	Austin	24.4	78.5	18.6	2.8
Tarrant	Fort Worth	24.0	79.7	17.7	2.4
Total		27.1	76.7	18.6	2.4

Mexican American Voting in Eighteen Rural Counties

	Turnout *(Percent of all voters)*	*Percent for Hill*	*Percent for Clements*	*Percent for Others*
Total	27.5	70.9	22.0	7.0

Source: Southwest Voter Registration Education Project 1978: 3–4.

Clements. The result was a new political narrative where partisan ideology submerged ethnic identities and set the terms for future racial compromise and policy outcomes.

This fateful turn in Texas politics had a profound impact on minority politics. Mexican Americans arose as full participants in state electoral politics, but without the power they expected. The same was true for Anglo liberals, a group with whom they had a long and frequently contentious relationship. Once the ideological struggle in the Democratic Party finally tilted in favor of the liberals, their gains were offset by the rapid growth of the Texas Republican Party. A brief reversal in this trend came during the administration of Governor Ann Richards (1991–1995).

Not coincidentally, the Mexican American Democrats and the Mexican American Legislative Caucus reported greater success in crafting and passing legislation that they favored. This newfound influence and recognition was short-lived but points to the potential for minority empowerment in Texas politics as demographic shifts accelerate and participation rates increase.

In the aftermath of Ann Richards's defeat, the Democratic Party's influence waned and the liberal cause suffered. Texas finally had a functioning two-party system, but Mexican American Democratic activists still found that it was almost impossible to solve some of the most pressing problems of their low-income constituents. The enormous problems facing Mexican Americans do not lend themselves to easy solutions, especially with a legislative process that is slow and cumbersome and the limitations of institutional avenues for change. Mexican American incorporation was decades in the making, but their movement into the two major parties was manifest in a relatively short period. La Raza Unida Party and other forms of overt ethnic advocacy were discredited. Racial discontent was channeled into the two major parties, in part because of the actions taken by Mexican American Democrats. Elected representatives and party activists did all they could to prevent a Republican takeover of state politics, but they soon found their purposes stymied by the very party system they defended. Moreover, the once intimate connection between civil rights advocacy and electoral politics had been severed. Members of groups like LULAC and the American GI Forum were drawn into electoral politics as Democrats or Republicans, not as ethnic group representatives.

CHAPTER 6

Tony Sánchez for Governor

Race politics in Texas was upended in 2002. That year Tony Sánchez, a South Texas businessman, won the Democratic Party's nomination for governor. His nomination was a powerfully symbolic act, an affirmation of racial inclusion and power sharing sought by political leaders and community organizations for over fifty years. It was the culmination of a long trend toward political incorporation. Mexican Americans now participated at every level of Democratic Party politics, from the precincts to the State Democratic Executive Committee. They formed an influential party caucus, were appointed to high-level positions in state government, and were elected increasingly to local and at times statewide office. Following these achievements, the party nominated Tony Sánchez to run for the state's highest office, a distinction that he won as the Republican Party was consolidating its grip on state politics and sending the state Democratic Party into the worst crisis in its history. When Bill Clements declined to run for another gubernatorial term in 1990, Ann Richards won a narrow victory and Democrats captured all the state's top positions, but the victory was short-lived. In the 1994 gubernatorial election Republican George W. Bush soundly defeated Richards. Party realignment was complete: the Republican Party had emerged as the state's dominant electoral force. In the following 1998 general election Republicans won every statewide race. The Republican Party would go on to sweep state elections again in 2002, 2006, and 2010 (Texas Secretary of State 1994, 1998, 2002b, 2006, 2010).

In this punishing climate the Texas Democratic Party aligned its politics with those of the national party. It was not the party of the New Deal or the Great Society but one dominated by centrists. Even so, its prospects of capturing statewide office diminished each year. Democratic leaders were

Photo 6.1. Governor George W. Bush with Carlos Truan, Irma Rangel, and others from Kingsville. Irma Rangel Collection, South Texas Archives, Texas A&M University–Kingsville, Box 230, Folder 4, Item 920.

desperate for a solution. Some senior activists thought that nominating a Mexican American to run for governor might reverse their party's declining fortunes, but the gambit was fraught with difficulties. First, the party would have to overcome racial animosities among whites. Anglo voters would have to be convinced that the prospect of a Mexican American governor was not only politically possible but also normatively acceptable. Second, few Mexican American politicians had enough name recognition to run a successful statewide campaign. The Democrats needed a seasoned candidate with the stature of former San Antonio mayor Henry Cisneros to step forward. Finally, there were financial considerations. The Democratic Party had little money, and placing a minority candidate at the top of the ticket could jeopardize fund-raising efforts for all candidates.

It would take an extraordinary politician to overcome these problems, but former Texas comptroller John Sharp, former lieutenant governor Ben Barnes, and Democratic political strategist Kelly Fero believed they knew who that person was. In 2001 they traveled to South Texas to visit oilman Tony Sánchez at his Webb County ranch and convince him to run for governor (Thorpe 2001). They told Sánchez that he would be a formidable candidate. He was Hispanic, politically moderate, and a successful businessman. He also happened to be one of the wealthiest men in the state (Reid 2001; Wilcox 2008). If Sánchez was willing to spend enough money, they said, he could break the Republican grip on Texas politics. The hope was that Sánchez could go on to consolidate a new Democratic Party coalition by energizing Latino voters while unifying other core Democratic groups like blacks, women, and liberal Anglos. Sánchez, it was argued, combined centrist politics with the regional loyalties necessary to forge a new Democratic coalition in Texas. One liberal observer gushed over Sánchez's potential: "[H]e's a longtime Democratic Party stalwart and he's also a gazillionaire and he's from the border" (Mabin 2002).

The exhilaration surrounding the Sánchez candidacy revealed a deeply troubled party. Tony Sánchez was not a party stalwart; instead he had a record of raising money for Republicans. He had little campaign experience, had a limited record of service to the Democratic Party, and was virtually unknown in party circles—much less by the general public (Robison 2001). But the idea of a wealthy, well-assimilated Mexican American heading the ticket sent Democratic hopes soaring. After three decades of losing at the polls, demoralized Democrats were ready to believe that race would be an asset rather than a liability in a high-stakes gubernatorial election. Indeed, for party regulars, discussions over Tony Sánchez's candidacy began to take on a matter-of-fact quality. The exit of conservatives from the party removed a long-standing impediment and, coupled with an increasing number of minority elected officials, made the notion that his race or ethnicity was not a problem more believable. Race and ethnicity no longer called to mind disruptive politics, demands for economic redistribution, or calls for cultural recognition. Democrats began to believe that Sánchez's racial identity would energize not only Mexican Americans but all of the party's base. Indeed Sánchez was the future of Texas politics: the political binder who would forge a powerful liberal coalition. This logic brought Democrats to the conclusion that race would not emerge as an issue during the general election precisely because Sánchez was "a Hispanic who doesn't scare people" (Reid 2001).

In the past Mexican American electoral activism had revolved around issues of community service, civil rights, and economic mobility. Not only did Tony Sánchez's candidacy materialize outside of those deliberations, but in many ways he resembled Anglo governors of the 1950s. He was a pro-business, multimillionaire oilman and banker with conservative political leanings and, like former Democratic governors Allan Shivers,

Price Daniel, and John Connally, sometimes worked for the Republican Party. He was a first-time candidate for public office whose primary qualification was success in the business world. Finally, Sánchez's political views were often nebulous or out of sync with the Democratic Party platform: he categorized himself as "raving moderate" and pledging not to introduce any new taxes (Shannon 2002c, 2002d). He declared that the state needed a change of leadership but took positions similar to those of sitting governor Rick Perry on almost every issue. These inconsistencies provoked one journalist to ask:

> What kind of Faustian bargain may . . . the Democrats be striking to get back into power? Tony Sánchez has been a lavish supporter of George W. Bush. During the last election, Sánchez even worked as a Pioneer, raising more than $100,000 for the Bush cause. According to the watchdog organization Center for Public Integrity, the Sánchez family has given Bush a total of $323,650 over the years, making them the third most generous patrons of Bush's political career, surpassed only by the contributions of Enron Corporation of Houston and MBNA Corporation of Delaware. (Thorpe 2001)

In other words, hopes for a Democratic Party revitalization were in the hands of a wealthy Republican Party fundraiser.

Tony Sánchez's inexperience and conservative inclinations were troubling to some, but no Democratic politician was willing to challenge him in the primary and face the prospect of running against a sitting Republican governor in the general election. The hope was that Sánchez would devote his time and money to devising a winning strategy and revive the Democratic Party. This leap of faith extended to the other two frontrunners for the top positions in the 2002 Democratic primary. That year the party nominated a multiracial team, with Sánchez running for governor, former Dallas mayor Ron Kirk as a black U.S. Senate candidate, and former comptroller John Sharp as an Anglo candidate for lieutenant governor. The great virtue of this lineup, the argument went, was that they reflected the racial composition of liberal voters and the current thinking of the national Democratic Party. Democratic strategists touted the three candidates as their "Dream Ticket," as diverse as the party base. The strategy was to use the time between a pro forma primary and the general election to frame Tony Sánchez as a moderate, postracial alternative to an unpopular governor who would propel the rest of the ticket to victory. That plan evaporated less than an hour before the primary filing deadline,

Photo 6.2. *Left to right*: Sylvia Rodriguez, Texas attorney general Dan Morales, and Linda Rodriguez. Courtesy of St. Philip's College Archives.

when former state attorney general Dan Morales declared his candidacy for the Democratic gubernatorial nomination (Yardley 2002).

Few Democrats knew Tony Sánchez, but Dan Morales enjoyed instant name recognition (Mager 2002). Based on experience alone, Morales was the stronger candidate, but he had made many enemies in the Democratic Party. During his two terms as state attorney general (1991 through 1998), he had cultivated a reputation as an aggressive crime fighter and a political conservative. Morales was best known for his legal interpretation of *Hopwood v. Texas* (1996). The case successfully challenged the University of Texas Law School's use of race as a factor in its admission policies. In his interpretation, Morales expanded the application of the District Court's decision to cover all institutional practices like financial aid, scholarships, fellowships, recruitment, and retention. As attorney general Morales also filed lawsuits against the federal government to secure reimbursement to the State of Texas for providing services to undocumented workers and families. It was a legal strategy that he said was designed to correct "the imbalance that exists between the federal government and the state government" (Cullen 1994). In the course of building his political career, Morales alienated most Mexican American politicians in the state. During his first run for the state attorney general's office, the Mexican American

Democrats endorsed his Anglo opponent, John Bryant. San Antonio congressmen Albert G. Bustamante and Henry B. González, San Antonio city councilman Walter Martinez, congressman Solomon Ortiz, state senators Carlos F. Truan and Gonzalo Barrientos, and judge Gilberto Hinojosa all went on record opposing Morales's candidacy. In a letter circulated during the primary campaign, they argued that Bryant was a better choice because of his record on civil rights, voter registration, and bilingual education (Carney 1989).

With two Mexican Americans as the frontrunners in its gubernatorial primary, the Democratic Party was poised to make history, but in the most inconsequential manner possible. The contest was between two Mexican American conservatives sniping at each other, one a multimillionaire oilman and the other a Harvard-educated former attorney general who said that he had never voted for a Democrat (Reid 2001; Burka 2002). Both were ambitious individuals who fit incongruously into the Democratic Party and offered little in the way of a clear message or vision (Cottle 2002; Shannon 2002e). Morales identified public health, domestic abuse, child abuse, drug use, and public education as his "top priority," moving from one to the other as the campaign wore on. Sánchez promised to "make things fairer" in Texas through pragmatic problem solving (King 2002a). Morales promised that his campaign would "tell it like it is" and touted his experience as attorney general as evidence of his ability to govern. Sánchez emphasized family values and pride in his Hispanic heritage (King 2002a; "Sánchez, Morales War" 2002). Sánchez insisted that he could "scrub the budget" for "waste and inefficiencies" but had difficulty identifying state programs where they might be found (King 2002b). He talked so much about why his mother, daughter, and wife were the three most important women in his life that one observer noted that he "forgot the Virgin Mary, but we'll forgive him" (Arnold Garcia 2000).

Instead of debating issues on their merits, the exchanges between Morales and Sánchez soon devolved into a series of ad hominem attacks and a bizarre conflict over ethnic authenticity (Falkenberg 2002; Davis and Connaughton 2005). Sánchez seized upon Morales's rejection of affirmative action or any other race-based policies, especially his decision in the 1996 *Hopwood* case that ended affirmative action in higher education ("Morales Defends" 2002). Sánchez also called Morales an ethnic turncoat, charging that he had benefited from affirmative action programs when he attended Harvard and then "pick[ed] up the ladder behind him" (Herman 2002). Morales shot back, accusing Sánchez of trying to divide the state by race and conducting a "patron-style" campaign typical of wealthy politicians "south of the border" (Shannon 2002f).

In an attempt to capitalize on Morales's unpopularity among Mexican Americans, Sánchez challenged him to a debate in Spanish. Morales responded by questioning Sánchez's political judgment, accusing him of insulting Mexican Americans by implying that they were not intelligent enough to learn English or patriotic enough to use English as their primary language ("Morales Makes Play" 2002). Morales argued that politicians had an obligation to communicate to as many voters as possible and reminded Sánchez that "only a very, very small minority of voters in Texas, some 3 to 4 percent, consider that Spanish is the only language that they understand" (Woodruff et al. 2002). He called Sánchez's insistence on a debate in Spanish "shameful pandering" and argued that issues like education and college admission should be debated and crafted using "race-neutral" criteria (Shannon 2002b). Finally, Morales said that Sánchez had few ideas for governing the state and charged that the oilman's only qualification for office was his "big fat wallet" ("Morales Aides" 2002).

The two candidates were locked into the kind of ethnic infighting not seen in Texas for decades. This time neither candidate was connected to community organizations or held any policy preferences informed by Mexican American identity. Unlike the debates within PASO in the 1950s or between Henry B. González and Chicano radicals during the 1960s and 1970s, this fight was between conservatives hurling personal invectives against one another. At one point during the Spanish-language debate, Sánchez accused Morales of being ashamed of his racial and ethnic heritage ("Historical Debate" 2002). Morales angrily replied that he was proud of his heritage but "prouder to be a Texan, prouder to be an American" (Badger 2002 2002b). Morales accused Sánchez of conducting an ethnically based campaign and, echoing the campaign rhetoric of former governor Bill Clements, told the South Texas businessman that he was not running "for governor of Mexico" (Jarvis and Connaughton 2005: 143).

Dan Morales lost the Democratic Party primary by a two-to-one margin, unable to overcome Sánchez's enormous advantage in resources and the overwhelming opposition of Democratic Party leaders. Morales's bid for the nomination was further hampered by allegations that he diverted state tobacco settlement funds to an associate while state attorney general. The animosity between the two men did not end with the primary contest, however, and Morales continued his assault on Sánchez. Morales predicted defeat for the Democrats in the general election: "I am very deeply troubled by the strategy of the Democratic leadership really to attempt to win statewide races in 2002 by way of generating enough Hispanic and African-American votes to overcome the number of Anglo votes . . . I think it is a flawed strategy, and I think ultimately it is doomed to failure."

The bitter struggle left both men angry, and Morales let it be known that the fundamental philosophical differences between himself and Sánchez were "still there" ("Morales Won't Rule Out Supporting Perry" 2002). The final twist in the surreal episode came when Morales endorsed Republican governor Rick Perry in the general election (Shannon 2002a).

Racializing Tony Sánchez

By 2002 identity politics in the Democratic Party had reached the point where Mexican American activists rarely pressed race-specific issues. They had developed a good working relationship with Anglo Democrats and two former Democratic governors based on mutual interests and reciprocity. But no such understanding existed between Mexican Americans and Republican governor Rick Perry. The governor and his surrogates were determined to prevent Sánchez from using his wealth to repair the damage inflicted on his image during the Democratic primary. In a break with past Republican Party outreach efforts, the Perry camp was willing to play the race card (Jarvis and Connaughton 2005). By the 2002 gubernatorial election the Republican Party dominated Texas politics and no longer needed to piece together a small margin of victory, as it had thirty years earlier. Hence Republicans felt no pressure to frame their conservative message in ethnic terms. Without that external constraint, Governor Perry launched a series of attack ads linking Tony Sánchez to Mexican drug dealers and accusing him of dodging the draft during the Vietnam War (Badger 2002a). The governor's ads further claimed that the drug lords in Mexico who orchestrated the murder and torture of a federal agent laundered their money through a bank owned by Sánchez. They asserted that Sánchez should have known about the drug money and asked if Texas voters could trust him (Gwynne 2002; "Perry Runs Ad" 2002). The drug ads were especially effective because they played on racial stereotypes and undermined Sánchez's appeal to conservatives as a successful businessman. One journalist characterized the ads as sinister and pernicious attacks that avoided overt racial appeals but communicated a racist message "just as clearly" (Slater 2002).

The Democratic Party gambled on Sánchez and the rest of the "Dream Team," but soon their campaigns were imploding. In the words of one journalist, Texas Democrats were dancing a "racial two-step," trying to rally Mexican American and black voters without offending white voters conscious of their inevitably approaching status as a numerical minority in Texas (Cienski 2002; McNeely 2002). For Sánchez the turn of events was a personal insult. He was an enormously successful businessman and politically conservative, but in 2002 the Republican Party that once had honored him as one of its major fundraisers had begun denigrating his character with a series of racist campaign ads. He was also subject to similar kinds of attacks from Republican Party leaders. When campaigning for Rick Perry, Republican senator Phil Gramm dismissed the Democratic Party ticket as a racial quota ticket ("Gramm Steals Spotlight" 2002; "Kirk Says" 2002; Parrott 2002). The chair of the Texas Republican Party wondered aloud why Sánchez had dropped the accent mark on his name, suggesting that he did so to increase his acceptability as a candidate. One journalist asked Sánchez if he cut his mustache for the same reason ("GOP Chair" 2002; Kolker 2002).

This campaign was a departure from the bipartisan tradition of racial outreach in Texas. Gubernatorial candidates of both parties from Price Daniel to Ann Richards invoked the bridging theme of a common political history between Anglos and Mexicans in Texas when trying to win Mexican American votes. Rick Perry dispensed with the myth of a unified Texas history and demonstrated the power of using race to demonize Mexicans, including one of the wealthiest men in the state. Instead of claiming a common history between Mexicans and Anglos during the Texas revolution, the narrative turned into an Anglo victory over Mexico. In his ads coupling Tony Sánchez with drug traffickers and money laundering, Perry compared himself to Sam Houston, the man who led Texas forces to defeat Mexican president Santa Ana in 1836 (Vertuno 2002). Partisan and ideological appeals were now more closely aligned, and Republican Party candidates no longer cloaked their politics behind the mantle of commitment to racial equality.

Almost sixty years after World War II Tony Sánchez, an accomplished and wealthy candidate for public office, was humiliated with an anti-Mexican campaign. But Sánchez was an important Mexican American politician with no links to a cadre of civil rights activists and organizations that could be mobilized on his behalf. Of course, the contest between Sánchez and Perry was not just about race. In the general election Mexican Americans gave Tony Sánchez 85 percent of their vote. His Spanish surname ramped up the percentage of Mexican American votes that Democrats typically receive, but as a group their support was soft. In the face of a media blitz in which Governor Perry likened himself to Sam Houston, only 32 percent of eligible Mexican American voters cast a ballot, lower than the 36 percent of all eligible Texas voters who made it to the polls (Texas Secretary of State 2002b; William C. Velasquez Institute 2004a). This weak ethnic support contrasts with the 1972 gubernatorial election, where frustration with the Democratic Party ran high and 50 to 60 percent of the Mexican American voters in some South Texas counties turned out to support the fledgling Raza Unida Party (Márquez and Espino 2010).

Although the Democrats hoped that Sánchez would boost the level of support among Mexican Americans, he had little in common with them other than his cultural background. His sparse record in community politics left him without a network of supporters that might have bolstered turnout. Even in South Texas, a traditional Democratic stronghold, Sánchez's performance was dismal. Sánchez won in Webb County, which included his hometown of Laredo, by a margin of 35,101 to 3,958, or over 89 percent of the vote. In other South Texas counties where Mexican American voters might be expected to rally around the embattled Democrat, however, Republican Rick Perry came very close to winning. In Nueces County, which includes Corpus Christi, Perry and Sánchez split the vote. Perry received 39 percent of the vote in Cameron County (Burka 2002). Winning such a small percentage of the vote in South Texas was an embarrassment for the Democratic Party, given that Tony Sánchez spent $76.3 million during the general campaign, almost $2 million of which went to purchase five thousand Spanish-language ads (Segal 2002; Morehouse and Jewell 2005).

Still, Sánchez's loss could not be attributed only to his weak ethnic ties and subsequent failure to mobilize a Mexican American constituency. Hobbled by a ruinous primary contest with Morales, all the Democrats could do was hope that Sánchez could use his wealth to find the formula that would defeat Rick Perry and somehow carry the rest of the Democratic ticket to victory. A survey conducted by the Scripps Howard Data Center on the day when Sánchez formally declared his candidacy, however, showed him trailing the unpopular incumbent governor by 30 percentage points ("As Sánchez Announces Candidacy" 2001). Sánchez closed some of the gap during the campaign; but Rick Perry easily won the general election, spending only $28 million (Beyle and Jensen 2009). Some racial voting was discernible in 2002, with Tony Sánchez receiving only 27 percent of the Anglo vote in the general election (Halter 2006). But Sánchez was no different from his fellow Democrats, who were no longer winning statewide elections—all who ran that year lost by big margins (Texas Secretary of State 2002b; Morton 2006: 282). As Charles S. Bullock and R. K. Gaddie (2005) found, "since 1996, no Democrat has approached

Photo 6.3. Representative Irma Rangel with Texas governor Rick Perry. Irma Rangel Collection, South Texas Archives, Texas A&M University–Kingsville, Box 228, Folder 1, Item 1.

majority support among Anglo voters and since 2000 no Democrat has commanded over 35 percent of the Anglo voter statewide." The Anglo vote, they discovered, was not significantly related to the candidate's race or ethnicity. John Sharp, the top Democratic vote getter in the 2002 statewide election, only managed to win 34 percent of the Anglo vote (Bullock and Gaddie 2005: 10–11). At the local level, where they were a large percentage of the population, Mexican American voters and candidates regularly carried the Democratic Party to victory. In his study of Mexican American electoral representation, Michael Rosenfeld (1998) found a "steady and significant level of representation" over time at the local level. Incorporation reached the point where Mexican Americans had achieved parity levels of representation in Arizona, California, and Colorado by the 1970s; while Texas was lagging behind the other southwestern states, parity was achieved by the 1980s (Rosenfeld 1998).

In the end Tony Sánchez's brief rise in Texas politics had less to do with racial identity politics than with a political party decline. He received the 2002 gubernatorial nomination because the Texas Democratic Party was in disarray and was grasping at straws for a way to restore its lost power. Sánchez's campaign was nothing more than "a grand illusion, an enormous smoke-and-mirrors machine fueled by a seemingly limitless supply of money . . . Stripped of the special effects, the race's predestined outcome came into focus. In spite of his promises to change Texas politics forever, Sánchez never had any more chance to beat Perry than [Democrat] Garry Mauro did to beat George W. Bush in 1998. The man behind the curtain turned out to be a very ordinary candidate" (Gwynne 2002). One observer argued that Sánchez was a very poor candidate whose inexperience emerged as an issue during the general election. Democrats were disappointed that he did not possess the skill set they expected for a gubernatorial candidate. He appeared reluctant to engage voters, lacked passion for the Democratic Party's issues, and did not work very hard on the campaign trail (Cottle 2002). With only Sánchez's enormous wealth to keep him in the public eye, Governor Perry taunted him: "[N]ever in the history of American politics has a political candidate spent so much money and said so little" (Gwynne 2002).

Conclusion

The fact that a Mexican American headed the ticket in 2002 was the culmination of demographic changes and years of political activism that trans-

Table 6.1. 2002 Democratic Primary Election for Governor

Candidate	Number of Votes	Percent
Bill Lyon	43,011	4.29
Dan Morales	330,873	32.98
Tony Sánchez	609,383	60.73
John Worldpeace	20,121	2.00
Total Votes	1,003,388	

Source: Texas Secretary of State 2002a.

Table 6.2. 2002 General Election Results

Candidate	Party	Number of Votes	Percent
Rick Perry (Incumbent)	Republican	2,632,591	57.81
Tony Sánchez	Democrat	1,819,798	39.96
Jeff Daiell	Libertarian	66,720	1.47
Rahul Mahajan	Green	32,187	0.71
Elaine Eure Henderson	Write-in	1,715	0.04
Earl W. (Bill) O'Neil	Write-in	976	0.02
Total Votes		4,553,987	

Source: Texas Secretary of State 2002b.

formed the Democratic Party. Texas politics were far different than they had been in the 1940s and 1950s, when state governors openly supported racial segregation. The modern Democratic Party's machinery was racially integrated and fielded minority candidates at all levels of government. Even in South Texas, where hard-fought conflicts over racial representation took place, Mexican American elected officials became the norm. At the same time Sánchez's nomination was a function of a party declining in influence and unable to field a candidate with statewide appeal. The years of activism, demographic shifts, changes in party rules, and identity bridging created the possibility that a Mexican American would soon take the Democratic Party's gubernatorial nomination. But the Democratic Party was now the minority party in Texas. Texas has had only two one-term Democratic governors after the election of Republican Bill Clements in

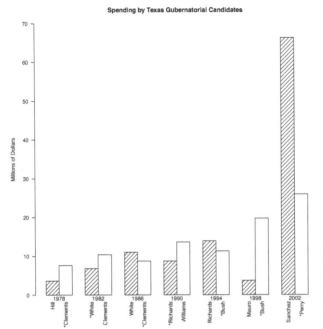

Figure 6.1. Spending by Texas Gubernatorial Candidates, 1978–2002

Photo 6.4. Tony Sánchez during his 2002 campaign for governor. The Associated Press.

1978. Tony Sánchez joined the ranks of Democrats Dolph Briscoe, Mark White, and Ann Richards, all of whom lost a gubernatorial election to conservative Republican opponents. Rick Perry easily defeated Tony Sánchez in 2002 and would go on to win reelection in 2006 and 2010, making him the longest-serving governor in Texas history.

The nomination of a Mexican American to head the Democratic Party ticket in 2002 was an important step toward full Mexican American incorporation into state politics. At the same time Sánchez was different from the others, embodying all the dilemmas and contradictions of racial incorporation. He was a wealthy South Texas oilman with little connection to the history of community and party activism that made a racial breakthrough possible. He won his party's nomination not through a groundswell of Mexican American or liberal support but because of his wealth and the unwillingness or inability of other Democratic Party leaders to mount a successful campaign against Governor Perry. Sánchez's entrance on the center stage of Texas politics occurred well after Mexican American activists had won some key victories in Texas politics. He was subjected to a series of racist attacks, but race ultimately played a relatively small role in his defeat. He lost at a time when all Democrats were drawing a minority of the Anglo vote and losing in statewide elections. Sánchez's liberal and racially integrated party was unable to prevail over an ideologically unified and racially homogeneous opposition. Short of the Republican Party nominating Tony Sánchez as its gubernatorial candidate, Texas was not going to have a Mexican American governor in 2002.

Mexican American activists have long debated the strategies necessary to obtain power and fix the problems that they faced as a group. They knew that racism had a powerful influence over the distribution of power, status, and income. By the 1960s the prevailing attitude was that coalition building with Anglos and African Americans in the Democratic Party was the most effective way to correct these disparities. Inevitable disagreements over any given course of action arose as activists navigated the complex terrain of race, class, and ideology. Those who first broke into Democratic Party politics, however, put a premium on descriptive representation because they believed that racial incorporation was part and parcel of a social justice agenda. Although the importance of integration waned over time, few envisioned a scenario where a Mexican American would win the Democratic Party's gubernatorial nomination by virtue of his wealth and Spanish surname. It was the anticlimactic end to fifty years of electoral activism.

CHAPTER 7

The Long and Grinding Road

The story of Mexican American political mobilization in the post–World War II era is one of success. The demand for racial incorporation resulted in representation at every level of partisan politics. By the 1980s Mexican Americans were being elected to public office at the state and local level in numbers equivalent to their proportion of the general population. But this transformation did not take place in a vacuum. Barriers to equal participation were rendered vulnerable to political pressure because of major economic and demographic upheavals taking place after the war. Industrialization and the mechanization of Texas agriculture drove thousands to cities and undermined the viability of Anglo-dominated political regimes in rural and urban areas. A growing urban population, accompanied by modest increases in income and educational levels, facilitated the creation of new organizations and strengthened existing political networks. Urbanization and industrialization in Texas created vulnerability in the racial order, which activists eagerly exploited. The movement toward equal access first occurred in cities with large Hispanic populations like San Antonio, El Paso, and Corpus Christi, but rural areas soon followed suit. Finally, federal legislation protecting voting rights and changes in Democratic Party rules gave activists additional tools with which to challenge racial discrimination and extend their influence in state politics. In this relatively short period Mexican Americans changed their status as outsiders in an Anglo-dominated one-party system to becoming working participants in a two-party state.

Racial incorporation was more than the ascent of one group overcoming adversity after decades of struggle. It was a process that shaped the scope and content of racial advocacy. From the beginning the meaning of racial and ethnic identity was a contested concept. Racial incorporation came about through a complex process of identity negotiation between Mexican Americans and Anglos. Competing visions of change, personality conflicts, the constraints of alliance building, institutional change, and the actions of Anglo politicians hoping to contain or redirect demands shaped the insurgency's course. The most significant consequence of these pressures was a growing separation between community and partisan organizing. The movement to integrate the Democratic Party was initiated and sustained by Mexican American civil rights organizations, but that connection weakened over time. The view that prevailed among partisan activists was that Mexican Americans' interests were better served if they could align the state party's policies with those of the national Democratic Party. This position drew fire from community activists as partisanship bound them to Anglo politicians who were openly antagonistic toward minority interests. The cost of membership for liberal Mexican Americans in Texas was high and fostered divisions, but those who balked at the demands of partisanship were marginalized or worked outside of the party structure.

The career of San Antonio politician Albert Peña is instructive in this regard. During the 1950s and 1960s he was an outspoken critic of the state Democratic Party and vehemently rejected compromises with reactionary politicians. He funneled that frustration into alternate modes of representation, working with civil rights organizations, unions, and dissident factions within the Democratic Party. He was the principal founder of the Political Association of Spanish-Speaking Organizations (PASO) and a driving force behind La Raza Unida Party in South Texas. Concurrent with his community organizing, Peña was an elected official and served the Democratic Party at the local, state, and national level. Despite this extraordinary record of service, Peña's work with La Raza Unida Party drew scorn from his Democratic colleagues, who condemned the community and party model of organizing that he pioneered as a counterproductive anachronism. Peña would lose his Bexar County commissioner's seat in 1972 to Albert Bustamante, a former aide to congressman Henry B. González. One of Bustamante's major criticisms of Peña was that he did not spend enough time serving his constituents. Politicians who prospered during this transition period were loyal Democrats, while those harboring an ethnically based agenda were co-opted, weeded out, or replaced by individuals more attuned to the norms of partisan loyalty.

Another finding of this study is that the politics of ethnic nationalism and incorporation into the two-party system proceeded along different trajectories. The Texas Democratic Party responded to political

pressure just as models of social assimilation predict, but evidence linking racial incorporation to the Chicano Movement is weaker than previously understood. During the late 1960s and early 1970s the drama
of La Raza Unida's rise and demolition of Anglo political machines in
South Texas drew considerable media attention, but the incorporation of
Mexican American Democrats into the party system began years before
the Chicano Movement. Although La Raza Unida's ethnic nationalism
may have prodded the Democrats, party reform at that time was steady.
Moreover, Mexican American Democrats rejected the rebellious social
movement; their work within the Democratic Party proceeded with little
spillover from the upheavals of the Chicano Movement. It is significant
that politicians like Paul Moreno and Tati Santiesteban of El Paso were
elected to public office in the mid-1960s with little or no racial acrimony.
Henry B. González was the target of a racial attack during his successful campaign for the San Antonio city council in 1953, but little of that
materialized during his subsequent campaigns for the Texas State Senate
and Congress. Even South Texas politicians like Irma Rangel and Carlos
Truan were elected to the state legislature with little controversy. Both
ran for office in the aftermath of La Raza Unida's most belligerent period,
at a time and place where their candidacy could have easily ignited racial
tensions. Instead they won office by campaigning as mainstream Democrats in Democratic Party strongholds. Irma Rangel was notable for her
smooth rise to power. In 1974 she returned to her South Texas hometown
after an extended absence, started a law practice, then ran for and won the
Democratic Party county chair. She was elected to the Texas House of
Representatives two years later.

The end of racial exclusion made Texas the state with the largest number of Latino officeholders in the country. In 1996 almost 1,700 Mexican Americans served in public office. By 2003 the number had grown
to 2,000, with more than 40 percent of all Latino officeholders in the
country serving in Texas, the bulk of whom were Democrats (Bullock
and Gaddie 2005: 6). The incorporation of Mexican American activists
and politicians into public life proceeded steadily even as vast socioeconomic disparities between the races remained intact. Electoral and community organizing gradually came to occupy distinct spheres of activism.
Civil rights organizations grew less influential in party affairs and were
replaced by ethnic caucuses and party leaders. By the twenty-first century
party activists were far less attached or accountable to community organizations than they had been in the 1950s. Mexican Americans are no longer
marginalized in party politics and are regularly elected to office in parts

of the state where they constitute a large proportion of the voting-age population. Identity, ideology, and party structure now play a powerful role in determining how Mexican Americans' interests are represented. In West Texas George McAlmon, the former El Paso County Democratic chair (1968–1972), witnessed a sea change in ethnic politics. He recalled that in the 1960s it was difficult and took a concerted community effort to elect a Mexican American to any office. When Raymond Telles became the first Mexican American mayor of El Paso in 1957, labor unions, liberals, and every Mexican American organization worked to assure a large ethnic turnout. He called those early mobilizations "noble efforts." Today, he said, "you can't get elected in El Paso unless you have a Spanish surname," but some Mexican Americans who run for public office "are total reactionaries" (McAlmon 2003).

These apparent incongruities are a product of uneven incorporation and assimilation. As racial barriers were broken, descriptive representation came to matter less as ideology and partisanship assumed greater importance. Rosenfeld (1998: 1127) argues that the divergence between racial and partisan interest is a net loss for Mexican Americans that left gaps in the group's political repertory. He believes that political organizations of the Chicano Movement era like La Raza Unida "were much more inclusive of immigrants, both legal and undocumented, in their rhetoric and in their political organizing than is the current spectrum of electorally oriented Mexican American civic organizations. The transition to electoral politics has meant a change from politics based on ethnicity to politics based on U.S. citizenship." Moreover, the absence of a powerful nationalist voice "left the Mexican American community with weakened defenses against attacks, such as California's Proposition 187 which explicitly targeted undocumented Mexican immigrants and also raised the level of xenophobia high enough to represent a threat to Mexican Americans in California" (Rosenfeld 1998: 1127).

The enduring power of racial discrimination and anti-immigrant movements in California, Arizona, and elsewhere inspires nostalgic readings of ethnically based movements. This study found that organized responses to racial injustices are subject to multiple forces that influence the course of an insurgency or suppress it altogether. Political organizing is a difficult and time-consuming task. Even when a group is united in its opposition to a state of affairs or strongly favors a given public policy, a sustained group-based response will not necessarily materialize. When movements emerge they are constrained by available resources, institutional biases, and the actions of powerful economic and political actors. For example, public opinion polls showed that Mexican Americans in Texas were over-whelmingly supportive of farmworker unionizing drives during the 1960s. But Mexican American activists and elected officials lacked the numbers and influence to enact protective legislation for farmworkers or curb the abuses that they suffered on Texas farms and ranches. The farm-worker movement in Texas met with resistance at the highest levels of government, and strikers were subjected to arrests and beatings at the hands of the Texas Rangers. The emerging Mexican American Democratic caucus was powerless to stop Anglo politicians like Governor Connally, who vehemently opposed farmworker unionization and basic reform like an agricultural minimum wage.

I also found that identity politics does not generate a predictable agenda of priorities. In fact identity is a highly contested and unwieldy organiz-ing tool. Soon after World War II, at a time when Mexican Americans were impoverished, subject to blatant acts of discrimination, and excluded from party politics, activists were divided over what constituted the prin-ciples of an ethnic agenda. They all understood the problems facing the community, but they had limited opportunities and difficult choices. Even in the 1950s the connection between ethnic identity and political strategy was never clear. Activists made decisions that sometimes placed them in opposition to one another, a dynamic that was further compli-cated as the Democratic Party actually began to change. Incorporation meant that Mexican American activists and politicians exercised greater freedom to place themselves in the spectrum of Texas politics, a testament to the practical demands of coalition politics and the elasticity of ethnic identities. The Mexican American Democrats (MAD) are a case in point. The first Mexican American caucus in the Texas Democratic Party pro-moted the interests of its members but could not define a set of political goals and principles as civil rights organizations did. MAD members were obligated to support their party's nominees for public office; beyond that, each member was the ultimate arbiter of his or her votes and actions.

Because it emerged from the shadow of the Texas Democratic Party, the Republican Party was forced to be more proactive and calculating when communicating its message to Mexican Americans. But the criteria for membership and demands upon Republican Party loyalists were essen-tially the same for everyone. John Tower's campaign for the U.S. Senate in 1961 created the template. By the time Republican Bill Clements was elected governor in 1978 the Republican Party's positions on race, politi-cal principles, and legislative priorities were completely unambiguous. Mexican Americans supporting the conservative governor accepted his program to keep government as small as possible and foster opportunities through the free market. The partisan divide offered no middle ground for ethnic activists, who increasingly couched their concerns for the welfare of poor Mexican Americans in strict partisan terms. After the 2002 gubernatorial election, South Texas rancher and Republican Party activist Frank Yturria criticized Mexican American leaders for their unwavering support of the Democratic Party. In light of Republican victories in statewide elections he asserted that South Texas legislators were rendered powerless to help their constituents:

> They are all going to be insignificant Democrats. They have no political influence, no power, no nothing. That is what "la palanca" [straight party ticket] has given the Rio Grande Valley. They all campaigned for Tony Sánchez and for the Democratic straight party ticket. What has it gotten them? It means now that Brownsville and the Rio Grande Valley will remain a poverty stricken area with Third World conditions. (Perez-Trevino 2002)

Tony Sánchez's disastrous performance in 2002 gave Yturria an opportunity to argue that Mexican Americans' interests were poorly served by their loyalty to the Democratic Party. What Yturria meant was that Mexican American liberals were in no position to implement their policies, given the Republican Party's control of state government. By that time partisan affiliation defined racial interests in Texas, rather than the other way around. Mexican Americans were no longer outsiders to state politics. They integrated the two-party system as partisans, not as agents of an abstractly defined group interest. San Antonio congressman Henry González best articulated this vision of social change in the 1950s when he argued that progress would only come about by working within the Democratic Party. He had little use for racially based social movements because he did not believe that it was possible to represent the interests of the Mexican American people outside of the institutional avenues for change. He dismissed those who argued for ethnic and racial solidarity as demagogues or "Professional Mexicans" ("González Calls" 1973).

González and his Democratic colleagues understood the advantages of partisan alliances as well as the danger of a Texas Republican Party takeover of state government. When the Republican Party consolidated its grip on state politics at the turn of the twenty-first century, liberals were left with few options except protest. In 2003 more than fifty Democratic representatives were absent when the Texas House convened, thus breaking the quorum needed to conduct business. Democrats boycotted the session to protest a congressional redistricting bill that would favor Republicans, a no-new-taxes budget that would devastate education and social services, and sweeping legislation limiting lawsuits. The same thing had occurred twenty-four years earlier when twelve Texas state senators, known as the "Killer Bees," boycotted the 1979 Senate. In 2003 Department of Public Safety Troopers, Texas Rangers, and the legislative sergeants-at-arms were sent to find the "Killer Ds" and bring them back to Austin. Their flight only delayed the eventual passage of the redistricting legislation in a Republican-dominated Texas legislature (Aynesworth 2003; McKee and Shaw 2005).

As their numbers grow, Mexican Americans will begin to exert more influence in the future; but it will be exercised through a liberal, multiracial alliance—not a hastily assembled "Dream Ticket." Nor is it likely to occur in the short term. After the 2002 gubernatorial election, Richard Murray (2004) argued that the Democratic Party's future electoral prospects were dim. The Republican Party built a powerful foundation of conservative ideas and money while the Democrats were disorganized and underfunded. Low rates of voter registration and turnout among the party's base were a function of low levels of participation by the poor and the working class, but the Democrats were doing a bad job of organizing their base and countering the Republicans' claims. Instead of functioning as an ideologically disciplined party, the Democratic Party was "an *expressive organization* for an unwieldy coalition of political activists" (Murray 2004: 6; emphasis in the original). He went on to argue that the "Dream Team" strategy of descriptive representation for every demographic and social group was a luxury that the Democratic Party could not afford. In order for Democrats to win, the party needed a way to contain demands for descriptive representation through an entity like the moderate Democratic Leadership Council. Its goal should be to assemble a progressive coalition based on the Democratic Party's core social and political values (Murray 2004: 8). In a world where the Republican Party regularly claims a significant percentage of the Mexican American vote and many Anglo voters are wary of multiracial coalitions, the price of descriptive representation will be continuing losses at the polls.

The value of descriptive versus substantive representation as a topic of debate goes back to the 1950s for Mexican American Democrats, but it was never a dispassionate reflection over what was best for the liberal cause in Texas. Mexican American activists wanted to see more Mexican Americans in party politics and elected to public office as well as favor-

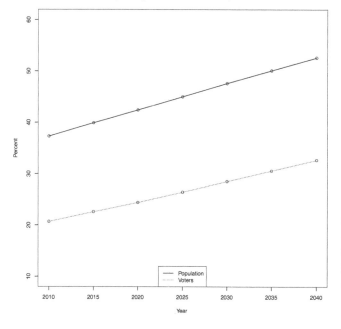

Figure 7.1.
Hispanic
Population
and Voters
in Texas,
2010–2040
(projected)

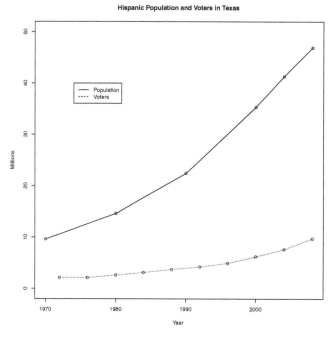

Figure 7.2.
Hispanic
Population
and Voters
in Texas,
1970–2000

able social policies, but they were also fighting for their civil rights. Setting aside the injuries that they suffered as members of a minority group when calculating the cost and benefits of a given strategy was a burden that Anglo liberals did not have to bear. During the 1950s and 1960s the contradictions of working within the Texas Democratic Party were particularly acute. Texas Democratic governors not only ignored Mexican American issues but aggressively worked against them and did their best to undermine the national party's candidates and goals. When PASO endorsed Governor Daniel for reelection in 1962, the rationale was that supporting a segregationist governor was in their best interests given the narrow range of choices.

The United States Census confirmed that Texas crossed a milestone when it became a minority-majority state in 2009. Mexican Americans constituted 37 percent of the state population, a figure projected to reach 58 percent in the year 2040. A shift in the state's politics is inevitable; but a youthful population, lower levels of income and education, and a significant number of noncitizens all depress the Mexican American electoral influence. Population increases in Texas and the rest of the country have been dramatic, but the relatively small number of Latino voters will keep them from exerting influence proportional to their size (William C. Velasquez Institute 2004b; Stanley 2008). The growing Mexican American population in Texas and the rest of the country fuels predictions that dramatic political change is not far behind. If voter registration and turnout are raised to the level of Anglo registration and turnout, what will that influence look like? Mexican Americans are a reliable Democratic voting bloc; but assimilation, mobility, and conservative social values have chipped away at that foundation. More Mexican Americans will be elected to political office, and the state's politics will be more in sync with the policy preferences and needs of the poor. As in the past, however, any growth in political power will be mediated through a maze of institutions, identities, and interests.

Bibliography

For maps showing population and employment shifts, see

http://www.lib.utexas.edu/maps/atlas_texas/pop_change_standard_tx.jpg
http://www.lib.utexas.edu/maps/atlas_texas/pop_spanish_lang_1970.jpg
http://www.lib.utexas.edu/maps/atlas_texas/agricultural_employment.jpg
http://www.lib.utexas.edu/maps/atlas_texas/large_manu_plants.jpg

Anonymous Sources by Title

"Abolish Rangers, Beat Connally, PASO Urges." 1967. *Houston Chronicle*, August 14. Texas Governor John Connally Records, LBJ Library. Box 744.

"After the Revolution: The Raza Unida Party Is Dead, and Crystal City Is Back to Normal. Or Is it?" 1982. *Texas Monthly* (September): 110.

"Albert Fuentes Makes His Case." 1964. *Texas Observer*, February 21.

"And Lest We Forget, Three Memos for Super Tuesday." 1992. *Economist*, March 7.

"Angry Blasts Climax Demo Control Fight." 1956. *Valley Evening Monitor*, May 4. Dr. Hector P. Garcia Papers, Special Collections and Archives, Texas A&M University–Corpus Christi, Mary and Jeff Bell Library.

"Anti-Connally Move Expected by PASO." 1967. *San Antonio Express*, August 10. Texas Governor John Connally Records, LBJ Library. Box 744.

"Appointments of Governor Dolph Briscoe." 1977. In *Mexican American Democrats First State Conference, June 1, 2, 3, 1977*. State conference booklet, n.p. Margo Gutiérrez Personal Files, University of Texas at Austin.

"Area Solon Favors 'American Power.'" 1970. *San Antonio Express*, September 29. Dolph Briscoe Papers, 1932–2010, Dolph Briscoe Center for American History, University of Texas at Austin. Box 265.

"As Sánchez Announces Candidacy, Poll Shows Perry Leading by 30 Points." 2001. Bulletin Broadfaxing Network, Inc., September 5. Retrieved from http://www.lexisnexis.com.

"AWR News Articles 1991–1993." ca. 1993. Ann W. Richards Papers, 1933–2010,

Dolph Briscoe Center for American History, University of Texas at Austin. Box 97–185/6(06839173).

"Baa, Baa, Baa." 1972. *Texas Observer*, April 28.

"Barrientos Expresses No Worry." ca. 1974. Newspaper clipping, no citation. Richard Moya Papers, Austin History Center, Austin Public Library.

"Barrientos Will Run against Wilson Forman." 1972. *La Fuerza*, January 27. Richard Moya Papers, Austin History Center, Austin Public Library.

"Belief That Truan Best for Senate Reinforced." 1976. *Corpus Christi Caller-Times*, June 4. Carlos Truan Papers, South Texas Archives and Special Collections, James C. Jernigan Library, Texas A&M University–Kingsville. Box 52.009.

"Berlanga's Selection: The Key Posts for Coastal Bend Legislators Give This Area More Clout." 1995. *Corpus Christi Caller*, February 3.

"Berlanga Used Politics, Friendships, Hustle to Get Ahead." 1991. *Laredo Morning Times*, March 18. "Berlanga, Hugo" Vertical File, Dolph Briscoe Center for American History, University of Texas at Austin.

"Bexar DOT Endorses Civil Rights Program." 1957. *Texas Observer*, September 13.

"Bexar GOP Head Gives Party Stand." ca. 1969. Henry B. González Papers (unprocessed), Dolph Briscoe Center for American History, University of Texas at Austin.

"Bexar's Efforts on Court Stand Fail." 1954. *Texas Observer*, May 21. Texas Democratic Party Papers, Archives and Information Services Division, Texas State Library and Archives Commission. Box 1977/96–12.

"Bexar's Renewed Coalition." 1961. *Texas Observer*, July 22.

"Bilingual Education Program Signed into Law by Briscoe." 1973. *Corpus Christi Caller*, June 14. Carlos Truan Papers, South Texas Archives and Special Collections, James C. Jernigan Library, Texas A&M University–Kingsville. Box 336.012.

"Bonillas: Hispanics for White." 1982. *San Antonio Light*, October 2. Records, Texas Governor Mark White, Archives and Information Services Division, Texas State Library and Archives Commission, "General: Hispanic Bonilla Sandoval." Box 1991/141–94.

"Briscoe Raps Grant, Again." 1976. *San Antonio Light*, December 24. Dolph Briscoe Papers, 1932–2010, Dolph Briscoe Center for American History, University of Texas at Austin. Box 293.

"Candidate Hits Record of Mattox." 1986. *Victoria Advocate*, April 26, 1986. "Barrera, Roy Jr." Vertical File, Dolph Briscoe Center for American History, University of Texas at Austin.

"Carlos F. Truan, Dean of the Texas Senate." ca. 1995. Carlos F. Truan Collection, South Texas Archives and Special Collections, James C. Jernigan Library, Texas A&M University–Kingsville. Box 1.001.

"Carr of Lubbock." 1966. *Texas Observer*, February 4. Henry B. González Papers, 1946–1998, Dolph Briscoe Center for American History, University of Texas at Austin. Box 2004–127/395.

"Carr Says Effectiveness Big Issue." 1966. *Daily Post*, September 22. Texas Observer Records, 1952–1990, Dolph Briscoe Center for American History, University of Texas at Austin.

"Castillo Beats Oakes in Controller's Race." 1971. *Houston Post*, December 8. Margo Gutiérrez Personal Files. University of Texas at Austin.

"Castillo Calls Race a Dogfight." 1974. *Dallas Morning News*, August 17. "Castillo, Leonel" Vertical File, Dolph Briscoe Center for American History, University of Texas at Austin.

"Challenge to the Valley Lords." 1955. *Texas Observer*, November 16.

"Chicano Leaders Have Plan for School Board." 1970. *Houston Chronicle*, September 11. Dolph Briscoe Papers, 1932–2010, Dolph Briscoe Center for American History, University of Texas at Austin. Box 265.

"Chronological History of M.A.D." 1977. In *Mexican American Democrats First State Convention, September 30 and October 1*. First state convention booklet, n.p. Margo Gutiérrez Personal Files, University of Texas at Austin.

"Clements' Hispanic Appointments." ca. 1983. Records, Texas Governor Mark White, Archives and Information Services Division, Texas State Library and Archives Commission, "Hispanics." M. W. Box 1991/141–94.

"Commite para el Banquete Honrando a el Senador Henry B. González." 1960. Fund-raising announcement. Dr. Hector P. Garcia Papers, Special Collections and Archives, Texas A&M University–Corpus Christi, Mary and Jeff Bell Library.

"Committee 'Friends of Senator Henry B. González.'" 1960. Membership list. Dr. Hector P. Garcia Papers, Special Collections and Archives, Texas A&M University–Corpus Christi, Mary and Jeff Bell Library.

"Connally Discontent Said Growing." 1967. Unidentified newspaper clipping, August 8. Texas Governor John Connally Records. LBJ Library. Box 744.

"Contribución para el Senador Henry González." ca. 1961. Announcement and attached pledge sheet. Dr. Hector P. Garcia Papers, Special Collections and Archives, Texas A&M University–Corpus Christi, Mary and Jeff Bell Library.

"The Convention Tilted Left." 1976. *Texas Observer*, July 2.

"Dallas County Returns." 1956. *Dallas Morning News*, July 28. Texas Governor Price Daniel Records, Archives and Information Services Division, Texas State Library and Archives Commission, Segregation. Box 596.

"Democratic Effort, Hispanic Vote Cited." ca. 1982. Unidentified newspaper clipping. Records, Texas Governor Mark White, Archives and Information Services Division, Texas State Library and Archives Commission, "General Hispanics." Box 1991/141–94.

"The Democratic Women of Bexar County 1953-77-78." n.d. Mexican American Democrats of Texas Records, 1962–1987, MS 29, UTSA Archives, Library, University of Texas at San Antonio. Box 8:8.

"Democrats Approach Harmony." 1976. *Texas Monthly* (October 1): 3.

"Democrats vs Dixiecrats: The Texas Story 1952 National Democratic Convention." n.d. Walter Gardner Hall—Papers, 1923–1990, MS 280, Woodson Research Center, Fondren Library, Rice University. Box 4, Folder 107.

"Demos for Tower Group Criticized by Carr Spokesman." 1966. *Corpus Christi Caller*, August 7. Henry B. González Papers, 1946–1998, Dolph Briscoe Center for American History, University of Texas at Austin. Box 2004-127/395.

"The Demos' Platform for Texas." 1960. *Texas Observer*, July 22.

"Demos to Hear State Senator." 1957. *Daily Texan*, September 29. "Austin,

Texas—Henry B. González" Vertical File, Dolph Briscoe Center for American History, University of Texas at Austin.

"Details Are Sought on González Charge." 1969. *Corpus Christi Caller*, April 2. Dr. Hector P. Garcia Papers, Special Collections and Archives, Texas A&M University–Corpus Christi, Mary and Jeff Bell Library.

"DOT Positions on State, U.S., World Issues." 1960. *Texas Observer*, February 26.

"DPS Officer Reports on Militant Activities." 1970. *Edinburg Daily Review*, July 28. Dolph Briscoe Papers, 1932–2010, Dolph Briscoe Center for American History, University of Texas at Austin. Box 265.

"The Dynamic Program of Henry González." ca. 1958. Campaign flyer, n.p. n.d. "Austin, Texas—Henry B. González" Vertical File, Dolph Briscoe Center for American History, University of Texas at Austin.

"Elect Leonel Castillo Chairman State Democratic Executive Committee." 1974. Campaign leaflet, July 17. Margo Gutiérrez Personal Files, University of Texas at Austin.

"Ethnic Caucus Not for Him González Says." 1971. *Houston Chronicle*, June 6. "González, Henry B." Vertical File, Dolph Briscoe Center for American History, University of Texas at Austin.

"Everything You Ever Wanted to Know about the September State Convention." 1972. *Texas Observer*, October 6.

"4 Incumbents Defeated in Light Turnout for Runoff Voting." 1976. *Amarillo Globe Times*, June 6. Carlos Truan Papers, South Texas Archives and Special Collections, James C. Jernigan Library, Texas A&M University–Kingsville. Box 52.010.

"Fuentes on Call to GOP." 1966. Unidentified newspaper clipping, February 1. Texas Observer Records, 1952–1990, Dolph Briscoe Center for American History, University of Texas at Austin.

"Fuentes Receptive to 'Firm' GOP Bid." 1966. Unidentified newspaper clipping, February 6. Texas Observer Records, 1952–1990, Dolph Briscoe Center for American History, University of Texas at Austin.

"GI Forum Thanks LBJ." 1959. *Texas Observer*, July 11.

"GI Forum Went 'All Out' in Buy Your Poll Tax Campaign." 1949. *Corpus Christi Sentinel*, February 4. Dr. Hector P. Garcia Papers, Special Collections and Archives, Texas A&M University–Corpus Christi, Mary and Jeff Bell Library.

"González Calls 'Atheism' Issue Legislation Folly." 1959. *Daily Texan*, April 17. "Austin, Texas—Henry B. González" Vertical File, Dolph Briscoe Center for American History, University of Texas at Austin.

"González Calls Raza Refuge for Scoundrels." 1973. *San Antonio Express*, August 27.

"González Campaigns as 'Consiberal' Demo." 1961. *Daily Texan*, March 30. "Austin, Texas—Henry B. Gonzalez" Vertical File, Dolph Briscoe Center for American History, University of Texas at Austin.

"The González Candidacy." 1958. *Texas Observer*, May 16. Henry B. González Papers, 1946–1998, Dolph Briscoe Center for American History, University of Texas at Austin. Box 2004–127/50.

"González Defends His Liberal Role." 1958. *Dallas News*, July 25. "Austin, Texas—

Henry B. González" Vertical File, Dolph Briscoe Center for American History, University of Texas at Austin.

"Gonzalez Enters Governor's Race as Guitars Play." 1958. *Daily Texan*, May 6. "Austin, Texas—Henry B. González" Vertical File, Dolph Briscoe Center for American History, University of Texas at Austin.

"González Flies to Help Wagner; Party Jubilant." 1961. *Houston Post*, November 6. "Austin, Texas—Henry B. González" Vertical File, Dolph Briscoe Center for American History, University of Texas at Austin.

"González for Governor." ca. 1958. Campaign flyer (n.p., n.d.). "Austin, Texas— Henry B. González" Vertical File, Dolph Briscoe Center for American History, University of Texas at Austin.

"González Says MAYO to Disrupt Celebration." 1969. *Corpus Caller-Times*, April 12. Dr. Hector P. Garcia Papers, Special Collections and Archives, Texas A&M University–Corpus Christi, Mary and Jeff Bell Library.

"González to Report on 'Anti-Gringoism.'" 1969. *Corpus Christi Caller*, April 8. Dr. Hector P. Garcia Papers, Special Collections and Archives, Texas A&M University–Corpus Christi, Mary and Jeff Bell Library.

"GOP Boss Non-Committal." 1966. Unidentified newspaper clipping, January 30. Texas Observer Records, 1952–1990, Dolph Briscoe Center for American History, University of Texas at Austin.

"GOP Chair Says Sánchez Changed Accent on Name." 2002. Associated Press State and Local Wire, June 15. Retrieved from http://www.lexisnexis.com.

"Gov. Briscoe Gets Plaque." 1973. *Corpus Christi Caller*, August 25. Dr. Hector P. Garcia Papers, Special Collections and Archives, Texas A&M University–Corpus Christi, Mary and Jeff Bell Library.

"Governor Clements and the Hispanic Leaders of Texas." 1981. April 3. Governor William P. Clements Jr. Records, Mexico and Latin American Relations Office [MALAR] Records, First Term, 1979–1983. Box 5, Folder 18.

"Governor Dolph Briscoe's Mexican-American Appointments." ca. 1979. Dolph Briscoe Papers, 1932–2010, Dolph Briscoe Center for American History, University of Texas at Austin. Box 208.

"Governor's Comments Get Favorable Response from Harlingen Gathering." 1979. *Valley Citizen*, February 1. Governor William P. Clements Jr. Records, Mexico and Latin American Relations Office [MALAR] Records, First Term, 1979–1983. Box 7, Folder 12.

"Governor Urged to Learn about Minorities Problems." 1970. *San Antonio Express-News*, September 4. Henry B. González Papers, 1946–1998, Dolph Briscoe Center for American History, University of Texas at Austin. Box 2004–127/395.

"Gramm Steals Spotlight with Dream-Team Race Comments." 2002. National Journal Group, Inc., June 10. Retrieved from http://www.lexisnexis.com.

"Group Votes to Oppose Governor." 1970. *Amarillo Daily News*, September 28. Dolph Briscoe Papers, 1932–2010, Dolph Briscoe Center for American History, University of Texas at Austin. Box 265.

"Gutierrez' Unbending Stance Splits Formerly 'United' Party." 1977. *Houston Post*, November 25. Dolph Briscoe Papers, 1932–2010, Dolph Briscoe Center for American History, University of Texas at Austin. Box 48.

"The Harris County PASO." ca. 1962. Political flyer. Dr. Hector P. Garcia Papers, Special Collections and Archives, Texas A&M University–Corpus Christi, Mary and Jeff Bell Library.

"HBG May Request Grand Jury Probe." 1969. *San Antonio News*, April 9. Joe J. Bernal Papers, Benson Latin American Collection, University of Texas Libraries, University of Texas at Austin. Box 38.

"Hispanic Chairman." ca. 1978. Internal campaign document, n.p., n.d. Governor William P. Clements Jr. Records, Mexico and Latin American Relations Office [MALAR] Records, First Term, 1979–1983. Box 14, Folder 30.

"Hispanic Groups Split in Their Gubernatorial Endorsements." 1982. *Houston Chronicle*, September 14. Governor William P. Clements Jr. Records, Mexico and Latin American Relations Office [MALAR] Records, First Term, 1979–1983. Box 5, Folder 16.

"Hispanic Leaders of Texas." 1980a. "Checklist," February 11. Governor William P. Clements Jr. Records, Mexico and Latin American Relations Office [MALAR] Records, First Term, 1979–1983. Box 5, Folder 18.

———. 1980b. Minutes, February 20. Governor William P. Clements Jr. Records, Mexico and Latin American Relations Office [MALAR] Records, First Term, 1979–1983. Box 5, Folder 18.

———. 1981. Minutes, July 28. Governor William P. Clements Jr. Records, Mexico and Latin American Relations Office [MALAR] Records, First Term, 1979–1983. Box 5, Folder 18.

"Historical Debate a 'Brawl.'" 2002. National Journal Group, Inc., March 4. Retrieved from http://www.lexisnexis.com.

"The History of M.A.D." 1977. In *Mexican American Democrats First State Conference*, June 1, 2, 3 (state conference booklet, n.p.). Margo Gutiérrez Personal Papers, University of Texas at Austin.

———. 1980. *Mexican American Democrats: Where We Are Heading in the Eighties* (Fourth State Annual Convention journal), September 19–20. Margo Gutiérrez Personal Papers, University of Texas at Austin.

"How to Be a Mod Con Delegate in 1978." 1978. Billie Carr Papers, 1956–2003, MS 373, Woodson Research Center, Fondren Library, Rice University. Box 12, Folder 4.

"Integration Works Fine, Senator Says." 1957. *Dallas News*, June 24. "Austin, Texas—Henry B. González" Vertical File, Dolph Briscoe Center for American History, University of Texas at Austin.

"Kirk Says Democrats' 'Dream Ticket' Not a Racial Quota System." 2002. Bulletin's Frontrunner. April 11. Retrieved from http://www.lexisnexis.com.

"Laredoans Pleased with Cadena's Appointment." 1965. *Laredo Times*, April 6. Texas Governor John Connally Records, LBJ Library. Box 496.

"Latin American Appointees of Governor Connally (as of 3–31–64)." 1964. Document, March 31. Texas Governor John Connally Records, LBJ Library. Box 1290.

"Latin American Appointees of Governor Connally." ca. 1965. Document, January. Texas Governor John Connally Records, LBJ Library. Box 1290.

"Latin Group Split on Endorsement." 1962. *Texas Observer*, February 16.

"Latinos and Votes: A Breakthrough?" 1962. *Texas Observer*, January 19.

"A Lecture to the Press." 1958. *Texas Observer*, January 31.

"Liberals and the Governor's Race." 1962. *Texas Observer*, January 5.

"The Liberal's Dilemma." 1955. *Texas Observer*, August 24.

"Local DOT Groups Name Choices." 1958. *Texas Observer*, May 23.

"The Longest Shot." 1972. *Texas Observer*, August 4. Dr. Hector P. Garcia Papers, Special Collections and Archives, Texas A&M University–Corpus Christi, Mary and Jeff Bell Library.

"LULAC Lauds Clements; White Gets Mayors' Nod." 1982. *San Antonio Light*, September 14. Governor William P. Clements Jr. Records, Mexico and Latin American Relations Office [MALAR] Records, First Term, 1979–1983. Box 7, Folder 8.

"Lulac Past President Supports Carr." 1966. *Edinburg Daily Review*, August 7. Henry B. González Papers, 1946–1998, Dolph Briscoe Center for American History, University of Texas at Austin. Box 2004–127/395.

"McKinnon Carries Refugio County; Truan Winner." 1976. Unidentified newspaper clipping, n.d. Carlos Truan Papers, South Texas Archives and Special Collections, James C. Jernigan Library, Texas A&M University–Kingsville. Box 52.012.

"Meanwhile Back at the Alamo." 1978. *Texas Observer*, September 22.

"Media Strategy." ca. 1978. Tower Media Strategy, memo (n.p., n.d.). Texas Observer Records, 1952–1990, Dolph Briscoe Center for American History, University of Texas at Austin.

"The Mexican American Chamber of Commerce." 1980. Text of speech delivered, May 5. Governor William P. Clements Jr. Records, Mexico and Latin American Relations Office [MALAR] Records, First Term, 1979–1983, Box 10, Folder 18.

"Mexican American Democrats Candidate Questionnaire." ca. 1982. Mark White for Governor. Records, Texas Governor Mark White, Archives and Information Services Division, Texas State Library and Archives Commission. "Hispanics," Box 1991/141–94.

"Mexican American Democrats Divided on Gubernatorial Endorsement." 1982. *Mexican American Democrat: Official Publication of the Mexican American Democrats of Texas* 1, no. 2 (April).

"Militant Latins Preach Hate, Say 5 Texas Congressmen." 1969. *El Sol*, May 2. Dr. Hector P. Garcia Papers, Special Collections and Archives, Texas A&M University–Corpus Christi, Mary and Jeff Bell Library.

"Minutes of the Hispanic Leadership Meeting." 1979 (October 10). Governor William P. Clements Jr. Records, Mexico and Latin American Relations Office [MALAR] Records, First Term, 1979–1983. Box 5, Folder 18.

"Mom's Counsel Changed Course of Barrera's Life." 1968. *San Angelo Standard Times*, March 10. "Roy Barrera" Vertical File, Dolph Briscoe Center for American History, University of Texas at Austin.

"Morales Aides Ponder Negative Ad Attack." 2002. Associated Press State and Local Wire, February 4. Retrieved from http://www.lexisnexis.com.

"Morales Defends His Affirmative Action Record." 2002. Bulletin Broadfaxing Network, Inc., January 8. Retrieved from http://www.lexisnexis.com.

"Morales Makes Play for White Voters with Affirmative Action Argument." 2002. Bulletin's Frontrunner. Retrieved from http://www.lexisnexis.com.

"Morales Won't Rule Out Supporting Perry." 2002. Bulletin Broadfaxing Network, Inc., June 20. Retrieved from http://www.lexisnexis.com.

"Negroes Back Ralph, Henry." *Texas Observer*, August 8.

"New Power for Texas Minorities." 1964. *Texas Observer*, November 13.

"The New Secretary of State." 1968. *Texas Observer*, March 31.

"News to Allan." 1956. *Valley Morning Star*, May 2. Dr. Hector P. Garcia Papers, Special Collections and Archives, Texas A&M University–Corpus Christi, Mary and Jeff Bell Library.

"The Only Way I Want to Win." 1959. *The Texas Observer*, July 4.

"Organizing Committee." ca. 1972. Dr. Hector P. Garcia Papers, Special Collections and Archives, Texas A&M University–Corpus Christi, Mary and Jeff Bell Library.

"Party Vote Bill Passes Committee." 1957. *Austin American-Statesman*, February 28. "Austin, Texas—Henry B. González" Vertical File, Dolph Briscoe Center for American History, University of Texas at Austin.

"PASO Backing Kennedy and Yarborough." 1968. *Houston Post*, March 17.

"PASO Firms Up Independence." 1966. *San Antonio Express*, January 24. Texas Governor John Connally Records, LBJ Library. Box 735.

"PASO Names Fuentes Successor." 1966. *San Antonio Express-News*, March 20. Texas Governor John Connally Records, LBJ Library. Box 744.

"PASO Opposes Smith, Bentsen; Slaps Dem Party." 1970. *Houston Chronicle*, September 29. Texas Observer Records, 1952–1990, Dolph Briscoe Center for American History, University of Texas at Austin.

"P.A.S.O. Political Association of Spanish-Speaking Organizations." n.d. Carlos Truan Collection, South Texas Archives and Special Collections, James C. Jernigan Library, Texas A&M University–Kingsville. Box 6.003.

"PASO Scores Connally; Urges Yarborough Bid." 1965. *Austin American-Statesman*, July 12. Texas Governor John Connally Records, LBJ Library. Box 744.

"Peña Questions González' Credentials to Speak for Poor." 1968. *San Antonio Express*, June 26. Dr. Hector P. Garcia Papers, Special Collections and Archives, Texas A&M University–Corpus Christi, Mary and Jeff Bell Library.

"Perry Runs Ad Linking Sánchez Bank to Drug Dealers Who Killed US Agent." 2002. October 28. Bulletin Broadfaxing Network, Inc. Retrieved from http://www.lexisnexis.com.

"Platform of the Democratic Party of Texas." 1964. State Democratic Convention, September 15. Texas Democratic Party Papers, Archives and Information Services Division, Texas State Library and Archives Commission. Box 1979/49-65.

"Political Association of Spanish Speaking Organizations Harris County." ca. 1962. Undated manuscript. Dr. Hector P. Garcia Papers, Special Collections and Archives, Texas A&M University–Corpus Christi, Mary and Jeff Bell Library.

"Poll Tax, Hymns, and Henry." 1958. *Texas Observer*, January 24. "Austin, Texas—

Henry B. González" Vertical File, Dolph Briscoe Center for American History, University of Texas at Austin.

"Poll Tax Issue GOP Victory." 1963. Unidentified newspaper clipping, April 23. Allan Shivers Papers, 1949–1984, Dolph Briscoe Center for American History, University of Texas at Austin.

"Poll Tax Retained by 72,563." 1963. Unidentified newspaper clipping, April 23. Allan Shivers Papers, 1949–1984, Dolph Briscoe Center for American History, University of Texas at Austin.

"President Pro Tempore Wins Easily." 1975. *Dallas Times Herald*, June 3. "Santiesteban, Tati" Vertical File, Dolph Briscoe Center for American History, University of Texas at Austin.

"Probe of 'Demo Club' Poll Tax Drive Awaits Ruling." 1956. *Valley Evening Monitor*, May 6. Dr. Hector P. Garcia Papers, Special Collections and Archives, Texas A&M University–Corpus Christi, Mary and Jeff Bell Library.

"Process Itself Biggest Winner in Saturday Vote." 1976. *Corpus Christi Caller-Times*, June 6. Carlos Truan Papers, South Texas Archives and Special Collections, James C. Jernigan Library, Texas A&M University–Kingsville. Box 52.010.

"Radio Jingles." ca. 1968. Undated transcription. Preston Smith Papers, 1930–1975 and undated, Southwest Collection/Special Collections Library, Texas Tech University, Lubbock.

"Rangel, Truan and Dreyer Capture Kleberg County Races." 1976. *Kingsville-Bishop Record News*, June 6. Irma Rangel Papers, South Texas Archives and Special Collections, James C. Jernigan Library, Texas A&M University–Kingsville. Box 4.003.

"Raza Unida Campaigns Aiding GOP." 1978. *Houston Post*, October 22. Dolph Briscoe Papers, 1932–2010, Dolph Briscoe Center for American History, University of Texas at Austin. Box 48.

"Reagan, Clements Honor G.I. Forum." 1982. *Hispanic Times of Texas*, July. Governor William P. Clements Jr. Records, Mexico and Latin American Relations Office [MALAR] Records, First Term, 1979–1983. Box 6, Folder 5.

"Resolution Would Praise González." 1969. *San Antonio Express*, April 9. Joe J. Bernal Papers, Benson Latin American Collection, University of Texas Libraries, University of Texas at Austin. Box 38.

"The Rodolfo Flores Family." n.d. Unidentified document. Dr. Hector P. Garcia Papers, Special Collections and Archives, Texas A&M University–Corpus Christi, Mary and Jeff Bell Library.

"San Antonio Judge Confident." 1986. *Victoria Advocate*, April 29. "Barrera, Roy Jr." Vertical File, Dolph Briscoe Center for American History, University of Texas at Austin.

"Sánchez, Morales War over Spanish-Language Radio." 2002. T Bulletin Broadfaxing Network, Inc. Retrieved from http://www.lexisnexis.com.

"Sandoval in DC." 1969. *Texas Observer*, March 28.

"The Sands Have Shifted." *Texas Observer*, October 24.

"Santiesteban Replaces Briscoe . . . for 4 Days." 1975. *Dallas Times Herald*, June 24. "Santiesteban, Tati" Vertical File, Dolph Briscoe Center for American History, University of Texas at Austin.

"Santiesteban's Day as Governor Noted." 1975. *Dallas Morning News*, December 13. "Santiesteban, Tati" Vertical File, Dolph Briscoe Center for American History, University of Texas at Austin.

"The Segregation Filibuster." 1957. *Texas Observer*, May 7.

"Segregationists' Program Unfolded." 1957. *Texas Observer*, January 29.

"Senator González Cites Roosevelt Leadership." 1958. *Dallas News*, February 24. "Austin, Texas—Henry B. González" Vertical File, Dolph Briscoe Center for American History, University of Texas at Austin.

"74th Legislative Priorities SHC Meeting." 1995. Draft, January 16. Carlos Truan Collection, South Texas Archives and Special Collections, James C. Jernigan Library, Texas A&M University–Kingsville. Box 539.011.

"Shivers Asks Probe of Democratic Club." 1956. *Valley Evening Monitor*, May 3. Dr. Hector P. Garcia Papers, Special Collections and Archives, Texas A&M University–Corpus Christi, Mary and Jeff Bell Library.

"Simply MAD in Politics." 1986. *Mexican American Democrat: Official Publication of the Mexican American Democrats of Texas*. Convention issue, February. Corpus Christi: MAD.

"Smith and Bentsen Opposed by PASO." 1970. *Del Rio News Herald*, September 28. Texas Observer Records, 1952–1990, Dolph Briscoe Center for American History, University of Texas at Austin.

"Smith, Bentsen Draw PASO Fire." 1970. *Dallas Times Herald*, September 28. Dolph Briscoe Papers, 1932–2010, Dolph Briscoe Center for American History, University of Texas at Austin. Box 265.

"Smith's Ex-Aide Backs Foe." 1970. *Houston Post*, October 8. Dolph Briscoe Papers, 1932–2010, Dolph Briscoe Center for American History, University of Texas at Austin. Box 265.

"Smith's Interest in Migrants Hit." 1968. *San Antonio Express*, October 4. E. Preston Smith Papers, 1930–1975 and undated, Southwest Collection/Special Collections Library, Texas Tech University, Lubbock.

"Spanish Land Grants Study Urged by HBG." 1969. *San Antonio Express*, March 14. Dolph Briscoe Papers, 1932–2010, Dolph Briscoe Center for American History, University of Texas at Austin. Box 265.

"State Officials Sued on Voting Rights Act." 1975. *El Paso Herald Post*, September 18. South West Vertical Files, El Paso Public Library. "Mexican Americans, Politics and Government."

"The Struggle for PASO." 1963. *Texas Observer*, June 14.

"Taxes-Services-Discrimination." Records, Texas Governor Mark White. Archives and Information Services Division, Texas State Library and Archives Commission, M.W. 1992/77–122.

"10 Chicanos Form Group for Tower." 1972. *Houston Post*, August 30. Dr. Hector P. Garcia Papers, Special Collections and Archives, Texas A&M University–Corpus Christi, Mary and Jeff Bell Library.

"Texans Divided in Racial Survey." 1955. *Texas Observer*, April 11.

"Texans Support All U.S. House Vets." 1970. *Big Spring Daily Herald*, May 4.

"Texas: Add It Up and You Get More Attacks." Hotline, National Journal Group, Inc., March 6, 2002. Retrieved from http://www.lexisnexis.com.

"Texas Demo Goal Is to Rebuild." 1973. *El Paso Herald Post*, June 27.

"Texas GOP Pays Tribute to Hispanics at Convention." 1982. *Hispanic Times of Texas* 2, no. 7 (August/September). Governor William P. Clements, Jr., Records, Mexico and Latin American Relations Office [MALAR] Records, First Term, 1979–1983. Box 6, Folder 5.

"Texas Latin Vote May Go for GOP." 1968. *Dallas Times Herald*, September 29. Texas Governor John Connally Records, LBJ Library. Box 735.

"Texas Liberals Argue, Act Like Outcasts." 1955. *Texas Observer*, May 30.

"Texas Referendum Committee." ca. 1956. Petition. Texas Governor Price Daniel Records, Archives and Information Services Division, Texas State Library and Archives Commission, Segregation. Box 596.

"Three Seek Post of State Rep. No. 1." 1966. *El Paso Herald Post*, May 2. Scrapbook, Tati Santiesteban Personal Papers.

"Touchy Meet May Cost Smith Support." 1970. *San Antonio Light*, August 30. Dolph Briscoe Papers, 1932–2010, Dolph Briscoe Center for American History, University of Texas at Austin. Box 265.

"Tower Aide Promoted to Top Position." 1978. *San Antonio Express*, August 22. Texas Observer Records, 1952–1990, Dolph Briscoe Center for American History, University of Texas at Austin.

"Tower Disputes Fuentes Reports." 1966. *San Antonio Express*, February 1. Texas Observer Records, 1952–1990, Dolph Briscoe Center for American History, University of Texas at Austin.

"Tower Endorsed." 1978. Press release. *John Tower News*, September 8 [Texans for Tower]. Texas Observer Records, 1952–1990, Dolph Briscoe Center for American History, University of Texas at Austin.

"Translation of the Ralph Yarborough Spanish Pamphlet." ca. 1956. Texas Governor Price Daniel Records, Archives and Information Services Division, Texas State Library and Archives Commission, Spanish Broadcasts. Box 216.

"Union Deposit Photos Probed." 1956. *Valley Evening Monitor*, May 4. Dr. Hector P. Garcia Papers, Special Collections and Archives, Texas A&M University–Corpus Christi, Mary and Jeff Bell Library.

"The Unpublished Facts about Waggoner Carr's Record of 'Effectiveness.'" 1966. Tower Campaign Research Staff, Austin, October 8. Texas Observer Records, 1952–1990, Dolph Briscoe Center for American History, University of Texas at Austin.

"U.S. Judge Garza on a Demonstrator—'I'd Probably Kick Him—?'" 1965. *Texas Observer*, September 3.

"Victorious Party Leaders." ca. 1965. Undated newspaper clipping with photo. Texas Governor John Connally Records, LBJ Library. Box 496.

"'Viva Smith' Base Has Its Opening." 1968. *Texas Observer*, September 25. E. Preston Smith Papers, 1930–1975 and undated, Southwest Collection/Special Collections Library, Texas Tech University, Lubbock.

"When Choosing a Party Vera Says Race Is No Barrier." 1978. *Del Rio News Herald*, August 31. Governor William P. Clements Jr. Records, Mexico and Latin American Relations Office [MALAR] Records, First Term, 1979–1983. Box 14, Folder 33.

"White Asks MAD to Help 'Finish What We Started.'" 1990. Southwest Newswire, January 13. Retrieved from http://www.lexisnexis.com.

"White House Conference on Latin Americans." ca. 1966. Unpublished manu-
script, n.p., n.d. Texas Governor John Connally Records, LBJ Library. Box
992.
"White Keeps Promise, Appoints Mexican American U.T. Regent." 1983. *Mexi-
can American Democrat: Official Publication of the Mexican American Democrats
of Texas* 2, no. 1 (April).
"Who Is Leonel Castillo?" ca. 1974. Leaflet. Mexican American Democrats of
Texas Records, 1962–1987, MS 29, UTSA Archives, Library, University of
Texas at San Antonio. Box 11:14.
"A Wide Open Primary in Duval." 1976. *Texas Observer*, February 27.
"Women, Liberal Coalition Defeated in Texas Demo Credentials Battle." 1974. *El
Paso Herald Post*, September 17. El Paso Public Library, Southwest Collection,
El Paso Vertical Files "Democratic Party."
"The Yarborough Defeat: Anti-Nigger, Anti-Mexican, Anti-Youth." *Texas Ob-
server*, May 15, 1970.
"Yarborough Gives Progress Plan." 1956. *Texas Observer*, June 6.

Sources by Author

Abbott, Carroll. 1972. *The Texas Delegation: A Handbook for Members of the Texas
National Democratic Delegation*. Austin: Ad Vantage Associates, Inc. Texas Ob-
server Records, 1952–1990, Dolph Briscoe Center for American History, Uni-
versity of Texas at Austin.
Abrams, Michael. 1982. "Hispanic Leaders Get Behind Clements." *Corpus Christi
Caller*, October 31. Governor William P. Clements Jr. Records, Mexico and
Latin American Relations Office [MALAR] Records, First Term, 1979–1983.
Box 7, Folder 8.
Adams, Mark, and Gertrude Adams. 1963. *A Report on Politics in El Paso*. Cam-
bridge: Joint Center for Urban Studies, Massachusetts Institute of Technology.
Aguirre, Humberto. 1970. Opening statement, Press Conference, August 7.
Dolph Briscoe Papers, 1932–2010, Dolph Briscoe Center for American His-
tory, University of Texas at Austin. Box 267.
Alba, Richard D., and Victor Nee. 2003. *Remaking the American Mainstream:
Assimilation and Contemporary Immigration*. Cambridge, Mass.: Harvard Uni-
versity Press.
Alderete, Chris. 1987. Memorandum to the Senate Hispanic Caucus, August
12. Carlos Truan Collection, South Texas Archives and Special Collections,
James C. Jernigan Library, Texas A&M University–Kingsville. Box 537.005.
Allred, James V. 1934. Letter Opinion 2953A, July 25. Texas State Library and
Archives Commission.
Alonzo, Roberto R. 1992a. "Letter from Chairman Roberto Alonzo." MAD of
Texas News, February 1992. Margo Gutiérrez Personal Papers.
———. 1992b. "Open Letter to MAD Members." Program for the Mexican
American Democrats of Texas State Democratic Convention 1992. Carlos
Truan Collection, South Texas Archives and Special Collections, James C. Jer-
nigan Library, Texas A&M University–Kingsville.

American GI Forum. 1950. Resolution. Second Annual Convention, McAllen, Texas, August 19, 20. Dr. Hector P. Garcia Papers, Special Collections and Archives, Texas A&M University–Corpus Christi, Mary and Jeff Bell Library.

Armendariz, Alex. 1972. Memorandum for Henry Ramirez, Committee for the Re-election of the President, June 19. Dr. Hector P. Garcia Papers, Special Collections and Archives, Texas A&M University–Corpus Christi, Mary and Jeff Bell Library.

Arnold, Ann. 1981. "GOP: Password to Clements' List." 1981. *Fort Worth Star-Telegram*, May 3. Governor William P. Clements Jr. Records, Mexico and Latin American Relations Office [MALAR] Records, First Term, 1979–1983. Box 1, Folder 18.

Associated Press. 1966. AP story. Texas Governor John Connally Records, August 4. LBJ Library. Box 744.

Attlesey, Sam. 1982. "White to Reward Minority Backers." 1982. *Dallas Morning News*, December 21. Moya (Richard) Papers (1969–1986), Austin History Center, AR.2002.024.

Aurispa, Eddie. 1981a. Memorandum to the Governor through Doug Brown, April 15. Governor William P. Clements Jr. Records, Mexico and Latin American Relations Office [MALAR] Records, First Term, 1979–1983, Box 5, Folder 13.

———. 1981b. Memorandum to the Governor through George Bayoud, July 21. Governor William P. Clements Jr. Records, Mexico and Latin American Relations Office [MALAR] Records, First Term, 1979–1983, Box 7, Folder 1.

———. 1981c. "Remarks by Eddie Aurispa Special Assistant to the Governor, Corpus Christi Mexican American Chamber of Commerce." March 14. Governor William P. Clements Jr. Records, Mexico and Latin American Relations Office [MALAR] Records, First Term, 1979–1983, Box 10, Folder 18.

———. 1982a. Memorandum to Hilary Doran, June 23. Governor William P. Clements Jr. Records, Mexico and Latin American Relations Office [MALAR] Records, First Term, 1979–1983. Box 3, Folder 1.

———. 1982b. Memorandum to Polly Sowell, April 14. Governor William P. Clements Jr. Records, Mexico and Latin American Relations Office [MALAR] Records, First Term, 1979–1983. Box 3, Folder 1.

———. 1982c. Memo to Jim Kaster, June 23. Governor William P. Clements Jr. Records, Mexico and Latin American Relations Office [MALAR] Records, First Term, 1979–1983. Box 3, Folder 1.

———. 1982d. "Remarks by Eddie Aurispa, Special Assistant to the Governor," September 30. Governor William P. Clements Jr. Records, Mexico and Latin American Relations Office [MALAR] Records, First Term, 1979–1983, Box 10, Folder 18.

Aynesworth, Hugh. 2003. "Democrats Close Texas House With a Walkout; Cops Sent to Bring Them In." *Washington Times*, May 13. Retrieved from http://www.lexisnexis.com.

Badger, T. A. 2002a. "Sánchez Accuses Perry of Raising Military Draft Questions." Associated Press State and Local Wire, May 17. Retrieved from http://www.lexisnexis.com.

———. 2002b. "Sánchez Urges Supporters to Get Out Vote; Morales Pushes

English Language Theme." Associated Press State and Local Wire, March 10. Retrieved from http://www.lexisnexis.com.

Badger, Tony. 1999. "Southerners Who Refused to Sign the Southern Manifesto." *Historical Journal* 42, no. 2: 517–534.

Bain, Kenneth, and Paul Travis. 1984. "South Texas Politics." *Southern Exposure* 12, no. 1: 49–52.

Balz, Dan. 1982. "GOP Incumbent Gains a Bit on Challenger." *Washington Post*, September 17. Retrieved from http://www.lexisnexis.com.

Banks, Jimmy. 1958a. "Gonzalez Almost Steals Show with Talk at DOT Convention." *Dallas News*, June 1. "Austin, Texas—Henry B. González" Vertical File, Dolph Briscoe Center for American History, University of Texas at Austin.

———. 1958b. "Senator Considers Legislation to End Gasoline Price Wars." *Dallas News*, March 21. "Austin, Texas—Henry B. González" Vertical File, Dolph Briscoe Center for American History, University of Texas at Austin.

———. 1958c. "Texas Assured of Good Show in Governor's Race." *Dallas News*, May 7. "Austin, Texas—Henry B. González" Vertical File, Dolph Briscoe Center for American History, University of Texas at Austin.

———. 1963. "Connally's Backers Sense Storm Clouds on Horizon." *Dallas Morning News*, July 14. Texas Governor John Connally Records, LBJ Library. Box 56.

———. 1967a. "PASO Attacks Connally, Rangers." *Dallas Morning News*, March 14. Texas Governor John Connally Records, LBJ Library. Box 744.

———. 1967b. "PASO Attacks Connally, Rangers." *Texas Observer*, August 14. Texas Observer Records, 1952–1990, Dolph Briscoe Center for American History, University of Texas at Austin.

Barragan, Polly Baca. 1972. Memorandum to Texas Spanish-Surnamed State Legislators and Key Mexican American Leaders, June 7. Dolph Briscoe Papers, 1932–2010, Dolph Briscoe Center for American History, University of Texas at Austin. Box 30, Folder 16.

Barrientos, Gonzalo. 1978. "Common Ground." *Texas Observer*, February 3.

———. 2009. Interview by Katherine Grace Mendez, May 22.

Barrientos, Gonzalo, et al. 1983. Letter to Mark White, June 23. Records, Texas Governor Mark White, Archives and Information Services Division, Texas State Library and Archives Commission, "Gonzalo Barrientos." Box 1992/77–122.

Barta, Carolyn. 1976. "Conservative Democrats Plan Strategy Talks." *Dallas Morning News*, September 2. Dolph Briscoe Papers, 1932–2010, Dolph Briscoe Center for American History, University of Texas at Austin. Box 415.

———. ca. 1976. "Guest Draws Challenge from Texas' Democrats." *Dallas Morning News* (n.d.). Dolph Briscoe Papers, 1932–2010, Dolph Briscoe Center for American History, University of Texas at Austin. Box 415.

Baskin, Robert E. 1961a. "Kennedy Writes González Letter." 1961. *Dallas News*, October 26. "Austin, Texas—Henry B. González" Vertical File, Dolph Briscoe Center for American History, University of Texas at Austin.

———. 1961b. "LBJ Effort Seen to Help González." *Dallas News*, October 31. "Austin, Texas—Henry B. González" Vertical File, Dolph Briscoe Center for American History, University of Texas at Austin.

Baum, Elmer. 1968. Minutes of Texas State Democratic Party meeting, October 21. Texas Democratic Party Papers, Archives and Information Services Division, Texas State Library and Archives Commission. Box 1979/49-65.

Beagle, Gail. 1958. "Henry B. González, Candidate for Governor, Says He Doesn't Believe in Waving False Flags." 1958. *Port Neches Chronicle*, July. Henry B. González Papers, 1946–1998, Dolph Briscoe Center for American History, University of Texas at Austin. Box 2004–127/50.

Belden, Joe. 1946. Release, October 27. Report #119, *The Texas Poll: The Statewide Survey of Public Opinion*. Dallas: Belden Associates. Nancy Belden Personal Papers.

———. 1948. Release, March 21. Report #192. *The Texas Poll: The Statewide Survey of Public Opinion*. Dallas: Belden Associates. Nancy Belden Personal Papers.

———. 1951. Release, September 2. Report #383. *The Texas Poll: The Statewide Survey of Public Opinion*. Dallas: Belden Associates. Nancy Belden Personal Papers.

———. 1957. Release, December 15. Report #556. *The Texas Poll: The Statewide Survey of Public Opinion*. Dallas: Belden Associates. Nancy Belden Personal Papers.

———. 1960a. Release, September 5. Report #591. *The Texas Poll: The Statewide Survey of Public Opinion*. Dallas: Belden Associates. Nancy Belden Personal Papers.

———. 1960b. "Stair-Step Plan Felt Most Desirable." *Dallas Morning News*, September 6. Texas Governor Price Daniel Records, Archives and Information Services Division, Texas State Library and Archives Commission, Segregation Folder. Box 356.

———. 1963. "Texas Poll Finds Massive Resistance to Social Integration over State," October 6. Report #641. *The Texas Poll: The Statewide Survey of Public Opinion*. Dallas: Belden Associates. Nancy Belden Personal Papers.

———. 1966. "Texans Favor $1.25 Minimum Wage for Farm Workers, Admitting Braceros from Mexico, Poll Shows," September 4. Report #713. *The Texas Poll: The Statewide Survey of Public Opinion*. Dallas: Belden Associates. Nancy Belden Personal Papers.

———. 1968a. "Acceptance of Negro Equality by White Texans Continues to Increase, Statewide Survey Shows," July 7. Report #750. *The Texas Poll: The Statewide Survey of Public Opinion*. Dallas: Belden Associates. Nancy Belden Personal Papers.

———. 1968b. "Connally's High Public Support Continues Despite His 'Lame Duck' Status," April 2. Report #743. *The Texas Poll: The Statewide Survey of Public Opinion*. Dallas: Belden Associates. Nancy Belden Personal Papers.

———. 1969. "White Texans Over-All Acceptance of Racial Integration Fails to Gain during Past Years, But Pattern Still Changing," September 14. Report #775. *The Texas Poll: The Statewide Survey of Public Opinion*. Dallas: Belden Associates. Nancy Belden Personal Papers.

———. 1973. "Most Texans Approve of Briscoe's Performance, Poll Finds," September 30. Report #852. *The Texas Poll: The Statewide Survey of Public Opinion*. Southland Center, Dallas: Belden Associates.

———. 1976. "Bicentennial Celebration for Texas Blacks: Highest-Ever Social

Acceptance by Whites, Poll Shows," March 15. Report #875. *The Texas Poll: The Statewide Survey of Public Opinion*. Dallas: Belden Associates. Nancy Belden Personal Papers.

Beltram, Hector C. 1982. Letter to Patrick Oles, January 26. Governor William P. Clements Jr. Records, Mexico and Latin American Relations Office [MALAR] Records, First Term, 1979–1983. Box 1, Folder 20.

Beltrán, Cristina. 2010. *The Trouble with Unity: Latino Politics and the Creation of Identity*. New York: Oxford University Press.

Benavides, John, et al. 1970. Letter to Preston Smith, August 28. E. Preston Smith Papers, 1930–1975 and undated, Southwest Collection/Special Collections Library, Texas Tech University, Lubbock.

Benham, Joe. 1961. "Maverick to Back González in Race." *Dallas Morning News*, June 14. "Austin, Texas—Henry B. González" Vertical File, Dolph Briscoe Center for American History, University of Texas at Austin.

Bernal, Joe J. 1968. Letter to John M. Bailey, Chairman, Democratic National Committee, January 30. Texas Observer Records, 1952–1990, Dolph Briscoe Center for American History, University of Texas at Austin.

———. 1969. Speech before the National Association of Community Development, March 10, Washington, D.C. Joe J. Bernal Papers, Benson Latin American Collection, University of Texas Libraries, University of Texas at Austin. Box 80.

———. 1970a. Speech before the National YWCA, April 14, Houston. Joe J. Bernal Papers, Benson Latin American Collection, University of Texas Libraries, University of Texas at Austin. Box 80.

———. 1970b. Speech on Honor America Day, July 4 San Antonio. Joe J. Bernal Papers, Benson Latin American Collection, University of Texas Libraries, University of Texas at Austin. Box 80.

———. ca. 1970. Statement on dissent (n.d.). Joe J. Bernal Papers, Benson Latin American Collection, University of Texas Libraries, University of Texas at Austin. Box 80.

———. 1974a. "Exhibit in Support of Bernal Challenge," September 29. Texas Democratic Party Papers, Archives and Information Services Division, Texas State Library and Archives Commission. Box 1979/49–123.

———. 1974b. Letter to Robert S. Strauss with text of challenge, September 30. Mexican American Democrats of Texas Records, 1962–1987, MS 29, UTSA Archives, Library, University of Texas at San Antonio. Box 9:2.

———. 1977a. "A Message from the Chairman." In *Mexican American Democrats First State Conference, June 1, 2, 3* (state conference booklet, n.p., letter not dated). Margo Gutiérrez Personal Files, University of Texas at Austin.

———. 1977b. "Mexican American Democrats." Margo Gutiérrez Personal Files.

———. 1977c. Open letter to Mexican American Democrats. In *Mexican American Democrats: First State Convention, September 30 and October 1* (first state convention booklet, n.p., letter not dated). Margo Gutiérrez Personal Files. University of Texas at Austin.

———. 2009. Interview by Katherine Grace Mendez, August 16.

Bernal, Joe J., and Leonel Castillo. 1974. Letter to Robert S. Strauss, September 24. Mexican American Democrats of Texas Records, 1962–1987, MS 29, UTSA Archives, Library, University of Texas at San Antonio. Box 9:2.

Beserra, Richard. 1972. Memorandum to Jean Westwood and Gary Hart, September 18. Alicia Chacon Personal Papers.

Bexar County Democrats. 1958a. Delegates to Democratic State Convention, September 9. Texas Democratic Party Papers, Archives and Information Services Division, Texas State Library and Archives Commission. Box 1997/96–10.

———. 1958b. Resolutions, August 2. Texas Democratic Party Papers, Archives and Information Services Division, Texas State Library and Archives Commission. Box 1997/96–10.

Beyle, Thad, and Jennifer Jensen. 2009. Gubernatorial Campaign Finance Database. Online (accessed June 10, 2009): http://www.unc.edu/~beyle/guber .html.

Blalock, Jeanie. 1984. "State Chairman Says Hispanics Turning to GOP." *Victoria Advocate*, August 19. Allan Shivers Papers, 1949–1984, Dolph Briscoe Center for American History, University of Texas at Austin.

Bloom, Jack M. 1987. *Class, Race, and the Civil Rights Movement*. Bloomington: Indiana University Press.

Boesch, Barry. 1976. "Whither La Raza Unida?" *Corpus Christi Caller*, September 5. "Raza Unida Party" Vertical File, Dolph Briscoe Center for American History, University of Texas at Austin.

Bomar, Pat. 1963. Unidentified newspaper clipping, July 7. Texas Governor John Connally Records, LBJ Library. Box 56.

Bonavita, Fred. 1970. "Republicans Out to Obtain Chicano Vote." *Houston Post*, August 2. Texas Observer Records, 1952–1990, Dolph Briscoe Center for American History, University of Texas at Austin.

———. 1974. "Democratic Conservatives Face Fight." *The Houston Post*, January 6.

———. 1979. "'Fugitives' Skip Senate Session; 'Arrest' Ordered." *Houston Post*, May 19. Carlos Truan Papers, South Texas Archives and Special Collections, James C. Jernigan Library, Texas A&M University–Kingsville.

Bonilla Campaign. 1966. Endorsement letter, April 13. *Corpus Christi Caller* (n.d.). Dr. Hector P. Garcia Papers, Special Collections and Archives, Texas A&M University–Corpus Christi, Mary and Jeff Bell Library.

Bonilla, Ruben. 1978. Letter to Bill Clements, November 30. Governor William P. Clements Jr. Records, Mexico and Latin American Relations Office [MALAR] Records, First Term, 1979–1983. Box 7, Folder 1.

———. 1982. "Statement of Ruben Bonilla Jr., Former National president of LULAC, Currently Their Legal Council, and Tony Bonilla, National President of LULAC," October 1. Records, Texas Governor Mark White, Archives and Information Services Division, Texas State Library and Archives Commission, "Hispanics." Box 1991/141–94.

Bonilla, Ruben, Jr. 1986. Memorandum to Executive Committee and Chapter Chairs, March 3. Mexican American Democrats of Texas Records, 1962–1987, MS 29, UTSA Archives, Library, University of Texas at San Antonio. Box 7:10.

———. 2003. Interview with author, August 26.

Bonilla, Tony. 1964. Letter to John Connally, February 21. Texas Governor John Connally Records, LBJ Library. Box 1055.

———. 1966. Press release, August 10. Texas Governor John Connally Records, LBJ Library. Box 1068.

———. 2003. Telephone interview with author, August 13.

———. 2007. Interview, KEDT Public Broadcasting. Online (accessed December 9, 2009): justiceformypeople.org/interview_bonilla.html.

Bonilla, William D. 1964. Letter to John Connally, February 21. Texas Governor John Connally Records, LBJ Library. Box 1069.

Box, Terry. 1977. "Uvalde Pays Lo Vaca; Del Rio Funds Ready." *Corpus Christi Caller*, October 13. Dolph Briscoe Papers, 1932–2010, Dolph Briscoe Center for American History, University of Texas at Austin. Box 48.

Brezosky, Lynne. 2002. "Morales Visits Laredo, But Just Barely." Associated Press, February 12. Retrieved from http://www.lexisnexis.com.

Bridges, Kenneth William. 2003. "Twilight of the Texas Democrats: The 1978 Governor's Race." Ph.D. diss. (History), University of North Texas.

Briggs, Vernon M., et al. 1977. *The Chicano Worker*. Austin: University of Texas Press.

Brischetto, Robert R. 1982. *Mexican American Voting in the 1982 Texas General Election*. San Antonio: Southwest Voter Registration Education Project.

———. 1983. *Mexican American Issues for the 1984 Presidential Election*. Southwest Voter Public Opinion Report #1. San Antonio: Southwest Voter Research Institute.

———. 1985. "Latino Political Participation: 1972–1984." Paper presented at the League of Women Voters Educational Fund Conference on Electoral Participation, July 18 (San Antonio: Southwest Voter Registration Education Project).

Brischetto, Robert R., and Annette A. Avina. 1986. "Trends in Ethnic Voting in Texas State Elections: 1978–1986." Paper presented to Leadership San Antonio Alumni Association, December 5 (San Antonio: Southwest Voter Registration Education Project).

Brischetto, Robert R., and Rodolfo de la Garza. 1985. *The Mexican American Electorate: Political Opinions and Behavior across Cultures in San Antonio*. San Antonio: Southwest Voter Registration Education Project and Austin: Center for Mexican American Studies.

Brischetto, Robert, et al. 1994. "Texas." In Chandler Davidson and Bernard Grofman, eds., *Quiet Revolution in the South: The Impact of the Voting Rights Act, 1965–1990*, 233–257. Princeton: Princeton University Press.

Briscoe, Dolph. 1972. Text of speech, June 1, Dallas. Texas Observer Records, 1952–1990, Dolph Briscoe Center for American History, University of Texas at Austin.

———. 1973a. Press release, August 28. Texas Observer Records, 1952–1990, Dolph Briscoe Center for American History, University of Texas at Austin.

———. 1973b. Text of speech before the 63rd Legislature, January 17. Texas Observer Records, 1952–1990, Dolph Briscoe Center for American History, University of Texas at Austin.

Brooks, Raymond, and Sam Wood. 1957. "Capitol A: Going Home?" *Austin American-Statesman*, November 22. "Austin, Texas—Henry B. González" Vertical File, Dolph Briscoe Center for American History, University of Texas at Austin.

———. 1958. "Capitol A." *Austin American-Statesman*, May 7. "Austin, Texas— Henry B. González" Vertical File, Dolph Briscoe Center for American History, University of Texas at Austin.

Browning, Harley, and S. Dale McLemore, eds. 1964. *A Statistical Profile of the Spanish Surname Population of Texas*. Austin: Bureau of Business Research, University of Texas.

Bullock, Charles S., III, and R. K. Gaddie. 2005. *An Assessment of Voting Rights Progress in Texas*. Washington, D.C.: Prepared for the American Enterprise Institute.

Burka, Paul. 1986a. "Henry B. and Henry C." *Texas Monthly* (January). "González, Henry B." Vertical File, Dolph Briscoe Center for American History, University of Texas at Austin.

———. 1986b. "The Strange Case of Mark White." *Texas Monthly* (October).

———. 2002. "Swept Away; The Election Day Rout Confirmed What We've Known, or Should Have Known, All Along: Texas Is a Republican State. And That's Not Going to Change Anytime Soon." *Texas Monthly* (December).

Byers, Bo. 1972. "How Much Will Briscoe Sway between Now and Election Day?" 1972. *Houston Chronicle*, July 13. Dolph Briscoe Papers, 1932–2010, Dolph Briscoe Center for American History, University of Texas at Austin. Box 294.

Byers, Bo, and Gayle McNutt. 1970. "Dem Liberals Bolt Convention." *Houston Chronicle*, September 16. Albert A. Peña Jr. Papers, 1952–1977 (bulk 1956– 1972), MS 37, UTSA Archives and Special Collections, Library, University of Texas at San Antonio. Box 8:18.

Calhoun, Ron. 1974a. "Bullock Vows Minority Recruitment." *Dallas Times Herald*, October 21. Dolph Briscoe Papers, 1932–2010, Dolph Briscoe Center for American History, University of Texas at Austin. Box 30.

———. 1974b. "Political War Brewing?" *Dallas Times Herald*, April 21. Texas Democratic Party Papers, Archives and Information Services Division, Texas State Library and Archives Commission. Box 1979–49/123.

Califano, Joseph A. 1966a. Memorandum for Chairman Macy, September 8. Office Files of White Aides, Office Files of Harry C. McPhearson, LBJ Library. Box 11 (1412) (file: "Mexican Americans").

———. 1966b. Memorandum to Jake Jacobson et al., September 15. LBJ Library, "LBJ Human Rights" HU2/MC 6/7/66–10/12/66. Box 23.

Cardenas, Blandina. 2004. Interview by Sudha Rajan, January.

Cárdenas, Leo. 1969. "Protest Taped on County Door." *San Antonio Express*, March 31. Dolph Briscoe Papers, 1932–2010, Dolph Briscoe Center for American History, University of Texas at Austin. Box 265.

Carl, Carlton. n.d. Undated list of events, October 15, 1968–February 8, 1972. E. Preston Smith Papers, 1930–1975 and undated, Southwest Collection/Special Collections Library, Texas Tech University, Lubbock.

Carney, Dan. 1989. States News Service, June 13. Retrieved from http://www.lexisnexis.com.

Carpenter, Scott. 1976. "$174,814 Spent to Date in Race for McKinnon's Senate Seat." *Corpus Christi Caller-Times*, June 3. Carlos Truan Papers, South Texas Archives and Special Collections, James C. Jernigan Library, Texas A&M University–Kingsville. Box 52.009.

Carr, Billie. 1974. Statement by Billie Carr, Democratic National Committee member. April 1974. Texas Democratic Party Papers, Archives and Information Services Division, Texas State Library and Archives Commission. Box 1979/49-123.

———. 1976. Letter to Bob Armstrong, May 26. Billie Carr Papers, 1956–2003, MS 373, Woodson Research Center, Fondren Library, Rice University. Box 12, Folder 2.

———. ca. 1976. Memo to the Democratic Party Compliance Review Commission. Texas Democratic Party Papers, Archives and Information Services Division, Texas State Library and Archives Commission. Box 1979/49-135.

———. ca. 1979a. "An Action Strategy for the Rebuilding of the Texas Democrats." Billie Carr Papers, 1956–2003, MS 373, Woodson Research Center, Fondren Library, Rice University. Box 13, Folder 4.

———. ca. 1979b. "Democrats Form a Firing Squad by Standing in a Circle." Billie Carr Papers, 1956–2003, MS 373, Woodson Research Center, Fondren Library, Rice University. Box 13, Folder 4.

———. ca. 1979c. Press release (n.p., n.d.). Billie Carr Papers, 1956–2003, MS 373, Woodson Research Center, Fondren Library, Rice University. Box 4, Folder 16.

———. 1982. "Billie Carr Reports . . ." Billie Carr Papers, 1956–2003, MS 373, Woodson Research Center, Fondren Library, Rice University. Box 11, Folder 22.

———. ca. 2001. *Harris County Newsletter* (n.p., n.d.). Billie Carr Papers, 1956–2003, MS 373, Woodson Research Center, Fondren Library, Rice University. Box 8, Folder 18.

———. n.d. "Texas Conventions: Past, Present, Future." Billie Carr Papers, 1956–2003, MS 373, Woodson Research Center, Fondren Library, Rice University. Box 1, Folder 1.

Carr, Waggoner. 1966. Letter to Henry B. González, September 24. Henry B. González Papers, 1946–1998, Dolph Briscoe Center for American History, University of Texas at Austin. Box 2004–127/395.

Case, Jeff D. 1976. "Barrientos Admits Idealism Loss." *Daily Texan*, August 29. "Barrientos, Gonzalo" Vertical File, Dolph Briscoe Center for American History, University of Texas at Austin.

Castillo, John. 1998. Oral history interview by José Ángel Gutiérrez, June 26, 1998. Center for Mexican American Studies No. 50.

Castillo, Leonel J. 1974a. Letter to Frances Farenthold, February 20. Billie Carr Papers, 1956–2003, MS 373, Woodson Research Center, Fondren Library, Rice University. Box 2, Folder 2.

———. 1974b. Letter to Harry Hubbard, September 23. Mexican American

Democrats of Texas Records, 1962–1987, MS 29, UTSA Archives, Library, University of Texas at San Antonio. Box 11:14.

———. 1974c. "Statement of Leonel Castillo." Texas Democratic Party Papers, Archives and Information Services Division, Texas State Library and Archives Commission. Box 1979/49–123.

———. 1975. "Amendment of the Voting Rights Act to Include Mexican Americans." Testimony of Leonel Castillo before the Subcommittee on Civil and Constitutional Rights. Benson Latin American Collection. F395, M5, C377.

Castro, Tony. 1974. "La Raza Unida Making Harris County Major Base." *Houston Post*, March 10. Texas Observer Records, 1952–1990. Dolph Briscoe Center for American History, University of Texas at Austin.

Cavazos, Eddie. 1991. News release, December 12. Carlos F. Truan Collection, South Texas Archives and Special Collections, James C. Jernigan Library, Texas A&M University–Kingsville.

Cen-Tex Advertising and Public Relations. 1967. Survey results. Preston Smith Papers, 1930–1975 and undated, Southwest Collection/Special Collections Library, Texas Tech University, Lubbock.

———. 1968. Survey results, August (handwritten report). Preston Smith Papers, 1930–1975 and undated, Southwest Collection/Special Collections Library, Texas Tech University, Lubbock.

Chacon, Alicia. 1996. Oral history interview by José Ángel Gutiérrez, June 22. Center for Mexican American Studies No. 002.

———. 2003. Interview with author, May 13, El Paso.

Chapa, Amancio. 2005. Interview by Sudha Rajan, January 9.

Chapa, Jaime. 1978. "Work Report on Campaign," October 30. Governor William P. Clements Jr. Records, Mexico and Latin American Relations Office [MALAR] Records, First Term, 1979–1983. Box 14, Folder 30.

Chastain, Wayne. 1958. "Bexar's Renewed Coalition." *Texas Observer*, May 2.

Cheavens, Dave. 1958. "González's Candidacy Fee Filed." *Austin American-Statesman*, May 6. "Austin, Texas—Henry B. González" Vertical File, Dolph Briscoe Center for American History, University of Texas at Austin.

Cherow-O'Leary, Rene. 1980. "MAD Leader Asks Carter for Action." August 8, 1980. *San Antonio Express News*. Mexican American Democrats of Texas Records, 1962–1987, MS 29, UTSA Archives, Library, University of Texas at San Antonio. Box 3:4.

Cienski, Jan. 2002. "Ethnicity, Money Are the Recipe for 'Dream Team': Battle for Texas: Democrats Court Blacks, Hispanics in Republican State." *National Post* (Canada), October 31. Retrieved from http://www.lexisnexis.com.

Clements, William P., Jr. 1979. "Remarks Prepared for Governor William P. Clements, Jr., Harlingen Area Chamber of Commerce–Texas Association of Business Annual Meeting." June 7. Governor William P. Clements Jr. Records, Mexico and Latin American Relations Office [MALAR] Records, First Term, 1979–1983. Box 10. Folder 18.

———. 1981a. "Remarks Prepared for Governor William P. Clements, Jr., Fifth Annual IMAGE de Tejas Convention," May 8. Governor William P. Clements Jr. Records, Mexico and Latin American Relations Office [MALAR] Records, First Term, 1979–1983. Box 10, Folder 18.

———. 1981b. "Remarks Prepared for Governor William P. Clements Jr., Luncheon Co-Sponsored by the Mexican American Business and Professional Association of San Antonio and the Mexican Chamber of Commerce," May 5. Governor William P. Clements Jr. Records, Mexico and Latin American Relations Office [MALAR] Records, First Term, 1979–1983. Box 10, Folder 18.

———. 1982a. "Remarks Prepared for Governor William P. Clements, Jr. Harlingen Mexican-American Chamber of Commerce Annual Awards Breakfast," April 16. Governor William P. Clements Jr. Records, Mexico and Latin American Relations Office [MALAR] Records, First Term, 1979–1983. Box 10, Folder 18.

———. 1982b. "Remarks Prepared for Governor William P. Clements, Jr. Texas Association of Mexican American Chambers of Commerce," July 30. Governor William P. Clements Jr. Records, Mexico and Latin American Relations Office [MALAR] Records, First Term, 1979–1983. Box 10, Folder 18.

———. ca. 1982. "Official Memorandum by William P. Clements, Jr., Governor of Texas." Governor William P. Clements Jr. Records, Mexico and Latin American Relations Office [MALAR] Records, First Term, 1979–1983. Box 7, Folder 12.

Cogburn, Ed, and Billie Carr. 1978. Open letter (n.d.). Billie Carr Papers, 1956–2003, MS 373, Woodson Research Center, Fondren Library, Rice University. Box 12, Folder 4.

Concerned Citizens of South Texas. ca. 1976. "Wake Up, South Texas!" Undated political ad. Carlos Truan Papers, South Texas Archives and Special Collections, James C. Jernigan Library, Texas A&M University–Kingsville. Box 31.017.

Conde, Carlos. 1968. "PASO Looks at Its Future. Talks of Going Republican." *Houston Chronicle*, August 11. Texas Governor John Connally Records, LBJ Library. Box 735.

Connally, John B. ca. 1962. "John Connally's Statement to PASO," August 4. Texas Governor John Connally Records, LBJ Library. Box 1361.

———. 1963. Letter to Eligio (Kika) de la Garza, August 2. Texas Governor John Connally Records, LBJ Library. Box 1069.

———. 1964. Letter to William Bonilla, March 3. Texas Governor John Connally Records, LBJ Library. Box 1055.

———. 1966. Letter to Marvin Watson, October 7. Texas Governor John Connally Records, LBJ Library. Box 992.

Cortez, R. A. 1947. Letter to L. A. Woods, September 6. Texas Governor Price Daniel Records, Archives and Information Services Division, Texas State Library and Archives Commission, Latin-American Matters. Box 54.

Cotera, Martha. 2004. Interview with Sudha Rajan, June.

Cotrell, Charles L., and Jerry Polinard. 1986. "Effects of the Voting Rights Act in Texas: Perceptions of County Election Administrators." *Publius* 16, no. 4: 67–80.

Cottle, Michelle. 2002. "Identity Crisis." *New Republic*, February 18.

Cox, Jack. ca 1963. "Poll Tax Repeal: Democracy or Licensing Illiterate?" Unidentified newspaper clipping. Allan Shivers Papers, 1949–1984, Dolph Briscoe Center for American History, University of Texas at Austin.

Crawford, Ann Fears, and Crystal Sasse Ragsdale. 1982. *Women in Texas: Their Lives, Their Experiences, Their Accomplishments*. Burnet, Tex.: Eakin Press.

Crespo, Manuel. 1956. Letter to Ed Idar Jr., February 7. Dr. Hector P. Garcia Papers, Special Collections and Archives, Texas A&M University–Corpus Christi, Mary and Jeff Bell Library.

Crossley, Mimi. 1972. "Castillo Hits Connally, Welch." *Houston Post*, October 15. "Castillo, Leonel" Vertical File, Dolph Briscoe Center for American History, University of Texas at Austin.

Cruz, Lauro. 1998. Oral history interview by José Ángel Gutiérrez, June 20. Center for Mexican American Studies No. 67.

Cuellar, Robert A. 1969. *A Social and Political History of the Mexican American Population of Texas, 1929–1963*. San Francisco: R and E Research Associates.

Culhane, Charles. 1969. "Militant Latins Preach Hate, Say 5 Texas Congressmen." *Fort Worth Star-Telegram*, April 29. Dolph Briscoe Papers, 1932–2010, Dolph Briscoe Center for American History, University of Texas at Austin. Box 265.

Cullen, James. 1994. "Transforming the Democrats." *Texas Observer*, June 17.

Dahl, Robert. 1964. *Who Governs?: Democracy and Power in an American City*. New Haven: Yale University Press.

Daniel Campaign. ca. 1956. "Spanish 5 Minute Talk—Price Daniel—'Runoff.'" Texas Governor Price Daniel Records, Archives and Information Services Division, Texas State Library and Archives Commission, Radio—Spanish Broadcasts. Box 216.

———. 1962. Campaign Memo No. 1, April 9. Dr. Hector P. Garcia Papers, Special Collections and Archives, Texas A&M University–Corpus Christi, Mary and Jeff Bell Library.

Daniel, Carey. 1955. Letter to Price Daniel, September 22. Texas Governor Price Daniel Records, Archives and Information Services Division, Texas State Library and Archives Commission, Segregation (File 2). Box 144.

———. 1958. Letter to Price Daniel, August 8. Texas Governor Price Daniel Records, Archives and Information Services Division, Texas State Library and Archives Commission, Segregation—1958—August. Box 428.

———. n.d. "Tom Jefferson for Segregation." *Dallas News*. Texas Governor Price Daniel Records, Archives and Information Services Division, Texas State Library and Archives Commission, Segregation (File 2). Box 144.

Daniel, Price. 1947a. Letter to Gus Garcia. August 21. Texas Governor Price Daniel Records, Archives and Information Services Division, Texas State Library and Archives Commission, Latin-American Matters. Box 54.

———. 1947b. Letter to Gus C. Garcia. August 22. Texas Governor Price Daniel Records, Archives and Information Services Division, Texas State Library and Archives Commission, Latin-American Matters. Box 54.

———. 1947c. Letter to Pauline R. Kibbe. April 16. Texas Governor Price Daniel Records, Archives and Information Services Division, Texas State Library and Archives Commission, Latin-American Matters. Box 54.

———. 1948. Letter to the Board of Directors, Texas State University for Negroes, July 31. Texas Governor Price Daniel Records, Archives and Information Services Division, Texas State Library and Archives Commission, Civil Rights. Box 52.

———. ca. 1948. Press release (n.d.). Texas Governor Price Daniel Records, Archives and Information Services Division, Texas State Library and Archives Commission, Segregation. Box 57.

———. 1949. Letter to Jose Maldonado et al., July 28. Texas Governor Price Daniel Records, Archives and Information Services Division, Texas State Library and Archives Commission, Segregation. Box 57.

———. 1955. Letter to Carey Daniel, September 29. Texas Governor Price Daniel Records, Archives and Information Services Division, Texas State Library and Archives Commission, Segregation (File 2). Box 144.

———. 1957. Statement from Governor Price Daniel, May 23. Texas Governor Price Daniel Records, Archives and Information Services Division, Texas State Library and Archives Commission, Segregation. Box 369.

———. 1958a. Letter to Reverend Carey Daniel, White Citizens Council of America, August 22. Texas Governor Price Daniel Records, Archives and Information Services Division, Texas State Library and Archives Commission, Segregation—1958—August. Box 428.

———. 1958b. Letter to Carey Daniel, October 16. Texas Governor Price Daniel Records, Archives and Information Services Division, Texas State Library and Archives Commission, Segregation Information. Box 504.

———. 1958c. Letter to Joe S. Sheldon. February 24. Texas Governor Price Daniel Records, Archives and Information Services Division, Texas State Library and Archives Commission. Republican Party Box 355.

———. 1958d. "Remarks of Governor Price Daniel Little School of the 400 Dedication (LULAC)," June 23. Texas Governor Price Daniel Records, Archives and Information Services Division, Texas State Library and Archives Commission, LULAC Education. Box 354.

Daniels, John A. 1965. Letter to John Connally, February 5. Texas Governor John Connally Records, LBJ Library. Box 496.

Davidson, Chandler. 1990. *Race and Class in Texas Politics*. Princeton: Princeton University Press.

Davis, Jim. 1979. "Clements Alien Plan Unpopular." *Corpus Christi Caller-Times*, June 23. Governor William P. Clements Jr. Records, Mexico and Latin American Relations Office [MALAR] Records, First Term, 1979–1983. Box 7, Folder 6.

Davis, Sharon E., and Stacey L. Connaughton. 2005. "Audiences Implicadas e Ignoradas in the English and Spanish Language 2002 Texas Gubernatorial Debates." *Howard Journal of Communications* 16: 131–148.

Davis, Will D. 1966. Memorandum to Democratic Party leaders, October 11. Henry B. González Papers, 1946–1998, Dolph Briscoe Center for American History, University of Texas at Austin. Box 2004–127/395.

De la Garza, Eligio (Kika). 1963a. Letter to John Connally, May 29. Texas Governor John Connally Records, LBJ Library. Box 1069.

———. 1963b. Letter to John Connally, June 14. Texas Governor John Connally Records, LBJ Library. Box 1069.

De la Garza, Kika, et al. 1966. Telegram to Frank Erwin, National Democratic Chairman from Texas, September 16. Henry B. González Papers, 1946–1998,

Dolph Briscoe Center for American History, University of Texas at Austin. Box 2004–127/395.

De la Garza, Rodolfo O., and Louis DeSipio. 1993. "Save the Baby, Change the Bathwater, and Scrub the Tub: Latino Electoral Participation after Seventeen Years of Voter Rights Act Coverage." *Texas Law Review* 71, no. 7: 1479–1539.

Democratic Coalition. 1963. *A Democratic Newsletter*, 1, no. 9, August 13. Frankie Carter Randolph Papers, 1858–1983, MS 372, Woodson Research Center, Fondren Library, Rice University. Box 2, Folder 10.

Democratic Committee for Responsible Government. 1974. Bulletin #3, April 17. Texas Democratic Party Papers, Archives and Information Services Division, Texas State Library and Archives Commission. Box 1979/49-123.

Democratic Committee on Platform and Resolutions. 1966. Minutes of the Committee on Platform and Resolutions, September 20. Texas Democratic Party Papers, Archives and Information Services Division, Texas State Library and Archives Commission. Box 1979/49.

Democratic National Committee. 1973. Final Report of the Drafting Committee to the Commission on Delegate Selection and Party Structure, October 7. Texas Democratic Party Papers, Archives and Information Services Division, Texas State Library and Archives Commission. Box 1979/49-123.

Democratic Party of Bexar County. 1958. Delegate list and list of resolutions passed by the Bexar County Democratic Convention, August 2. Texas Democratic Party Papers, Archives and Information Services Division, Texas State Library and Archives Commission. Box 1997/96-10.

Democratic Rebuilding Committee. 1970a. Press release, September 16. Albert A. Peña Jr. Papers, 1952–1977 (bulk 1956–1972), MS 37, UTSA Archives and Special Collections, Library, University of Texas at San Antonio. Box 8:18.

———. 1970b. Press release, September 29. Albert A. Peña Jr. Papers, 1952–1977 (bulk 1956–1972), MS 37, UTSA Archives and Special Collections, Library, University of Texas at San Antonio. Box 8:18.

Democrats of Texas. 1957a. "Background—Up to Now." *Democratic Reporter*, 1, no. 1, September 9. Texas Governor Price Daniel Records, Archives and Information Services Division, Texas State Library and Archives Commission, Democrats of Texas. Box 295.

———. 1957b. A Code of Ethics for Democratic Party Procedures, November 23. Creekmore Fath Papers, 1938–1992 and undated, Southwest Collection/Special Collections Library, Texas Tech University, Lubbock. Box 2, Folder 3.

———. 1957c. *Statewide Meeting: The Story of the Democrats of Texas*. Lubbock: Chaparral Press.

———. 1958. Minutes, Executive Board Meeting, January 31. Creekmore Fath Papers, 1938–1992 and undated, Southwest Collection/Special Collections Library, Texas Tech University, Lubbock. Box 2, Folder 3.

———. ca. 1958. *Research Bulletin* No. 1. Creekmore Fath Papers, 1938–1992 and undated, Southwest Collection/Special Collections Library, Texas Tech University, Lubbock. Box 2, Folder 3.

———. 1959. "Democrats of Texas" Executive board and steering committee member roster. Frankie Carter Randolph Papers, 1858–1983, MS 372, Woodson Research Center, Fondren Library, Rice University. Box 3, Folder 3.

————. n.d. "Recommendations of the Issues Committee Endorsed by the Steering Committee." Creekmore Fath Papers, 1938–1992 and undated, Southwest Collection/Special Collections Library, Texas Tech University, Lubbock. Box 2, Folder 16.

Dickens, Edwin Larry. 1969. "The Political Role of Mexican Americans in San Antonio Texas." Ph.D. dissertation, Texas Tech University, 1969.

Dickson, Fagan. 1952. "Report by Fagan Dickson on New Braunfels Meeting of State Executive Committee before a Democratic Meeting in Dallas on April 21, 1952 [*sic*]." Walter Gardner Hall—Papers, 1923–1990, MS 280, Woodson Research Center, Fondren Library, Rice University. Box 4, Folder 80.

Diehl, Kemper. 1982a. "Hispanics Are No Longer Society's 'Sleeping Giant.'" *San Antonio Express*, May 16. Moya (Richard) Papers (1969–1986), Austin History Center, AR.2002.024.

————. 1982b. "When the Chips Are Down, Democrats Stick Together." *San Antonio Express*, June 27. Governor William P. Clements Jr. Records, Mexico and Latin American Relations Office [MALAR] Records, First Term, 1979–1983. Box 6, Folder 4.

Dixie, Chris. ca. 1977. "A Message from the Chairman of HCD." Harris County Democrats newsletter. Billie Carr Papers, 1956–2003, MS 373, Woodson Research Center, Fondren Library, Rice University. Box 4, Folder 15.

Don Politico. 1968. "1968 May Be 'Year of Latino.'" *San Antonio Light*, July 28. E. Preston Smith Papers, 1930–1975 and undated, Southwest Collection/Special Collections Library, Texas Tech University, Lubbock.

————. 1969. "Who's Running the Good Race?" *San Antonio Light*, April 6. "González, H. B." Vertical File, Dolph Briscoe Center for American History, University of Texas at Austin.

Dorsey, Margaret E. 2006. *Pachangas: Borderlands Music, U.S. Politics and Transnational Marketing*. Austin: University of Texas Press.

Drake, Jack H. 1966a. Letter to Terrell Blodgett, June 3. Texas Governor John Connally Records, LBJ Library. Box 992.

————. 1966b. Letter to Terrell Blodgett, June 6. Texas Governor John Connally Records, LBJ Library. Box 992.

Draper, Alan. 1994. *Conflict of Interests: Organized Labor and the Civil Rights Movement in the South, 1954–1968*. Ithaca: Industrial Labor Relations Press.

Draper, Robert. 1996. "Dan Morales: Taking On the Tobacco Industry and Other Foes, Texas' Attorney General Is Smokin'—At Last." *Texas Monthly*, September.

Dribben, Melissa. 1982. "Clements Backs COPS' Proposals." *Houston Post*, June 19. Governor William P. Clements Jr. Records, Mexico and Latin American Relations Office [MALAR] Records, First Term, 1979–1983. Box 3, Folder 1.

Duarte, E. B. 1957. Letter to Creekmore Fath, November 29. Creekmore Fath Papers, 1938–1992 and undated, Southwest Collection/Special Collections Library, Texas Tech University, Lubbock. Box 1, Folder 5.

Dubose, Louis. 1994. "High Court Endorsements." *Texas Observer*, February 11.

Duckworth, Allen. 1957. "Bill Would Require Party Registration." *Dallas News*, January 25. "Austin, Texas—Henry B. González" Vertical File, Dolph Briscoe Center for American History, University of Texas at Austin.

———. 1958. "González Poses Threat to Daniel." *Dallas News*, May 6. "Austin, Texas—Henry B. González" Vertical File, Dolph Briscoe Center for American History, University of Texas at Austin.

———. ca. 1961. "González Wins House Seat in Election at San Antonio." *Dallas News* n.d. "Austin, Texas—Henry B. González" Vertical File, Dolph Briscoe Center for American History, University of Texas at Austin.

Dugger, Ronnie. 1956. "NAACP Is Closed Down in Texas: The Judge and John Ben Were Friends in Boyhood." *Texas Observer*, October 31.

———. 1957. "The Segregation Filibuster of 1957." *Texas Observer*, May 7.

———. 1958. "González on Road, Rough, Tireless." *Texas Observer*, July 18.

———. 1962. "The Imminent Threat to Texas Liberalism." *Texas Observer*, January 19.

———. 1963. "Texas: Two-Fisted, Three Party State." *New York Times Magazine*, November 3. Texas Governor John Connally Records, LBJ Library. Box 56.

———. 1979. Letter to Billie Carr, May 5. Billie Carr Papers, 1956–2003, MS 373, Woodson Research Center, Fondren Library, Rice University. Box 12, Folder 5.

———. 1980a. "González of San Antonio. Part III: The South Texas Cauldron Guns, Disease, Politics, Victory." *Texas Observer*, May 9. "González, Henry B." Vertical File, Dolph Briscoe Center for American History, University of Texas at Austin.

———. 1980b. "González of San Antonio. Part V: The Politics of Fratricide." *Texas Observer*, December 12. "González, Henry B." Vertical File, Dolph Briscoe Center for American History, University of Texas at Austin.

———. 1982. "And Now the Democrats." *Texas Observer*, November 26.

Dugger, Ronnie, and Tom Philpot. 1974. *Daily Texan*, November 1. "Barrientos, Gonzalo" Vertical File, Dolph Briscoe Center for American History, University of Texas at Austin.

Duncan, Bill. 1966. "Legislative Runoff Race Splits Latin Community." *Corpus Christi Caller*, June 3. Dr. Hector P. Garcia Papers, Special Collections and Archives, Texas A&M University-Corpus Christi, Mary and Jeff Bell Library.

Duncan, Dawson. 1957a. "Senator González' Filibuster Blocks Action on Troop Bill." *Dallas News*, November 22. "Austin, Texas—Henry B. González" Vertical File, Dolph Briscoe Center for American History, University of Texas at Austin.

———. 1957b. "Senator González' Filibuster Blocks Action on Troop Bill." *Texas Observer*, November 22. "Austin, Texas—Henry B. González" Vertical File, Dolph Briscoe Center for American History, University of Texas at Austin.

———. 1958. "Racial Integration Appears as Issue." *Dallas News*, May 6. "Austin, Texas—Henry B. González" Vertical File, Dolph Briscoe Center for American History, University of Texas at Austin.

Dusek, Ron. 1982. "Platform Bypasses Hispanic Group." *El Paso Times*, July 9. Governor William P. Clements Jr. Records, Mexico and Latin American Relations Office [MALAR] Records, First Term, 1979–1983. Box 6, Folder 4.

Dyer, James A., et al. 1988. "New Voters, Switchers, and Political Realignment in Texas." *Western Political Quarterly* 41, no. 1 (March): 155–167.

———. 1998. "Party Identification and Public Opinion in Texas, 1984–1994." In

Anthony Champagne and Edward J. Harpham, eds., *Texas Politics: A Reader*, Second Edition, 107–122. New York: W. W. Norton, 1998.

Ed Yardang and Associates. 1978. Radio Ad #6-146-78-B, September 5. Governor William P. Clements Jr. Records, Mexico and Latin American Relations Office [MALAR] Records, First Term, 1979–1983. Box 14, Folder 31.

———. ca. 1978. "Our Children" and "New Movement" (undated television ad transcripts and illustrations). Governor William P. Clements Jr. Records, Mexico and Latin American Relations Office [MALAR] Records, First Term, 1979–1983. Box 14, Folder 31.

Elect Preston Smith Governor of Texas Campaign. 1968. Press release, October 10. Texas Observer Records, 1952–1990, Dolph Briscoe Center for American History, University of Texas at Austin.

Elizondo, Juan B. 1997. "A Senator's Niche." *Austin American-Statesman*, June 20. "Barrientos, Gonzalo" Vertical File, Dolph Briscoe Center for American History, University of Texas at Austin.

Falkenberg, Lisa. 2002. "Race, Ethnicity Prominent Factors This Election Season." Associated Press State and Local Wire, March 4. Retrieved from http://www.lexisnexis.com.

Fath, Creekmore. 1957. Letter to R. P. Sánchez, October 2. Creekmore Fath Papers, 1938–1992 and undated, Southwest Collection/Special Collections Library, Texas Tech University, Lubbock. Box 1, Folder 4.

Fikac, Peggy. 1993. "Caucus Angry over Opposition to Cavazos." *Valley Morning Star*, February 18. Irma Rangel Collection (A2003-042), South Texas Archives and Special Collections, James C. Jernigan Library, Texas A&M University–Kingsville. Box 4.018.

Fish, Rick. 1973. "Senator Sees Himself as Example for Young." *Austin American-Statesman*, May 13. Dolph Briscoe Papers, 1932–2010, Dolph Briscoe Center for American History, University of Texas at Austin. Box 265.

———. 1974. "Barrientos: From Cotton Picker to Texas Legislator." *Austin American-Statesman*, November 24. "Barrientos, Gonzalo" Vertical File, Dolph Briscoe Center for American History, University of Texas at Austin.

Fitzgerald, Kathleen. 1986. "Bidding for Influence." *Texas Observer*, October 24.

Flynn, Ken. 1979. "Border Problems Discussion with Clements Is Planned." *El Paso Herald Post*, September 25. Governor William P. Clements Jr. Records, Mexico and Latin American Relations Office [MALAR] Records, First Term, 1979–1983. Box 5, Folder 18.

Foley, Eugene P. 1966. Memo to Joseph A. Califano Jr., September 6. LBJ Library, "LBJ Human Rights" HU2/MC 6/7/66–10/12/66. Box 23.

Foley, Neil. 1997. *The White Scourge: Mexicans, Blacks, and Poor Whites in Texas Cotton Culture*. Berkeley: University of California Press.

Ford, Jon. 1967. "Carr Slaps Criticism." *San Antonio Express*, August 15. Texas Governor John Connally Records, LBJ Library. Box 735.

———. 1968. "Unit Rule Use by Demos Defended by Will Davis." *San Antonio Express*, August 13. Albert A. Peña Jr. Papers, 1952–1977 (bulk 1956–1972), MS 37, UTSA Archives and Special Collections, Library, University of Texas at San Antonio. Box 4:30.

———. 1969. "Floyd Blasts Bernal for Del Rio Protest." *San Antonio Express*,

April 1. Dolph Briscoe Papers, 1932–2010, Dolph Briscoe Center for American History, University of Texas at Austin. Box 265.

———. 1970a. "Aguirre: He Worked Too Hard." *San Antonio Express*, August 8. Henry B. González Papers, 1946–1998, Dolph Briscoe Center for American History, University of Texas at Austin. Box 2004–127/395.

———. 1970b. "Revising Words Simple—Problem Still There." *Corpus Christi Caller-Times*, August 30. Dolph Briscoe Papers, 1932–2010, Dolph Briscoe Center for American History, University of Texas at Austin. Box 265.

———. 1972a. "Briscoe's Inept Moves May Prove Costly." *Dallas Morning News*, July 16. Dolph Briscoe Papers, 1932–2010, Dolph Briscoe Center for American History, University of Texas at Austin. Box 294.

———. 1972b. "Briscoe Switches His Vote. Backs Wallace, Then McGovern." *San Antonio Express*, July 13. Dolph Briscoe Papers, 1932–2010, Dolph Briscoe Center for American History, University of Texas at Austin. Box 294.

———. 1974. "Minorities Employment Plan Gets Approval of Governor." *Austin American-Statesman*, February 13. Texas Observer Records, 1952–1990, Dolph Briscoe Center for American History, University of Texas at Austin.

Fox-Piven, Frances, and Richard Cloward. 1979. *Poor People's Movements: Why They Succeed, How They Fail*. New York: Vintage.

Fraga, Luis R., et al. 2010. *Latino Lives in America: Making It Home*. Philadelphia: Temple University Press.

Freeman, Don. 1958. "Gonzalez Reports Gifts Turned Down." *Dallas News*, June 25. "Austin, Texas—Henry B. González" Vertical File, Dolph Briscoe Center for American History, University of Texas at Austin.

Fuchs, Lawrence H. 1990. *The American Kaleidoscope: Race, Ethnicity, and the Civic Culture*. Middletown: Wesleyan University Press.

Fuentes, Albert, Jr. ca. 1963. "Statement by Albert Fuentes Jr., State Executive Secretary, PASO of Texas." Texas Observer Records, 1952–1990, Dolph Briscoe Center for American History, University of Texas at Austin.

Galvan, Cynthia Wise. 1994. Memorandum to Senate Hispanic Caucus Members, June 27. Carlos Truan Collection, South Texas Archives and Special Collections, James C. Jernigan Library, Texas A&M University–Kingsville. Box 537.016.

Garces, Ramon. 1956. "Laredo's Mayor Defends System." *Texas Observer*, April 11.

———. 1957. "Latin Vote Grows." *Texas Observer*, April 2.

———. 1967. "LULACS Protest Picketing." *Laredo Times*, May 31. Texas Governor John Connally Records, LBJ Library. Box 1055.

———. ca. 1967. "Connally Cites Latins' Progress: Governor Cheered at LULAC Banquet." Undated newspaper clipping, *Laredo Times*. Texas Governor John Connally Records, LBJ Library. Box 1055.

García, Arcenio. 2003. Interview by Sudha Rajan, October 29.

Garcia, Arnold. 2000. "Sánchez Would Put a New Face on 2002." Cox News Service, July 26. Retrieved from http://www.lexisnexis.com.

Garcia, G. G. ca. 1978. Memorandum to Luis Vera Jr. (undated). Governor William P. Clements Jr. Records, Mexico and Latin American Relations Office [MALAR] Records, First Term, 1979–1983. Box 14, Folder 33.

———. 1979a. Letter to Governor Clements, October 1. Governor William P.

Clements Jr. Records, Mexico and Latin American Relations Office [MALAR] Records, First Term, 1979–1983. Box 5, Folder 14.

———. 1979b. Memorandum to Jim Adams through Doug Brown, December 18. Governor William P. Clements Jr. Records, Mexico and Latin American Relations Office [MALAR] Records, First Term, 1979–1983. Box 4, Folder 14.

———. 1979c. Memorandum to the Governor through Allen B. Clark, February 15. Governor William P. Clements Jr. Records, Mexico and Latin American Relations Office [MALAR] Records, First Term, 1979–1983. Box 4, Folder 14.

———. 1979d. Memorandum to the Governor through Allen B. Clark, March 13. Governor William P. Clements Jr. Records, Mexico and Latin American Relations Office [MALAR] Records, First Term, 1979–1983. Box 4, Folder 14.

———. 1979e. Memorandum to the Governor through Allen B. Clark, April 24. Governor William P. Clements Jr. Records, Mexico and Latin American Relations Office [MALAR] Records, First Term, 1979–1983. Box 4, Folder 14.

———. 1979f. Memorandum to the Governor through Allen B. Clark, June 12. Governor William P. Clements Jr. Records, Mexico and Latin American Relations Office [MALAR] Records, First Term, 1979–1983. Box 4, Folder 14.

———. 1979g. Memo to Governor Clements, December 21. Governor William P. Clements Jr. Records, Mexico and Latin American Relations Office [MALAR] Records, First Term, 1979–1983. Box 1, Folder 19.

———. 1979h. Memo to Tobin Armstrong, September 20. Governor William P. Clements Jr. Records, Mexico and Latin American Relations Office [MALAR] Records, First Term, 1979–1983. Box 1, Folder 19.

———. 1980a. Memo to Susan Heckman, April 8. Governor William P. Clements Jr. Records, Mexico and Latin American Relations Office [MALAR] Records, First Term, 1979–1983. Box 5, Folder 19.

———. 1980b. Memo to Tobin Armstrong, July 7. Governor William P. Clements Jr. Records, Mexico and Latin American Relations Office [MALAR] Records, First Term, 1979–1983. Box 1, Folder 19.

Garcia, Gilbert C. 1969. Interviewed by Robert Cuellar, March 3. Oral History Program, University of North Texas, Denton.

Garcia, Gus. 1947a. Letter to Price Daniel, August 13. Texas Governor Price Daniel Records, Archives and Information Services Division, Texas State Library and Archives Commission, Latin-American Matters. Box 54.

———. 1947b. Letter to Price Daniel, August 15. Texas Governor Price Daniel Records, Archives and Information Services Division, Texas State Library and Archives Commission, Latin-American Matters. Box 54.

———. 1963. Letter to Ralph Yarborough. January 29. Dr. Hector P. Garcia Papers, Special Collections and Archives, Texas A&M University–Corpus Christi, Mary and Jeff Bell Library.

Garcia, Hector P. 1950. Letter to American GI Forum members, January 12. Dr. Hector P. Garcia Papers, Special Collections and Archives, Texas A&M University–Corpus Christi, Mary and Jeff Bell Library. Unprocessed files.

———. 1951. "¡Una suplica a nuestra gente en un punto de honor!" Open letter to American GI Forum members (n.p., n.d.). My translation. Dr. Hector P. Garcia Papers, Special Collections and Archives, Texas A&M University–Corpus Christi, Mary and Jeff Bell Library.

———. ca. 1952a. Text of speech, first talk (n.p., n.d.). My translation. Dr. Hector P. Garcia Papers, Special Collections and Archives, Texas A&M University–Corpus Christi, Mary and Jeff Bell Library. Unprocessed files.

———. ca. 1952b. Text of speech, third talk (n.p., n.d.). My translation. Dr. Hector P. Garcia Papers, Special Collections and Archives, Texas A&M University–Corpus Christi, Mary and Jeff Bell Library. Unprocessed files.

———. 1953a. Letter to Byron Skelton. June 23. Dr. Hector P. Garcia Papers, Special Collections and Archives, Texas A&M University–Corpus Christi, Mary and Jeff Bell Library.

———. 1953b. Letter to Ed Idar, June 29. Dr. Hector P. Garcia Papers, Special Collections and Archives, Texas A&M University–Corpus Christi, Mary and Jeff Bell Library.

———. 1953c. Letter to Homer Garza, July 30. Dr. Hector P. Garcia Papers, Special Collections and Archives, Texas A&M University–Corpus Christi, Mary and Jeff Bell Library.

———. 1954. Letter to Gerald Saldana, March 13. Dr. Hector P. Garcia Papers, Special Collections and Archives, Texas A&M University–Corpus Christi, Mary and Jeff Bell Library. Unprocessed files.

———. 1956. Letter to the editor, *Lubbock Morning Avalanche*, July 18. Dr. Hector P. Garcia Papers, Special Collections and Archives, Texas A&M University–Corpus Christi, Mary and Jeff Bell Library.

———. 1957a. Campaign letter, April 2. Dr. Hector P. Garcia Papers, Special Collections and Archives, Texas A&M University–Corpus Christi, Mary and Jeff Bell Library.

———. 1957b. "El Doctor Hector Garcia hablando por la candidatura de Ralph Yarborough para gobernador," July 27. Dr. Hector P. Garcia Papers, Special Collections and Archives, Texas A&M University–Corpus Christi, Mary and Jeff Bell Library.

———. 1961. "Atención todos mis amigos y votantes de el estado de Texas y amigos nuestros de todos los Estados Unidos." Dr. Hector P. Garcia Papers, Special Collections and Archives, Texas A&M University–Corpus Christi, Mary and Jeff Bell Library.

———. 1967. Letter to Henry B. González, July 21. Henry B. González Papers, 1946–1998, Dolph Briscoe Center for American History, University of Texas at Austin. Box 2004/127-88.

———. 1972a. "Atención todos los votantes de el estado de Texas," May 25. Dr. Hector P. Garcia Papers, Special Collections and Archives, Texas A&M University–Corpus Christi, Mary and Jeff Bell Library.

———. 1972b. "Atención votantes de el condado de Nueces," May 26. Dr. Hector P. Garcia Papers, Special Collections and Archives, Texas A&M University–Corpus Christi, Mary and Jeff Bell Library.

———. 1972c. Open letter to Mexican American voters, May 20. Dr. Hector P. Garcia Papers, Special Collections and Archives, Texas A&M University–Corpus Christi, Mary and Jeff Bell Library.

———. 1974. "Letter from Our Readers," November 3. Dr. Hector P. Garcia

Papers, Special Collections and Archives, Texas A&M University–Corpus Christi, Mary and Jeff Bell Library.

Garcia, Hector, et al. 1966. Form letter in support of Al González, February 28. LBJ Library, "LBJ Human Rights" HU2/MC 6/7/66–10/12/66. Box 22.

García, Ignacio M. 1989. *United We Win*. Albuquerque: University of New Mexico Press.

———. 2000. *¡Viva Kennedy! Mexican Americans in Search of Camelot*. College Station: Texas A&M University Press.

———. 2002. *Hector P. Garcia: In Relentless Pursuit of Justice*. Houston: Arte Público Press.

Garcia, John. 1986. "The Voting Rights Act and Hispanic Political Representation in the Southwest." *Publius* 16, no. 4: 49–66.

García, Mario T. 1982. Interview with Lucy Acosta. "Interview no. 653." Institute of Oral History, University of Texas at El Paso.

———. 1989. *Mexican Americans: Leadership, Ideology, and Identity, 1930–1960*. New Haven: Yale University Press.

———. 1994. *Memories of Chicano History: The Life and Narrative of Bert Corona*. Berkeley: University of California Press.

———. 1998. *The Making of a Mexican American Mayor: Raymond Telles of El Paso*. El Paso: Texas Western Press.

Garcia, Michelle. 1999. "My Talk with Henry B." 1999. *Austin American-Statesman*, January 3.

Garcia, Ruben R. 1979. Memorandum to Omar Harvey, April 24. Governor William P. Clements Jr. Records, Mexico and Latin American Relations Office [MALAR] Records, First Term, 1979–1983. Box 4, Folder 14.

Garcia, Ruperto. 1981. "Bonillas Awaken LULAC." *Texas Observer*, September 11.

Garcia, Sylvia. ca. 1982. Letter to Eddie Aurispa, February 23. Governor William P. Clements Jr. Records, Mexico and Latin American Relations Office [MALAR] Records, First Term, 1979–1983. Box 1, Folder 20.

Garrett, Glenn E. 1966. Letter to Terrell Blodgett, June 6. Texas Governor John Connally Records, LBJ Library. Box 992.

Garrett, Robert T. 1978. "GOP Candidates Trying to Win the Minority Vote." *Dallas Times Herald*, October 16. Texas Observer Records, 1952–1990, Dolph Briscoe Center for American History, University of Texas at Austin.

Garza, Pedro Ruiz. 1986. "Bonilla and Hernandez: A Study in Contrasts." In *Mexican American Democrat: Official Publication of the Mexican American Democrats of Texas* (convention issue: February).

Giovanola, Anouck. 2005. "Irma Rangel." Women's Legal History Project, Stanford University. Online (accessed July 26, 2007): http://womenslegalhistory.stanford.edu/papers05/RangelI-Giovanola05.pdf.

Glazer, Sarah Jane. 1972a. *John Young: Democratic Representative From Texas*. New York: Grossman Publishers.

———. 1972b. *Olin E. Teague: Democratic Representative from Texas*. New York: Grossman Publishers.

Goldberg, Robert A. 1983. "Racial Change on the Southern Periphery: The Case of San Antonio, Texas, 1960–1965." *Journal of Southern History* 49, no. 3: 349–374.

Gomes, Lydia. 1972. *Eligio de la Garza: Democratic Representative from Texas.* New York: Grossman Publishers.

González, Arnold. ca. 1982. "Remarks by Rep. Arnold González Introducing Mark White" (n.d.). Records, Texas Governor Mark White, Archives and Information Services Division, Texas State Library and Archives Commission, "General–Blacks." Box 1991/141–94.

González, Guile. 1972. "Muñiz, La Raza Slate Endorsed by Bonilla," July 14. Dr. Hector P. Garcia Papers, Special Collections and Archives, Texas A&M University–Corpus Christi, Mary and Jeff Bell Library.

González, Henry B. 1956. Letter to Price Daniel. September 3. Texas Governor Price Daniel Records, Archives and Information Services Division, Texas State Library and Archives Commission, González, Henry B. Box 350.

———. ca. 1958. Text of untitled, undated speech. Henry B. González Papers, 1946–1998, Dolph Briscoe Center for American History, University of Texas at Austin. Box 2004–127/50.

———. 1960. Letter to Maury Maverick Jr., November 26. Henry B. González Papers, 1946–1998, Dolph Briscoe Center for American History, University of Texas at Austin. Box 2004–127/88.

———. 1964. Letter to John Connally, December 3. Texas Governor John Connally Records, LBJ Library. Box 496.

———. 1966a. "González Upholds Demo Record." *Texas Observer*, August 5.

———. 1966b. Letter to Hector P. Garcia, December 5. Dr. Hector P. Garcia Papers, Special Collections and Archives, Texas A&M University–Corpus Christi, Mary and Jeff Bell Library.

———. 1966c. Letter to Waggoner Carr, September 6. Henry B. González Papers, 1946–1998, Dolph Briscoe Center for American History, University of Texas at Austin. Box 2004–127/395.

———. 1967a. "Hope and Promise: Americans of Spanish Surname." Dr. Hector P. Garcia Papers, Special Collections and Archives, Texas A&M University–Corpus Christi, Mary and Jeff Bell Library.

———. 1967b. Letter to George I. Sánchez, February 8. Henry B. González Papers, 1946–1998, Dolph Briscoe Center for American History, University of Texas at Austin. Box 2004–127/91.

———. 1967c. Letter to Hector P. Garcia, February 1. Dr. Hector P. Garcia Papers, Special Collections and Archives, Texas A&M University–Corpus Christi, Mary and Jeff Bell Library.

———. 1967d. Letter to Mario Compean, December 7. Henry B. González Papers, 1946–1998, Dolph Briscoe Center for American History, University of Texas at Austin. Box 2004–127/395.

———. 1967e. Letter to O. J. Valdez, May 8. Henry B. González Papers, 1946–1998, Dolph Briscoe Center for American History, University of Texas at Austin. Box 2004–127/395.

———. 1968. Statement of Congressman Henry B. González, Press Conference, April 28. Henry B. González Papers (unprocessed), Dolph Briscoe Center for American History, University of Texas at Austin.

———. 1969a. Letter to George R. Rivas, September 8. Dr. Hector P. Garcia

Papers, Special Collections and Archives, Texas A&M University–Corpus Christi, Mary and Jeff Bell Library.

———. 1969b. Letter to Herman Gallegos, September 10. Henry B. González Papers (unprocessed), Dolph Briscoe Center for American History, University of Texas at Austin.

———. 1969c. Letter to Mitchell Sviridoff, May 26. Henry B. González Papers (unprocessed), Dolph Briscoe Center for American History, University of Texas at Austin.

———. 1981. Letter to Henry Cisneros, April 6. Texas Observer Records, 1952–1990, Dolph Briscoe Center for American History, University of Texas at Austin.

Goodwyn, Larry. 1963a. Letter to Justine O'Donnell, July 30. Walter Gardner Hall—Papers, 1923–1990, MS 280, Woodson Research Center, Fondren Library, Rice University. Box 6, Folder 106.

———. 1963b. Letter to state Democratic leaders, December 18. Frankie Carter Randolph Papers, 1858–1983, MS 372, Woodson Research Center, Fondren Library, Rice University. Box 2, Folder 10.

———. 1963c. Letter to Walter Hall, February 21. Frankie Carter Randolph Papers, 1858–1983, MS 372, Woodson Research Center, Fondren Library, Rice University. Box 6, Folder 99.

———. 1963d. Letter to Walter Hall, March 26. Frankie Carter Randolph Papers, 1858–1983, MS 372, Woodson Research Center, Fondren Library, Rice University. Box 6, Folder 99.

———. 1963e. Letter to Walter Hall, September 11. Walter Gardner Hall—Papers, 1923–1990, MS 280, Woodson Research Center, Fondren Library, Rice University. Box 6, Folder 106.

———. ca. 1963. "New Shapes in Texas Politics" (report for the Democratic Coalition). Frankie Carter Randolph Papers, 1858–1983, MS 372, Woodson Research Center, Fondren Library, Rice University. Box 6, Folder 99.

Gordon, Milton. 1964. *Assimilation in American Life*. New York: Oxford University Press.

Governor Bill Clements Campaign. 1983. "Governor Clements Actions on Issues Affecting the Hispanic Community." Records, Texas Governor Mark White, Archives and Information Services Division, Texas State Library and Archives Commission. Box 1991/141–94.

———. ca. 1983. "Hispanic Judicial Appointments." Governor William P. Clements Jr. Records, Mexico and Latin American Relations Office [MALAR] Records, First Term, 1979–1983. Box 1, Folder 13.

Graves, Debbie. 1982. "53% More Aid Asked for Poor School Districts." *Austin American-Statesman*, December 22. Governor William P. Clements Jr. Records, Mexico and Latin American Relations Office [MALAR] Records, First Term, 1979–1983. Box 3, Folder 1.

Gray, Walter. ca. 1967. "About 200 Picket as Gov. Connally Arrives." Undated newspaper clipping from *Laredo Times*. Texas Governor John Connally Records, LBJ Library. Box 1055.

Grebler, Leo, et al. 1970. *The Mexican American People: The Nation's Second Largest Minority*. New York: Free Press.

Green, George N. 1979. *The Establishment in Texas Politics: The Primitive Years, 1938–1957*. Westport: Greenwood Press.

Guarino, David. 1978. "SDEC's San Antonio Session." *Texas Observer*, February 17.

Guerra, Fidencio M. 1956. Letter to J. J. Pickle, June 2. Texas Governor Price Daniel Records, Archives and Information Services Division, Texas State Library and Archives Commission, Spanish Brochures. Box 355.

Guest, Calvin. ca. 1974. Memorandum (undated). Texas Democratic Party Papers, Archives and Information Services Division, Texas State Library and Archives Commission. Box 1979/49-123.

———. 1978. Letter to Karl Sandstrom, February 5, 1978. Billie Carr Papers, 1956–2003, MS 373, Woodson Research Center, Fondren Library, Rice University. Box 5, Folder 3.

Guglielmo, Thomas A. 2006. "Fighting for Caucasian Rights: Mexicans, Mexican Americans, and the Transnational Struggle for Civil Rights in World War II Texas." *Journal of American History* 92, no. 4: 1212–1237.

Gutierrez, Hector, Jr. 1982a. Letter to Eddie Aurispe [*sic*], February 12. Governor William P. Clements Jr. Records, Mexico and Latin American Relations Office [MALAR] Records, First Term, 1979–1983. Box 10, Folder 18.

———. 1982b. Letter to William P. Clements, February 12, 1982. Governor William P. Clements Jr. Records, Mexico and Latin American Relations Office [MALAR] Records, First Term, 1979–1983. Box 10, Folder 18.

Gutiérrez, José Ángel. 1999. *The Making of a Chicano Militant: Lessons from Cristal*. Madison: University of Wisconsin Press.

Gwynne, S. C. 2002. "Grand Illusion; Rich, Moderate, and Hispanic: For a While, Tony Sánchez Seemed Like a Competitive Candidate for Governor. Then the Smoke Cleared." *Texas Monthly*, December.

Hager, Hoyt. 1955. "Kelley Skirts Debate on Poll-Tax Campaign." *Corpus Christi Caller*, December 22. Dr. Hector P. Garcia Papers, Special Collections and Archives, Texas A&M University–Corpus Christi, Mary and Jeff Bell Library.

Hall, Walter G. 1958. "Keynote Address before [the] Convention of the Democrats of Texas." Austin, May 31. Texas Democratic Party Papers, Archives and Information Services Division, Texas State Library and Archives Commission. Box 1979/49-135.

Halter, Gary M. 2006. *Government and Politics of Texas: A Comparative View*. Boston: McGraw-Hill.

Haney-López, Ian. 2003. *Racism on Trial: The Chicano Fight for Justice*. Cambridge, Mass.: Belknap Press of Harvard University Press.

Hannan, Bob. 1976. "Zavala Grant Fails to Get Support." *San Angelo Standard*, November 18. Dolph Briscoe Papers, 1932–2010, Dolph Briscoe Center for American History, University of Texas at Austin. Box 293.

Harris County Democrats. 1973. Newsletter (July). Billie Carr Papers, 1956–2003, MS 373, Woodson Research Center, Fondren Library, Rice University. Box 4, Folder 11.

Hatefield, Tom, and Carol Hatefield. 1960. "An Offensive Campaign." *Texas Observer*, June 10.

Hawthorne, Miles. 1972. *Ray Roberts: Democratic Representative from Texas*. New York: Grossman Publishers.

Heard, Robert. 1981. *The Miracle of the Killer Bees: 12 Senators Who Changed Texas Politics*. Austin: Honey Hill Pub. Co.

———. 1982. "COPS Issues Ultimatum to Texas's Top 3 Leaders." *San Antonio Express*, December 22. Governor William P. Clements Jr. Records, Mexico and Latin American Relations Office [MALAR] Records, First Term, 1979–1983. Box 3, Folder 1.

Henderson, Lana. 1974. "Senator Asks Mexican Americans to Face Reality." *Dallas Times Herald*, September 29. "Santiesteban, Tati" Vertical File, Dolph Briscoe Center for American History, University of Texas at Austin.

Hendricks, David. 1974. "Barrientos: An Advocate for People." *Daily Texan*, December 5. "Barrientos, Gonzalo" Vertical File, Dolph Briscoe Center for American History, University of Texas at Austin.

Henry, John C. 1982. "Bonilla Brothers Support White Despite Rifts on Hispanic Issues." *Austin American-Statesman*, October 2. Governor William P. Clements Jr. Records, Mexico and Latin American Relations Office [MALAR] Records, First Term, 1979–1983. Box 7, Folder 8.

———. 1983. "Ex-Legislator Powers to Be White's Top Assistant." *Austin American-Statesman*, January 5. Moya (Richard) Papers (1969–1986), Austin History Center, AR.2002.024.

Herman, Ken. 2002a. "Democrats Face Off in Texas." Cox News Service, January 14. Retrieved from http://www.lexisnexis.com.

———. 2002b. "Divisive Primary Campaign in Store for Texas Democrats." Cox News Service, January 12. Retrieved from http://www.lexisnexis.com.

Hernández, Andrew. 1978. *Mexican American Voting in the 1978 Texas Democratic Primary*. San Antonio, Texas: Southwest Voter Registration Education Project.

———. 1982. *Mexican American Voting in the 1982 Democratic Primary: A Southwest Voter Registration Education Project Research Report*. San Antonio: Southwest Voter Registration Education Project.

Herrera, John J. 1966. Resume of John J. Herrera, June. EEOC, FG 655, White House Central Files, LBJ Library.

Hickie, Jane. 1974. Letter to John C. White, June 10. Texas Democratic Party Papers, Archives and Information Services Division, Texas State Library and Archives Commission. Box 1979/49-123.

Hight, Bruce. 1991. "After Years of Climbing, Barrientos Reaches State Senate's Upper Echelon." *Austin American-Statesman*, January 27. "Barrientos, Gonzalo" Vertical File, Dolph Briscoe Center for American History, University of Texas at Austin.

House Committee on the Judiciary. March 24, 1975. Mexican American Democrats of Texas Records, 1962–1987, MS 29, UTSA Archives, Library, University of Texas at San Antonio. Box 10:4.

Howell, Joy. 1975. "Controller, Students Debate Party Politics." *Daily Texan*, November 21. "Castillo, Leonel" Vertical File, Dolph Briscoe Center for American History, University of Texas at Austin.

Hubbard, Harry. 1974. Letter to Leonel J. Castillo, October 1. Mexican American

Democrats of Texas Records, 1962–1987, MS 29, UTSA Archives, Library, University of Texas at San Antonio. Box 11:14.

———. 1976. Open letter to union members, Texas AFL-CIO, May 19. Carlos Truan Papers, South Texas Archives and Special Collections, James C. Jernigan Library, Texas A&M University–Kingsville. Box 31.017.

Hunter, Jason. 1998. "Barrientos Says Legislature Can Better Help Minorities." *Daily Texan*, November 18. "Barrientos, Gonzalo" Vertical File, Dolph Briscoe Center for American History, University of Texas at Austin.

Hutcheson, Ron. 1982. "Clements, White Seek Hispanic Vote." *Fort Worth Star-Telegram*, September 14. Governor William P. Clements Jr. Records, Mexico and Latin American Relations Office [MALAR] Records, First Term, 1979–1983. Box 5, Folder 16.

Idar, Ed, Jr. 1952a. Letter to Ed Cazares, October 31. Dr. Hector P. Garcia Papers, Special Collections and Archives, Texas A&M University–Corpus Christi, Mary and Jeff Bell Library.

———. 1952b. "Message from State Chairman Ed Idar, Jr." Fourth Annual Convention American GI Forum of Texas. Dr. Hector P. Garcia Papers, Special Collections and Archives, Texas A&M University–Corpus Christi, Mary and Jeff Bell Library.

———. 1953a. Letter to Henry B. González, August 26. Dr. Hector P. Garcia Papers, Special Collections and Archives, Texas A&M University–Corpus Christi, Mary and Jeff Bell Library.

———. 1953b. Letter to M. Cieplinski, June 13. Dr. Hector P. Garcia Papers, Special Collections and Archives, Texas A&M University–Corpus Christi, Mary and Jeff Bell Library.

———. 1955a. Letter to Senator Dennis Chavez, December 12. Dr. Hector P. Garcia Papers, Special Collections and Archives, Texas A&M University–Corpus Christi, Mary and Jeff Bell Library.

———. 1955b. Open letter to American GI Forum officers, August 3. Dr. Hector P. Garcia Papers, Special Collections and Archives, Texas A&M University–Corpus Christi, Mary and Jeff Bell Library.

———. 1960/1961. Confidential memorandum, December 19, 1960; epilogue April 14, 1961 (two documents attached in collection). Dr. Hector P. Garcia Papers, Special Collections and Archives, Texas A&M University–Corpus Christi, Mary and Jeff Bell Library.

———. 1961. Letter to Hector P. Garcia, December 19. Dr. Hector P. Garcia Papers, Special Collections and Archives, Texas A&M University–Corpus Christi, Mary and Jeff Bell Library.

———. 1962. Letter to George Sánchez, May 17. Dr. Hector P. Garcia Papers, Special Collections and Archives, Texas A&M University–Corpus Christi, Mary and Jeff Bell Library.

———. 1963. Letter to R. P. Sánchez, June 18. Dr. Hector P. Garcia Papers, Special Collections and Archives, Texas A&M University–Corpus Christi, Mary and Jeff Bell Library.

———. 1969. Interviewed by Robert Cuellar, February 20. Oral History Program, University of North Texas, Denton.

Ignatiev, Noel. 1995. *How the Irish Became White*. New York: Routledge.

Inter-Agency Committee on Mexican American Affairs. 1967. *The Mexican American: A New Focus on Opportunity*. Washington, D.C.: U.S. Government Printing Office.

Inter-Organizational Committee. 1947. Laredo, Alba Club, and University Chapter of the American Veterans Committee Report, August 22. Texas Governor Price Daniel Records, Archives and Information Services Division, Texas State Library and Archives Commission, Latin-American Matters. Box 54.

Ivins, Molly. 1972. "Ya Basta!" *Texas Observer*, August 25.

———. 1995. "View from Mexico: Deciding Who Gets Credit." *Corpus Christi Caller*, October 13. Irma Rangel Collection (A2003–042), South Texas Archives and Special Collections, James C. Jernigan Library, Texas A&M University–Kingsville. Box 8.010.

Ivins, Molly, and Joe Franz. 1974. "La Raza Unida." *Texas Observer*, November 29.

Jacobson, Matthew Frye. 1999. *Whiteness of a Different Color*. Cambridge, Mass.: Harvard University Press.

Jalonick, Mary Clare. 2002. "Minority 'Dream Ticket' in Texas Excites Democrats in Bush Country." *CQ Weekly Online* (August 10): 2180–2181. Online (accessed June 5, 2009): http://library.cqpress.com.ezproxy.library.wisc.edu /cqweekly/weeklyreport107–000000487572.

Jarvis, Sharon E., and Stacy L. Connaughton. 2005. "Audiences Implicadas e Ignoradas in the English and Spanish Language 2002 Texas Gubernatorial Debates." *Howard Journal of Communications* 16, no. 2: 131–148.

Jenkins, J. Craig. 1985. *The Politics of Insurgency*. New York: Columbia University Press.

Johnson, Benjamin Heber. 2003. *Revolution in Texas: How a Forgotten Rebellion and Its Bloody Suppression Turned Mexicans into Americans*. New Haven: Yale University Press.

Johnson, Bob. 1966. "A Rootin'-Tootin' Liberal." *Houston Post*, October 3. Texas Observer Records, 1952–1990, Dolph Briscoe Center for American History, University of Texas at Austin.

Johnson, Ed. 1964. "Texas' Latins Bid for Better Lot with Ballots." *Fort Worth Star-Telegram*, April 5. Dr. Hector P. Garcia Papers, Special Collections and Archives, Texas A&M University–Corpus Christi, Mary and Jeff Bell Library.

Jones, Franklin. 1956. "We Need More Republicans." *Texas Observer*, September 26.

Jones, Garth. 1976. "Prominent Liberals Take Senate Spots, House Incumbents Fall to Challengers." *Valley Morning Star*, June 7. Carlos Truan Papers, South Texas Archives and Special Collections, James C. Jernigan Library, Texas A&M University–Kingsville. Box 52.011.

———. 1978. "Party's Liberals Have Kind Word for Calvin Guest." *Fort Worth Star-Telegram*, January 8. "Guest, Calvin" Vertical File, Dolph Briscoe Center for American History, University of Texas at Austin.

Jones, Lee. 1961. "Henry González Has Become a Colorful Figure," November 5. "Austin, Texas—Henry B. González" Vertical File, Dolph Briscoe Center for American History, University of Texas at Austin.

Jones, Robert N. 1949. Letter to Lyndon Johnson, November 13. Dr. Hector P.

Garcia Papers, Special Collections and Archives, Texas A&M University–Corpus Christi, Mary and Jeff Bell Library.

Jordan, Barbara. 1975. "Representative Barbara Jordan Asks Congress to Extend Voting Rights Act to Texas." Press statement, Office of Representative Barbara Jordan, February 26. Texas Observer Records, 1952–1990, Dolph Briscoe Center for American History, University of Texas at Austin.

Katznelson, Ira. 2005. *When Affirmative Action Was White: An Untold History of Racial Inequality in Twentieth-Century America*. New York: W. W. Norton and Co.

Kazen, Philip A. 1965. Letter to John B. Connally, April 7. Texas Governor John Connally Records, LBJ Library. Box 496.

———. 1966. Letter to John B. Connally, June 15. Texas Governor John Connally Records, LBJ Library. Box 992.

Kennedy Johnson State Campaign Headquarters. ca. 1960. Press release. Allan Shivers Papers, 1949–1984, Dolph Briscoe Center for American History, University of Texas at Austin.

Key, V. O., Jr. 1984. *Southern Politics in State and Nation*. Knoxville: University of Tennessee Press.

Keyssar, Alexander. 2000. *The Right To Vote: The Contested History of Democracy in the United States*. New York: Basic Books.

Kiehl, Ekmper. 1971. "González: Minorities Must 'Join Mainstream' to End 'Injustices.'" *San Antonio Express*, January 6. Dr. Hector P. Garcia Papers, Special Collections and Archives, Texas A&M University–Corpus Christi, Mary and Jeff Bell Library.

Kinch, Sam, Jr. 1976. "Briscoe, Guest Lost Control?" *Dallas Morning News*, June 26. Dolph Briscoe Papers, 1932–2010, Dolph Briscoe Center for American History, University of Texas at Austin. Box 415.

King, Michael. 2002a. "The Banker vs. the Prosecutor. As the Primary Campaign Winds to an Abrupt Close, What Do We Know about Sánchez and Morales?" *Austin Chronicle*, March 8.

———. 2002b. "Tony and Dan Go Mano a . . . Hand? Dem Gubernatorial Debate Less Than Meets the Eye." *Austin Chronicle*, March 8.

Knaggs, John R. 1986. *Two Party Texas: The John Tower Era, 1961–1984*. Austin: Eakin Press.

———. 2005. Interview with author, July 27, Austin.

Knoles, Don. 1957. "González Condemns Texas Political Trends." *Daily Texan*, October 2. "Austin, Texas—Henry B. González" Vertical File, Dolph Briscoe Center for American History, University of Texas at Austin.

Kolker, Claudia. 2002. "Texas Candidates Debate in Spanish; Latinos Hold Key in Governor Race." *Boston Globe*, March 3. Retrieved from http://www.lexisnexis.com.

Lacy, Virginia P., and Joseph Permetti. 1978. Open letter, March 15. Billie Carr Papers, 1956–2003, MS 373, Woodson Research Center, Fondren Library, Rice University. Box 12, Folder 4.

Lamare, James W., et al. 2007. "Texas: Lone Star (Wars) State." In Charles S. Bullock III and Mark J. Rozell, eds., *The New Politics of the Old South: An Intro-*

duction to Southern Politics, 285–300. Lanham: Rowman and Littlefield Publishing Group.

Lee, Bill. 1969. "Liberal González Details His Quarrel with Latin Radicals." *Houston Chronicle*, May 18. "González, H. B." Vertical File, Dolph Briscoe Center for American History, University of Texas at Austin.

Lee, Jennifer, and Frank Bean. 2007. "Reinventing the Color Line: Immigration and America's New Racial/Ethnic Divide." *Social Forces* 86, no. 2: 561–586.

Lieberson, Stanley, and Mary Waters. 1990. *From Many Strands: Ethnic and Racial Groups in Contemporary America*. New York: Russell Sage Foundation.

Lindee, Susan. 1982. "White Says He'll Work with COPS." *San Antonio Express*, November 8. Governor William P. Clements Jr. Records, Mexico and Latin American Relations Office [MALAR] Records, First Term, 1979–1983. Box 3, Folder 1.

Long, Larry H. 1968. "Patterns of Migration for Short Periods, 1930 to 1960." In Harley Browning and Larry H. Long, eds., *Population Mobility: Focus on Texas*, 135–168. Austin: Bureau of Business Research, University of Texas.

Long, Stuart. 1964. "Mexicans Target of Vote Seekers." *Corpus Christi Caller-Times*, February 9. Texas Governor John Connally Records, LBJ Library. Box 56.

———. 1966. "Fuentes Talk Muddles State Political Scene." *Corpus Christi Caller-Times*, January 30. Texas Observer Records, 1952–1990, Dolph Briscoe Center for American History, University of Texas at Austin.

Looney, J. C. 1966. Letter to Terrell Blodgett, June 1. Texas Governor John Connally Records, LBJ Library. Box 992.

López, David. 1963. "Bonilla-Garcia Exchange Marks GI Forum Meeting." *Corpus Christi Caller*, August 14. Dr. Hector P. Garcia Papers, Special Collections and Archives, Texas A&M University–Corpus Christi, Mary and Jeff Bell Library.

Lucio, Eddie, Jr. 1995. Letter to Carlos Truan, October 18. Carlos F. Truan Collection, South Texas Archives and Special Collections, James C. Jernigan Library, Texas A&M University–Kingsville. Box 537.016.

Luders, Joseph E. 2010. *The Civil Rights Movement and the Logic of Social Change*. New York: Cambridge University Press.

Ludlin, Ron. 1977. Memorandum to Rudy R. Flores, March 30. Governor William P. Clements Jr. Records, Mexico and Latin American Relations Office [MALAR] Records, First Term, 1979–1983. Box 4, Folder 14.

Luna, Gregory. 1991. Oral history interview by José Ángel Gutiérrez, July 1. Center for Mexican American Studies No. 51.

Mabin, Connie. 2002. "Mexican-American Seeks to Make History as Texas' First Hispanic Governor." Associated Press. Retrieved from http://www.lexisnexis.com.

———. 2003. "Texas House Democrats Break Quorum." Associated Press, May 12. Retrieved from http://www.lexisnexis.com.

Machado, Melinda. 1982. "Parties, Politics, and Prose . . ." *Austin Light*, November 11. Moya (Richard) Papers (1969–1986), Austin History Center, AR.2002.024.

———. 1983. "White Repaying Hispanic Vote." *Austin Light*, February 3. Moya (Richard) Papers (1969–1986), Austin History Center, AR.2002.024.

Macias, Thomas. 2006. *Mestizo in America: Generations of Mexican Ethnicity in the Suburban Southwest*. Tucson: University of Arizona Press.

Macy, John W. 1966. Memorandum for the president, October 14. Office Files of White Aides, Office Files of John Macy, LBJ Library. Box 890 (file: "Latin Americans-Endorsements Contacts").

———. 1968. Memorandum for the president, July 12. Office Files of White Aides, Office Files of John Macy, LBJ Library. Box 890 (file: "Education of Bilingual Children").

Mager, Phil. 2002. "Analysis: Hispanics Alter Texas Politics." United Press International, January 15. Retrieved from http://www.lexisnexis.com.

Maldonado, José, et al. ca. 1949. Letter to Price Daniel (n.d.), Texas Governor Price Daniel Records, Archives and Information Services Division, Texas State Library and Archives Commission, Segregation. Box 57.

Malone, Dan, and Ann Arnold. 1981. "Minority Appointees Rarities." *Fort Worth Star-Telegram*, May 5. Governor William P. Clements Jr. Records, Mexico and Latin American Relations Office [MALAR] Records, First Term, 1979–1983. Box 1, Folder 18.

Mark White Committee. ca. 1982a. Press release, March 1. Records, Texas Governor Mark White, Archives and Information Services Division, Texas State Library and Archives Commission, "General—Blacks." Box 1991/141–94.

———. ca. 1982b. "There Have Been Some Questions in This Gubernatorial Campaign about Commitments to Equality. Let's Look at the Record." Records, Texas Governor Mark White, Archives and Information Services Division, Texas State Library and Archives Commission, "General—Blacks." Box 1991/141–94.

Mark White for Governor. 1982a. "Mark White for Governor from a Black Perspective," August 5. Records, Texas Governor Mark White, Archives and Information Services Division, Texas State Library and Archives Commission, "General—Blacks." Box 1991/141–94.

———. 1982b. Press release, September 13. Records, Texas Governor Mark White, Archives and Information Services Division, Texas State Library and Archives Commission. "General—Blacks." Box 1991/141–94.

Márquez, Benjamin. 1993. *LULAC: The Evolution of a Mexican American Political Organization*. Austin: University of Texas Press.

———. 2003. *Constructing Identities in Mexican American Political Organizations: Choosing Issues, Taking Sides*. Austin: University of Texas Press.

Márquez, Benjamin, and Rodolfo Espino. 2010. "La Raza Unida Party in Texas Politics: An Analysis of Racial Appeals and Third Party Voting in the 1972 Texas Gubernatorial Election." *Ethnic and Racial Studies* 33, no. 2 (February): 290–312.

Márquez, Benjamin, and James Jennings. 2000. "Representation by Other Means: Mexican American and Puerto Rican Social Movement Organizations." *PS: Political Science and Politics* 33, no. 3 (September): 541–546.

Martin, Louis. 1965. Letter to John Macy, September 2. Office Files of White Aides, Office files of John Macy, LBJ Library. Box 890 (file: "Latin Americans—Candidates").

Martínez, George. 1997. Oral history interview by José Ángel Gutiérrez, October 24. Center for Mexican American Studies No. 121.

Martínez, María. 1998. Oral history interview by José Ángel Gutiérrez, October 26. Center for Mexican American Studies No. 133.

Martinez-Ebers, Valerie, and Manochehr Dorraj, eds. 2010. *Perspectives on Race, Ethnicity, and Religion*. New York: Oxford University Press.

Marx, Anthony W. 1998. *Making Race and Nation: A Comparison of South Africa, the United States, and Brazil*. New York: Cambridge University Press.

Mathis, Richard. 1968. "The Process of Urbanization in Texas." In Harley L. Browning and Larry H. Long, eds., *Population Mobility: A Focus on Texas*, 105–134. Austin: Bureau of Business Research, University of Texas at Austin.

Maverick, Maury, Jr. 1960. Letter to Henry B. González, November 25, 1960. Henry B. González Papers, 1946–1998, Dolph Briscoe Center for American History, University of Texas at Austin. Box 2004–127/88.

———. 1961. Letter to Henry B. González, November 4. Henry B. González Papers, 1946–1998, Dolph Briscoe Center for American History, University of Texas at Austin. Box 2004–127/88.

———. ca. 1968a. "Summary of Brief Supporting the Texas Democrats for an Open Convention." Albert A. Peña Jr. Papers, 1952–1977 (bulk 1956–1972), MS 37, UTSA Archives and Special Collections, Library, University of Texas at San Antonio. Box 4:30.

———. ca. 1968b. "Summary of Brief Supporting the Texas Democrats for an Open Convention versus the John Connally Delegation" (undated document). Albert A. Peña Jr. Papers, 1952–1977 (bulk 1956–1972), MS 37, UTSA Archives and Special Collections, Library, University of Texas at San Antonio. Box 8:16.

———. 1975. Interview by Chandler Davidson, October 27. Interview A-0323. Southern Oral History Program Collection (#4007). Online (accessed January 26, 2010): http://docsouth.unc.edu/sohp/A-0323/A-0323.html.

Maverick, Maury, et al. 1952. "Before the Credentials Committee of the Democratic National Executive Committee, at Chicago, July, 1952: In the Matter of the Texas Delegations. Brief on Behalf of the Delegation of Which Mr. Maury Maverick and Major J. R. Parten Are Chairmen." Dolph Briscoe Center for American History, University of Texas at Austin.

McAdam, Douglas. 1982. *Political Process and the Development of Black Insurgency, 1930–1970*. Chicago: University of Chicago Press.

McAlmon, George. 2003. Interview with author, May 17, El Paso.

McCall, Brian. 2009. *The Power of the Texas Governor: Connally to Bush*. Austin: The University of Texas Press.

McCarthy, John D., and Mayer N. Zald. 1973. "Resource Mobilization and Social Movements: A Partial Theory." *American Journal of Sociology* 82, no. 6: 1212–1241.

McCleskey, Clifton, and Bruce Merrill. 1973. "Mexican American Political Behavior in Texas." *Social Science Quarterly* 53, no. 4: 785–798.

McCrory, James. 1963. "PASO Leadership Decision Today." *San Antonio Express*, June 9. Texas Governor John Connally Records, LBJ Library. Box 735.

————. 1965. "Yarborough Governor Race Asked." *San Antonio Express*, July 12. Texas Governor John Connally Records, LBJ Library. Box 744.

————. 1966a. "PASO Aide Rips Fuentes, Quits." *San Antonio Express*, January 23. Texas Governor John Connally Records, LBJ Library. Box 735.

————. 1966b. "Tower, Carr Lose PASO Nod." *San Antonio Express*, August 21. Henry B. González Papers, 1946–1998, Dolph Briscoe Center for American History, University of Texas at Austin. Box 2004–127/395.

————. 1967. "Bernal Fires New Blast at Connally." *San Antonio Express*, October 24. Texas Governor John Connally Records, LBJ Library. Box 744.

————. 1968. "Texas Demo Delegation Challenged." *San Antonio Express*, August 14. Albert A. Peña Jr. Papers, 1952–1977 (bulk 1956–1972), MS 37, UTSA Archives and Special Collections, Library, University of Texas at San Antonio. Box 4:30.

————. 1969. "Rodriguez May Get U.S. Post" (unidentified newspaper clipping), April 23. Henry B. González Papers (unprocessed), Dolph Briscoe Center for American History, University of Texas at Austin.

————. 1970a. "Bernal Says Smith Has Done Good Job." *San Antonio Express*, August 31. Texas Observer Records, 1952–1990, Dolph Briscoe Center for American History, University of Texas at Austin.

————. 1970b. "14 Mexican-Americans Appreciate Smith's Visit." *San Antonio Express*, September 2. Texas Observer Records, 1952–1990, Dolph Briscoe Center for American History, University of Texas at Austin.

————. 1970c. "Gov. Smith Due to Strengthen Ethnic Fences." *San Antonio Express*, August 27. Henry B. González Papers, 1946–1998, Dolph Briscoe Center for American History, University of Texas at Austin. Box 2004–127/395.

————. 1970d. "Mexican American Poll on Smith Views Planned." *San Antonio Express News*, September 4. Henry B. González Papers, 1946–1998, Dolph Briscoe Center for American History, University of Texas at Austin. Box 2004–127/395.

————. 1970e. "Smith Shaken by S. A. Meeting." *San Antonio Express*, August 28. Dolph Briscoe Papers, 1932–2010, Dolph Briscoe Center for American History, University of Texas at Austin. Box 265.

————. 1974. "Foes Don't Dare Run against Popular HBG." *San Antonio News*, January 9. "González, Henry B." Vertical File, Dolph Briscoe Center for American History, University of Texas at Austin.

————. 1976a. "Guest Sure He Will Keep Post." *San Antonio Express*, September 16. "Guest, Calvin" Vertical File, Dolph Briscoe Center for American History, University of Texas at Austin.

————. 1976b. "Rural Counties Clinch Top Demo Spot for Guest." *San Antonio Express-News*, September 19.

————. ca. 1976. "Guest Sure He Will Keep Post" (undated article). Dolph Briscoe Papers, 1932–2010, Dolph Briscoe Center for American History, University of Texas at Austin. Box 415.

————. 1978. "Top Tower Post Goes to Hispanic." *San Antonio Express*, August 23. Texas Observer Records, 1952–1990, Dolph Briscoe Center for American History, University of Texas at Austin.

————. 1980a. "Demo Hispanic Delegates Plan Building Own Platform." *San*

Antonio Express, August 9. Mexican American Democrats of Texas Records, 1962–1987, MS 29, UTSA Archives, Library, University of Texas at San Antonio. Box 3:4.

———. 1980b. "Hot Texas Delegates Cool Down." *San Antonio Express News*, August 15. Mexican American Democrats of Texas Records, 1962–1987, MS 29, UTSA Archives, Library, University of Texas at San Antonio. Box 3:4.

———. 1980c. "Mexican-American Vote Called Vital for Carter." *San Antonio Express News*, August 1980. Mexican American Democrats of Texas Records, 1962–1987, MS 29, UTSA Archives, Library, University of Texas at San Antonio. Box 3:4.

———. 1980d. "Texas Delegates Arriving in N.Y." *San Antonio Express*, August 9. Mexican American Democrats of Texas Records, 1962–1987, MS 29, UTSA Archives, Library, University of Texas at San Antonio. Box 3:4.

McGovern, George. 1972. Letter to Herman Badillo, September 28. Dr. Hector P. Garcia Papers, Special Collections and Archives, Texas A&M University–Corpus Christi, Mary and Jeff Bell Library.

McGrath, Jack. 1975a. "State Objects to Registrars." *San Antonio Express*, April 23. Records, Texas Governor Mark White, Archives and Information Services Division, Texas State Library and Archives Commission, "General—Blacks." Box 1991/141–94.

———. 1975b. "Voting Rights: Texas May Be Next." *San Antonio Express*, April 28. Texas Observer Records, 1952–1990, Dolph Briscoe Center for American History, University of Texas at Austin.

McKee, Seth C., and Daron R. Shaw. 2005. "Redistricting in Texas: Institutionalizing Republican Ascendancy." In Peter F. Galderisi, ed. *Redistricting in the New Millennium*, 294. Lanham: Rowman and Littlefield Publishers.

McLemore, David. 1982. "Bonilla Gives Endorsement to Temple." *Dallas Morning News*, February 19. Governor William P. Clements Jr. Records, Mexico and Latin American Relations Office [MALAR] Records, First Term, 1979–1983. Box 7, Folder 8.

McNeely, Dave. 2002. "Texas Democrats Analyze Loss." Cox News Service, December 5. Retrieved from http://www.lexisnexis.com.

McPherson, Harry C. 1966. Confidential memo for the president, December 1. Office Files of White Aides, Office Files of Harry C. McPherson, LBJ Library. Box 11 (1412) (file: "Mexican Americans").

Mexican American Democrats. 1974. "A Challenge to the Composition of the Texas Delegation to the 1974 Conference on Democratic Party Organization and Policy by Mexican American Democrats." Joe J. Bernal Papers, Benson Latin American Collection, University of Texas Libraries, University of Texas at Austin. Democratic Party—Texas: State Democratic Exec. Committee (Party Rules). Box 107.

———. ca. 1974. "Confidential Strategy Notes" (n.d.). Joe J. Bernal Papers, Benson Latin American Collection, University of Texas Libraries, University of Texas at Austin. Democratic Party—Texas: State Democratic Exec. Committee (Party Rules). Box 107.

———. 1982. "Mexican American Democrats Candidate Questionnaire." Records, Texas Governor Mark White, Archives and Information Services

Division, Texas State Library and Archives Commission, "Hispanics." Box 1991/141–94.

———. n.d. "Rules and By-Laws of the Mexican-American Democrats Caucus of the Democratic Party of Texas." Dr. Hector P. Garcia Papers, Special Collections and Archives, Texas A&M University–Corpus Christi, Mary and Jeff Bell Library.

Mexican American Republicans of Texas. 1981. "MAR Work-Plan: A Proposal to the Republican National Committee," February 23. Governor William P. Clements Jr. Records, Mexico and Latin American Relations Office [MALAR] Records, First Term, 1979–1983. Box 84, Folder 63.

Mexican American Youth Organization. ca. 1968. Untitled document. Henry B. González Papers (unprocessed), Dolph Briscoe Center for American History, University of Texas at Austin.

Meza, Choco González. 1978. "Mexican American Voting in the 1978 Texas General Election," December 1. San Antonio: Southwest Voter Registration Education Project.

Miller, Jarvis E. 1982. Memorandum to William P. Clements Jr., July 8. Governor William P. Clements Jr. Records, Mexico and Latin American Relations Office [MALAR] Records, First Term, 1979–1983. Box 3, Folder 1.

Miller, Kathi. ca. 1974. "Comptroller Candidates Trade Verbal Punches Here." Unidentified newspaper clipping. Dolph Briscoe Papers, 1932–2010, Dolph Briscoe Center for American History, University of Texas at Austin. Box 30.

Millet, Anne L. 1972. *W. R. Poage: Democratic Representative from Texas*. New York: Grossman Publishers.

Milner, Jay. 1962. "The Young GOP Turks." *Texas Observer*, March 30.

Moderate Conservative Democratic Caucus. ca. 1978. "To All Moderate and Conservative Texas Democrats" (n.d.). Billie Carr Papers, 1956–2003, MS 373, Woodson Research Center, Fondren Library, Rice University. Box 12, Folder 4.

Montejano, David. 1987. *Anglos and Mexicans in the Making of Texas, 1836–1986*. Austin: University of Texas Press.

Montemayor, Manuel J. 1979. Letter to Ruben Bonilla, March 15. Governor William P. Clements Jr. Records, Mexico and Latin American Relations Office [MALAR] Records, First Term, 1979–1983. Box 7, Folder 1.

Montemayor, Paul. 1962. Open letter to American GI Forum Members, March. Dr. Hector P. Garcia Papers, Special Collections and Archives, Texas A&M University–Corpus Christi, Mary and Jeff Bell Library.

Montgomery, Dave. 1976. "Demo Chief Faces Fight." *Dallas Times Herald*, June 21. Dolph Briscoe Papers, 1932–2010, Dolph Briscoe Center for American History, University of Texas at Austin. Box 415.

Montoya, Juan. 1978. "Mexican American Solons Supporting Hill and Krueger." *Laredo Citizen*, November 2. Carlos Truan Papers, South Texas Archives and Special Collections, James C. Jernigan Library, Texas A&M University–Kingsville. Box 52.018.

Montoya, Richard T. 1980. Letter to Julio Moran, May 21. Governor William P. Clements Jr. Records, Mexico and Latin American Relations Office [MALAR] Records, First Term, 1979–1983. Box 7, Folder 16.

———. 1981a. Letter to Oscar Moran, July 7. Governor William P. Clements Jr. Records, Mexico and Latin American Relations Office [MALAR] Records, First Term, 1979–1983. Box 5, Folder 18.

———. 1981b. Memorandum to William P. Clements through Allen B. Clark Jr., April 3. Governor William P. Clements Jr. Records, Mexico and Latin American Relations Office [MALAR] Records, First Term, 1979–1983. Box 5, Folder 18.

———. 1982. Memo to Governor Clements through Hilary Doran, January 22. Governor William P. Clements Jr. Records, Mexico and Latin American Relations Office [MALAR] Records, First Term, 1979–1983. Box 5, Folder 13.

Moody, Mary. 1975. "Castillo Says He Will Seek Re-election." *Houston Chronicle*. March 26. "Castillo, Leonel" Vertical File, Dolph Briscoe Center for American History, University of Texas at Austin.

Morales, Dan. ca. 1995. "Molly Ivins Can Say That, But Is It Correct?" Newspaper editorial, unidentified source. Irma Rangel Collection (A2003–042), South Texas Archives and Special Collections, James C. Jernigan Library, Texas A&M University–Kingsville, Box 8.010.

———. 1997. "Hopwood Opens New Era in Pursuit of Diversity." *Austin American-Statesman*, February 7.

Morales, Johnny. 1968a. Handwritten report, September 3. Preston Smith Papers, 1930–1975 and undated, Southwest Collection/Special Collections Library, Texas Tech University, Lubbock.

———. 1968b. Memorandum (handwritten, no recipient), July 11. Preston Smith Papers, 1930–1975 and undated, Southwest Collection/Special Collections Library, Texas Tech University, Lubbock.

———. 1968c. Poll results (handwritten report), August 8. Preston Smith Papers, 1930–1975 and undated, Southwest Collection/Special Collections Library, Texas Tech University, Lubbock.

———. 1968d. "Trip to Valley Area" (handwritten report), August 18. Preston Smith Papers, 1930–1975 and undated, Southwest Collection/Special Collections Library, Texas Tech University, Lubbock.

———. ca. 1968. "San Antonio Report" (handwritten report, undated). Preston Smith Papers, 1930–1975 and undated, Southwest Collection/Special Collections Library, Texas Tech University, Lubbock.

Morante, José. 1958. Untitled corrido in "Don Politico Says." *San Antonio Light*, May 11.

Morehead, Richard M. ca. 1968. "Candidates Woo Latins' Vote." *Austin American-Statesman* (undated newspaper clipping). E. Preston Smith Papers, 1930–1975 and undated, Southwest Collection/Special Collections Library, Texas Tech University, Lubbock.

Morehouse, Sarah M., and Malcolm E. Jewell. 2005. "The Future of Political Parties in the States." In *Book of the States* vol. 37, 331–345. Lexington, Ky.: Council of State Governments.

Moreno, Paul. 2004. Interview with author, May 28, El Paso.

Morgan, Darla. 1982. "Ruben Bonilla Fires LULAC Official." *Corpus Christi Caller*, October 20. Governor William P. Clements Jr. Records, Mexico and

Latin American Relations Office [MALAR] Records, First Term, 1979–1983. Box 7, Folder 8.

Morgan, Ricardo P. 1956. Letter to Hector P. Garcia, May 29. Dr. Hector P. Garcia Papers, Special Collections and Archives, Texas A&M University–Corpus Christi, Mary and Jeff Bell Library.

Morris, Aldon D. 1984. *The Origins of the Civil Rights Movement: Black Communities Organizing for Change*. New York: Free Press.

Morton, Rebecca B. 2006. *Analyzing Elections*. New York: W. W. Norton.

Moss, Marquita. 1968. "Barrera Sworn In as State Secretary." *Dallas Morning News*, March 13. "Barrera, Roy" Vertical File, Dolph Briscoe Center for American History, University of Texas at Austin.

Moya, Richard, et al. 1974. Open letter to Mexican American Democrats, September 3. Margo Gutiérrez Personal Files, University of Texas at Austin.

Muñiz Governor '72. 1972. "Ramsey Muñiz: On the Issues." Press release, State Campaign Headquarters (n.p., n.d.). Texas Observer Records, 1952–1990, Dolph Briscoe Center for American History, University of Texas at Austin.

Muñoz and Associates. 1982. "Mexican American Politics in Texas: A Proposal of Action to Elect Mark White Governor of Texas in the General Election in November 1982." Records, Texas Governor Mark White, Archives and Information Services Division, Texas State Library and Archives Commission, "Hispanics." Box 1991/141–194.

Muñoz, Carlos, Jr. 1989. *Youth, Identity, Power: The Chicano Movement*. New York: Verso.

Murguia, Edward. 1982. *Chicano Intermarriage: A Theoretical and Empirical Study*. San Antonio: Trinity University Press.

Murray, Richard. 2004. "Texas Democrats in the 21st Century: Will They Go Quietly into that Good Night? . . . Or Be the Comeback Kids of the 2006 Elections?" Online (updated May 26, 2004; accessed September 15, 2010): http:// texasweekly.com/documents/MurrayMemo.pdf.

Navarro, Armando. 2005. *Mexicano Political Experience in Occupied Aztlan: Struggles and Change*. Walnut Creek, Calif.: Altamira Press.

Newton, Billy. 1977. "Rangel—Area Needs to Draw New Industry." *Corpus Christi Caller*, December 26. Irma Rangel Papers, South Texas Archives and Special Collections, James C. Jernigan Library, Texas A&M University–Kingsville. Box 1.002.

Nobles, Doug. 1967. Memorandum for Chairman Macy, January 28. Office Files of White Aides, Office Files of John Macy, LBJ Library. Box 889 (file: "Latin Americans").

Noblet, Michael W. 1974. "The Events Which Occurred during the Permanent Nominations Committee of the 1974 Texas Democratic Convention," October 1. Billie Carr Papers, 1956–2003, MS 373, Woodson Research Center, Fondren Library, Rice University. Box 11, Folder 26.

Norman, Mike. 1981. "Senate Panel Will Not Hear Mrs. Pickard." *Corpus Christi Caller*, January 21. Irma Rangel Papers, South Texas Archives and Special Collections, James C. Jernigan Library, Texas A&M University–Kingsville. Box 2.006.

North, David S. 1966a. Memorandum for Joseph Califano, September 28. LBJ Library, "LBJ Human Rights" HU2/MC 6/7/66–10/12/66. Box 23.

———. 1966b. Memorandum for Mr. Califano, September 8. Office Files of White Aides, Office Files of Harry C. McPherson, LBJ Library. Box 11 (1412) (file: "Mexican Americans").

———. 1966c. Memorandum for Mr. Levinson. September 13. LBJ Library, "LBJ Human Rights" HU2/MC 6/7/66–10/12/66. Box 23.

O'Brien, Larry F. 1972. Letter to Roy Orr, Chairman State Democratic Executive Committee, June 7. Dolph Briscoe Papers, 1932–2010, Dolph Briscoe Center for American History, University of Texas at Austin. Box 30, Folder 16.

Office of Governor Preston Smith. 1970. Press release, September 2. E. Preston Smith Papers, 1930–1975 and undated, Southwest Collection/Special Collections Library, Texas Tech University, Lubbock.

Office of Lt. Governor Preston Smith. 1968. Press release, September 13. Preston Smith Papers, 1930–1975 and undated, Southwest Collection/Special Collections Library, Texas Tech University, Lubbock.

Office of the Governor. 1981. Executive Order Establishing the Governor's Task Force on Equal Opportunities for Women and Minorities, August 1981. Governor William P. Clements Jr. Records, Mexico and Latin American Relations Office [MALAR] Records, First Term, 1979–1983. Box 4, Folder 3.

Office of the Spanish Speaking. 1972. "Directory and Alternates 1972 Democratic National Convention." Mexican American Democrats of Texas Records, 1962–1987, MS 29, UTSA Archives, Library, University of Texas at San Antonio. Box 11:12.

Oropeza, Lorena. 2005. *¡Raza Si! ¡Guerra No! Chicano Protest and Patriotism during the Viet Nam Era*. Berkeley: University of California Press.

Orozco, Cynthia E. n.d. "Mexican American Democrats." *Handbook of Texas Online* (published by the Texas State Historical Association). Online (accessed July 27, 2012): http://www.tshaonline.org/handbook/online/articles/wmm02.

Ortiz, Juan X. ca. 1968. Editorial (n.p., n.d.). Preston Smith Papers, 1930–1975 and undated, Southwest Collection/Special Collections Library, Texas Tech University, Lubbock.

Palmer, Dana. 1981. "Truan Sure to Oust Regent." *Corpus Christi Caller*, January 21. Irma Rangel Papers, South Texas Archives and Special Collections, James C. Jernigan Library, Texas A&M University–Kingsville. Box 2.006.

Palomo, Juan R. ca. 1982. "No Clear Gubernatorial Endorsement Given by Mexican-American Group." *Brownsville Herald*, (n.d.). Records, Texas Governor Mark White, Archives and Information Services Division, Texas State Library and Archives Commission, "Hispanics." Box 1991/141–94.

Pangburn, Pat. 1974. Letter to Calvin R. Guest, April 22. Texas Democratic Party Papers, Archives and Information Services Division, Texas State Library and Archives Commission. Box 1979/49-123.

Parish, Jim. ca. 1974. "Tony Bonilla to Work Vigorously for South Texas University System." Unidentified newspaper clipping. Dolph Briscoe Papers, 1932–2010, Dolph Briscoe Center for American History, University of Texas at Austin. Box 293.

Parks, Scott. 1976a. "Issues May Take Back Seat in McKinnon–Truan Choice." *Corpus Christi Caller-Times*, June 4. Carlos Truan Papers, South Texas Archives and Special Collections, James C. Jernigan Library, Texas A&M University–Kingsville. Box 52.009.

———. 1976b. "McKinnon Denies Knowing of Controversial Ad." *Corpus Christi Caller-Times*, June 3. Carlos Truan Papers, South Texas Archives and Special Collections, James C. Jernigan Library, Texas A&M University–Kingsville. Box 52.009.

———. 1976c. "Political Ad." *Corpus Christi Caller-Times*, June 5. Carlos Truan Papers, South Texas Archives and Special Collections, James C. Jernigan Library, Texas A&M University–Kingsville. Box 52.009.

Parrott, Susan. 2002. "Gramm's Remarks Called Insulting." Associated Press State and Local Wire, June 8, BC cycle. Retrieved from http://www.lexisnexis.com.

Peace, John. 1957. Letter to Ronnie Dugger, March 4. Texas Democratic Party Papers, Archives and Information Services Division, Texas State Library and Archives Commission. Box 1979/96–10.

———. 1963. Letter to John Connally, November 1. Texas Governor John Connally Records, LBJ Library. Box 1286.

Pearson, Ray. 1966. Letter to Terrell Blodgett, June 1. Texas Governor John Connally Records, LBJ Library. Box 992.

Pearson, Spencer. 1966a. "Bonilla Calls Foe Puppet of Garcia." *Corpus Christi Caller*, May 27. Dr. Hector P. Garcia Papers, Special Collections and Archives, Texas A&M University–Corpus Christi, Mary and Jeff Bell Library.

———. 1966b. "González Calls Foe Man of 'Many Faces.'" *Corpus Christi Caller*, June 3. Dr. Hector P. Garcia Papers, Special Collections and Archives, Texas A&M University–Corpus Christi, Mary and Jeff Bell Library.

———. ca. 1966. "Hector Garcia, Labor Men Accused of Unfair Tactics." *Corpus Christi Caller* (n.d.). Dr. Hector P. Garcia Papers, Special Collections and Archives, Texas A&M University–Corpus Christi, Mary and Jeff Bell Library.

———. 1972. "Reaction Mixed to Briscoe Act." *Corpus Christi Caller*, July 13. Texas Observer Records, 1952–1990, Dolph Briscoe Center for American History, University of Texas at Austin.

Peña, Albert A., Jr. 1959. Letter to Mrs. R. D. Randolph, January 5. Creekmore Fath Papers, 1938–1992 and undated, Southwest Collection/Special Collections Library, Texas Tech University, Lubbock. Box 1, Folder 11.

———. 1968. Testimony by County Commissioner Albert Peña before National Democratic Party Credentials Committee, August 21. Albert A. Peña Jr. Papers, 1952–1977 (bulk 1956–1972), MS 37, UTSA Archives and Special Collections, Library, University of Texas at San Antonio. Box 4:29.

———. 1970a. Keynote address, Annual Texas P.A.S.O. State Convention, September 27. Henry B. González Papers, 1946–1998, Dolph Briscoe Center for American History, University of Texas at Austin. Box 2004–127/395.

———. 1970b. "Peña on La Raza." *Texas Observer*, October 16.

———. 1971. Letter to the State Democratic Executive Committee, July 14. Albert A. Peña Jr. Papers, 1952–1977 (bulk 1956–1972), MS 37, UTSA Archives and Special Collections, Library, University of Texas at San Antonio. Box 8:16.

———. 1972a. McGovern endorsement, April 26. Albert A. Peña Jr. Papers, 1952–1977 (bulk 1956–1972), MS 37, UTSA Archives and Special Collections, Library, University of Texas at San Antonio. Box 11:14.

———. 1972b. "Statement of the Honorable Albert Peña Jr. before the Subcommittee on the Rules of the State Democratic Executive Committee in Austin, Texas, on January 12, 1972." Dolph Briscoe Papers, 1932–2010, Dolph Briscoe Center for American History, University of Texas at Austin. Box 64: "Party Rules."

———. 1996. Oral history interview by José Ángel Gutiérrez. July 2. Center for Mexican American Studies No. 015.

Peña, Albert, et al. 1969. "Making Politics Relevant to the Daily Life Needs of the More Than 11 Million Mexican and Other Spanish Speaking Americans Living in the U.S.A. Requires Political Representation at All Decision Making Levels and the Building of a Strong, Independent Political Infrastructure Controlled by Them." Text of presentation material, July 26. Texas Observer Records, 1952–1990, Dolph Briscoe Center for American History, University of Texas at Austin.

Perez-Trevino, Emma. 2002. "GOP Says Palanca Party Finished." Irma Rangel Collection (A2003–042), South Texas Archives and Special Collections, James C. Jernigan Library, Texas A&M University–Kingsville, Box 236.008.

Peters, Steve. 1974. "El Paso Issue Settled on Floor." *El Paso Times*, September 18. El Paso Public Library, Southwest Collection, El Paso Vertical Files: "Democratic Party."

———. 1978. "Tower's Ads Called 'Patronizing.'" *El Paso Times*, September 2. Texas Observer Records, 1952–1990, Dolph Briscoe Center for American History, University of Texas at Austin.

Pickle, J. J. 1956. Letter to Fidencio M. Guerra, June 30. Texas Governor Price Daniel Records, Archives and Information Services Division, Texas State Library and Archives Commission, Spanish Brochures. Box 355.

Piña, Trinidad, Jr. 1979. Letter to G. G. Garcia, March 7. Governor William P. Clements Jr. Records, Mexico and Latin American Relations Office [MALAR] Records, First Term, 1979–1983. Box 7, Folder 20.

Pinkerton, James. 1983. "Quintanilla Appointed White Department Head." *Austin American-Statesman*, January 27. Moya (Richard) Papers (1969–1986), Austin History Center, AR.2002.024.

Piven, Frances Fox, and Richard A. Cloward. 1979. *Poor People's Movements: Why They Succeed, How They Fail*. New York: Pantheon Books.

Politico, Don. 1982. "It Was No Easy Feat, But Clements Has COPS in the Palm of His Hand." *San Antonio Light*, June 27. Governor William P. Clements Jr. Records, Mexico and Latin American Relations Office [MALAR] Records, First Term, 1979–1983. Box 3, Folder 1.

Porterfield, Bill. 1965. "Paso's Peña Goes Out with Fiery Blast at Connally." *Houston Chronicle*, July 11. Texas Governor John Connally Records, LBJ Library. Box 744.

Portes, Alejandro, and Rubén G. Rumbaut. 2001. *Legacies: The Story of the Immigrant Second Generation*. New York: Russell Sage Foundation.

Price Daniel for Governor Headquarters. ca. 1956. Press release, Special to Texas

Weeklies. Texas Governor Price Daniel Records, Archives and Information Services Division, Texas State Library and Archives Commission, Segregation. Box 215.

Pullen, Dale. 1972. *George H. Mahon: Democratic Representative from Texas*. New York: Grossman Publishers.

Pycior, Julie Leininger. 1993. "From Hope to Frustration: Mexican Americans and Lyndon Johnson in 1967." *Western Historical Quarterly* 24, no. 4 (November): 469–494.

———. 1997. *LBJ and Mexican Americans: The Paradox of Power*. Austin: University of Texas Press.

Quintanilla, Humberto L. 1974. Letter to John C. White, March 21. Texas Democratic Party Papers, Archives and Information Services Division, Texas State Library and Archives Commission. Box 1979/49-123.

———. ca. 1974. "State Democratic Parties [*sic*] Responsibilities." Texas Democratic Party Papers, Archives and Information Services Division, Texas State Library and Archives Commission. Box 1979/49-123.

Raba, Ernest A. 1965. Letter to Phil Kazen, January 6. Texas Governor John Connally Records, LBJ Library. Box 496.

Ragsdale, Virginia L. 1958a. Letter to Creekmore Fath, July 28. Creekmore Fath Papers, 1938–1992 and undated, Southwest Collection/Special Collections Library, Texas Tech University, Lubbock. Box 1, Folder 9.

———. 1958b. Letter to Ralph Yarborough, June 7. Creekmore Fath Papers, 1938–1992 and undated, Southwest Collection/Special Collections Library, Texas Tech University, Lubbock. Box 1, Folder 9.

Ramos, Rudy L. 1966. Letter to Lyndon B. Johnson, April 27. Office Files of White Aides. Office Files of John Macy, LBJ Library. Box 890 (file: "Latin Americans-General").

Randolph, R. D. 1958a. Open letter to Texas Democrats, September. Texas Governor Price Daniel Records, Archives and Information Services Division, Texas State Library and Archives Commission, Democrats of Texas. Box 294.

———. 1958b. Press release, January 20. Texas Governor Price Daniel Records, Archives and Information Services Division, Texas State Library and Archives Commission, Democrats of Texas. Box 435.

Rangel, Irma. ca. 1982. Untitled, undated document. Irma Rangel Collection (A2003–042), South Texas Archives and Special Collections, James C. Jernigan Library, Texas A&M University–Kingsville. Box 13A.010.

———. 1995. Letter to the editor, October 20. Irma Rangel Collection (A2003–042), South Texas Archives and Special Collections, James C. Jernigan Library, Texas A&M University–Kingsville. Box 8.010.

———. 1996. Oral history interview José Ángel Gutiérrez, April 10. Center for Mexican American Studies No. 62.

Ray, Steve. ca. 1993. "Cavazos Sworn In as TEC Chairman." Unidentified newspaper clipping. Irma Rangel Collection (A2003–042), South Texas Archives and Special Collections, James C. Jernigan Library, Texas A&M University–Kingsville. Box 4.019.

Reid, Jan. 2001. "Sánchez's New Deal." *Texas Monthly* (November).

Reinhold, Robert. 1985. "Mexican Americans in Texas Move into Political Main-

stream." *New York Times*, September 15. Retrieved from http://www.lexisnexis
.com.

Reno, Edie, and Anne Zill. 1972. *Henry B. González: Democratic Representative
from Texas*. New York: Grossman Publishers.

Republican National Hispanic Assembly. 1982. News release, October 29. Texas
Observer Papers, Editorial Files, The Races 1982, Dolph Briscoe Center for
American History, University of Texas at Austin.

Republican Party of Texas. ca. 1982. News release. Texas Observer Papers, Editorial Files, The Races 1982, Dolph Briscoe Center for American History, University of Texas at Austin.

Rio Grande Democratic Club. ca. 1955. "Texas Needs Four Million Voting Citizens." Dr. Hector P. Garcia Papers, Special Collections and Archives, Texas
A&M University–Corpus Christi, Mary and Jeff Bell Library.

Rips, Geoffrey. 1983. "Mexican Americans Jalaron la Palanca, Democrats Say
Ole!" *Texas Observer*, January 14.

———. 1985. "How It Ended." *Texas Observer*, June 14.

Rivas, George R. 1968. Text of speech delivered at conference (no title), San
Antonio, January 6. Texas Observer Records, 1952–1990, Dolph Briscoe Center for American History, University of Texas at Austin.

Robison, Clay. 2001. "Gov. Sánchez or Clayton Williams II?" *Houston Chronicle*,
April 20.

Robles, Belen B. 1966. Letter to Joseph Califano, September 13. LBJ Library,
"LBJ Human Rights" HU2/MC 6/7/66–10/12/66. Box 23.

Rodriguez, Eugene, Jr. 1976. *Henry B. Gonzalez: A Political Profile*. New York:
Arno Press.

Rodriguez, Gene, Jr. 1985. "Hispanics and the Democratic Party," February 17.
Mexican American Democrats of Texas Records, 1962–1987, MS 29, UTSA
Archives, Library, University of Texas at San Antonio. Box 8:2.

Rodriguez, Javier. 1987. "That Was the Cry 15 Years Ago: La Raza Unida's De-
scendants Now Hold Office across the State." *San Antonio Light*, November 29.

Rodriguez, Sylvia. ca. 1978. Text of presentation at the Robert A. Taft Institute
of Government. Mexican American Democrats of Texas Records, 1962–1987,
MS 29, UTSA Archives, Library, University of Texas at San Antonio. Box
7:10.

Roediger, David R. 2006. *Working toward Whiteness: How America's Immigrants
Became White: The Strange Journey from Ellis Island to the Suburbs*. New York:
Basic Books.

———. 2007. *The Wages of Whiteness: Race and the Making of the American Working Class*. London: Verso.

Rosenfeld, Michael. 1998. "Mexican Immigrants and Mexican American Politi-
cal Assimilation." In *Migration between Mexico and the United States: Binational
Study*, 1117–1131. Washington, D.C.: U.S. Commission on Immigration
Reform.

Salinas, Olivia. 1979. Letter to Ruben Bonilla, April 5. Governor William P.
Clements Jr. Records, Mexico and Latin American Relations Office [MALAR]
Records, First Term, 1979–1983. Box 7, Folder 1.

Sánchez, George I. 1958. Letter to Mrs. R. D. Randolph, October 8. Creekmore Fath Papers, 1938–1992 and undated, Southwest Collection/Special Collections Library, Texas Tech University, Lubbock. Box 1, Folder 8.

———. 1961. Letter to James W. Boren, March 16. Dr. Hector P. Garcia Papers, Special Collections and Archives, Texas A&M University–Corpus Christi, Mary and Jeff Bell Library.

———. 1962a. Letter to Ed Idar Jr., January 29. Dr. Hector P. Garcia Papers, Special Collections and Archives, Texas A&M University–Corpus Christi, Mary and Jeff Bell Library.

———. 1962b. Letter to Ed Idar Jr., May 16. Dr. Hector P. Garcia Papers, Special Collections and Archives, Texas A&M University–Corpus Christi, Mary and Jeff Bell Library.

———. 1962c. Letter to Gregorio E. Coronado, February 17. Dr. Hector P. Garcia Papers, Special Collections and Archives, Texas A&M University–Corpus Christi, Mary and Jeff Bell Library.

———. 1962d. Letter to Hector Garcia, March 6. Dr. Hector P. Garcia Papers, Special Collections and Archives, Texas A&M University–Corpus Christi, Mary and Jeff Bell Library.

———. 1962e. Letter to Hector P. Garcia, April 24. Dr. Hector P. Garcia Papers, Special Collections and Archives, Texas A&M University–Corpus Christi, Mary and Jeff Bell Library.

———. ca. 1962. Letter to Hector Garcia, May 27. Dr. Hector P. Garcia Papers, Special Collections and Archives, Texas A&M University–Corpus Christi, Mary and Jeff Bell Library.

———. 1967. Letter to Henry B. González. February 6. Henry B. González Papers, 1946–1998, Dolph Briscoe Center for American History, University of Texas at Austin. Box 2004–127/91.

———. n.d. "Statement of PASO Principles." Henry B. González Papers, 1946–1998, Dolph Briscoe Center for American History, University of Texas at Austin. Box 2004–127/50.

Sánchez, Robert P. 1956. Letter to Fred Schmidt, May 2. Dr. Hector P. Garcia Papers, Special Collections and Archives, Texas A&M University–Corpus Christi, Mary and Jeff Bell Library.

———. 1957a. Letter to Creekmore Fath, September 28. Creekmore Fath Papers, 1938–1992 and undated, Southwest Collection/Special Collections Library, Texas Tech University, Lubbock. Box 1, Folder 4.

———. 1957b. Letter to Creekmore Fath, November 4. Creekmore Fath Papers, 1938–1992 and undated, Southwest Collection/Special Collections Library, Texas Tech University, Lubbock. Box 1, Folder 4.

———. 1970. Letter to Albert Peña, May 8. Albert A. Peña Jr. Papers, 1952–1977 (bulk 1956–1972), MS 37, UTSA Archives and Special Collections, Library, University of Texas at San Antonio. Box 8 : 18.

San Miguel, Guadalupe, Jr. 1987. *"Let All of Them Take Heed": Mexican Americans and the Campaign for Educational Equality in Texas, 1910–1981.* Austin: University of Texas Press.

Santiesteban, Tati. 2003. Interview with author, May 15, 2003, El Paso.

Schneider, Megan. 2008. Interview with Marc Campos, April 18. Houston Oral History Project. Online (accessed January 13, 2010): http://digital.hous tonlibrary.org/oral-history/marc-campos.php.

Scott, Stefanie, and Diana R. Fuentes. 1993. "House Mexican Americans Battle Back to Help Cavazos." *San Antonio Express-News*, February 18. Irma Rangel Collection (A2003–042), South Texas Archives and Special Collections, James C. Jernigan Library, Texas A&M University–Kingsville. Box 4.018.

Segal, Adam. 2002. "Records Broken: Spanish-Language Television Advertising in the 2002 Election." Hispanic Voter Project, November 21. Johns Hopkins University, Washington, D.C.

Senate Hispanic Caucus. 1995. Draft letter to Texas Congressional Delegation, October 18. Carlos Truan Collection, South Texas Archives and Special Collections, James C. Jernigan Library, Texas A&M University–Kingsville. Box 537.016.

Sepúlveda, Juan. 2003. *The Life and Times of Willie Velasquez: Su Voto Es Su Voz*. Houston: Arte Público Press.

Shafer, Byron E., and Richard Johnston. 2006. *The End of Southern Exceptionalism: Class, Race, and Partisan Change in the Postwar South*. Cambridge, Mass.: Harvard University Press.

Shannon, Kelly. 2002a. "Democrat Dan Morales to Endorse Perry." Associated Press, October 8. Retrieved from http://www.lexisnexis.com.

———. 2002b. "Morales Says Spanish Lacks 'Status' of English." Associated Press State and Local Wire. February 28. Retrieved from http://www.lexisnexis .com.

———. 2002c. "Sánchez Takes Stand against New Taxes, Criticizes Morales." Associated Press State and Local Wire, February 19. Retrieved from http://www .lexisnexis.com.

———. 2002d. "Sánchez Tries to Grow into Politics from Business World." Associated Press State and Local Wire, October 17. Retrieved from http://www .lexisnexis.com.

———. 2002e. "Spanish Debate Sets Stage for Stretch Run of Governor's Race." Associated Press, March 2. Retrieved from http://www.lexisnexis.com.

———. 2002 f. "Texas Gubernatorial Candidate Accuses Opponent of Running 'Patron-Style' Campaign." Associated Press, March 8. Retrieved from http:// www.lexisnexis.com.

Shapiro, Dave. 1970. Letter to Oscar Pérez, August 11. Albert A. Peña Jr. Papers, 1952–1977 (bulk 1956–1972), MS 37, UTSA Archives and Special Collections Library, University of Texas at San Antonio. Box 8:18.

Sheeler, Kristina K. Horn. 2000. "Women's Public Discourse and the Gendering of Leadership Culture: Ann Richards and Christine Todd Whitman Negotiate the Governorship." Ph.D. dissertation, Department of Communication and Culture, Indiana University.

Sheldon, Joe. 1958. Letter to Price Daniel Sr., February 13. Texas Governor Price Daniel Records, Archives and Information Services Division, Texas State Library and Archives Commission, Republican Party. Box 355.

Shipp, Dixie. 1974. "Barrientos Captures Rep. Foreman's Seat." *Austin American-*

Statesman, June 2. Richard Moya Papers, Austin History Center, Austin Public Library.

Shivers, Allan. 1952a. "Remarks of Governor Allan Shivers." Broadcast speech, Austin, October 2. Allan Shivers Papers, 1949–1984, Dolph Briscoe Center for American History, University of Texas at Austin.

———. 1952b. "Remarks of Governor Allan Shivers." State Democratic Executive Committee Meeting, New Braunfels, Texas, April 18. Walter Gardner Hall—Papers, 1923–1990, MS 280, Woodson Research Center, Fondren Library, Rice University. Box 4, Folder 80.

———. 1956. Press memorandum. Office of the Governor, February 23. Allan Shivers Papers, 1949–1984, Dolph Briscoe Center for American History, University of Texas at Austin.

———. 1960a. "Remarks of Allan Shivers." Southern TV Network. Charleston, South Carolina, October 31. Allan Shivers Papers, 1949–1984, Dolph Briscoe Center for American History, University of Texas at Austin.

———. 1960b. "Remarks of Allan Shivers." Speech, Austin, November 7. Allan Shivers Papers, 1949–1984, Dolph Briscoe Center for American History, University of Texas at Austin.

Shockley, John Staples. 1979. *Chicano Revolt in a Texas Town*. Notre Dame: University of Notre Dame Press.

Silex, Humberto. 1967. Press release, Republican Party of Texas, July 15. Texas Observer Records, 1952–1990, Dolph Briscoe Center for American History, University of Texas at Austin.

Sinkin, William R. 1966. "Conversation between Waggoner Carr and William Sinkin on September 10, 1966," September 13. Henry B. González Papers, 1946–1998, Dolph Briscoe Center for American History, University of Texas at Austin. Box 2004–127/395.

Slater, Wayne. 1994. "Richards' Appointees Counted among Her Victories, Headaches, Women, Minorities Gain; Critics Call Many Unqualified." *Dallas Morning News*, September 2.

———. 2002. "Subtly, Surely, Working Race into the Races." *Dallas Morning News*, October 15. Retrieved from http://www.lexisnexis.com.

Smith, Erna. 1974. "Barrientos Takes Place 4: Demo Overcomes Todd, Gutiérrez." *Daily Texan*, November 6. "Barrientos, Gonzalo" Vertical File, Dolph Briscoe Center for American History, University of Texas at Austin.

Smith, Lee Matt. 1969. Letter to Pancho Medrano (with attached report), November 17. Texas Observer Records, 1952–1990, Dolph Briscoe Center for American History, University of Texas at Austin.

Smith, Mark. 1972. "Smith v. Gutierrez." *Texas Observer*, September 22.

Smith, Preston. 1970. Letter to Tati Santiesteban, July 29. Dolph Briscoe Papers, 1932–2010, Dolph Briscoe Center for American History, University of Texas at Austin. Box 265.

Smyser, Craig. 1977. "Many Think Raza Unida Is Finished as Political Party." *Houston Chronicle*, February 20. Dolph Briscoe Papers, 1932–2010, Dolph Briscoe Center for American History, University of Texas at Austin. Box 48.

Sosa, Lionel. 2009. "Politics and the Latino Future: A Republican Dream." In

Henry Cisneros and John Rosales, eds., *Latinos and the Nation's Future*, 115–124. Houston: Arte Público Press.

Southwest Voter Registration Education Project. 1978. *Mexican American Voting in the 1978 Texas General Election* (Research report/Southwest Voter Registration Education Project). San Antonio: Southwest Voter Registration Education Project.

———. 1982. *Mexican American Voting in the 1982 Texas General Election* (Research report/Southwest Voter Registration Education Project). San Antonio: Southwest Voter Registration Education Project.

———. 1983. *The National Hispanic Voter Registration Campaign*. San Antonio: Southwest Voter Registration Education Project.

Sowell, Polly, and Rich Thomas. 1982. Memo to William P. Clements, August 12. Governor William P. Clements Jr. Records, Mexico and Latin American Relations Office [MALAR] Records, First Term, 1979–1983. Box 3, Folder 1.

Stanley, Harold W. 2008. "Latino Population Growth, Political Clout, and the South, 2008." Online (accessed September 16, 2010): http//sppc2010.org/Papers/Stanley.SPPC.2010.paper.pdf.

State Democratic Executive Committee. 1964a. "Minutes." State Democratic Executive Committee, Austin, October 13. Texas Democratic Party Papers, Archives and Information Services Division, Texas State Library and Archives Commission. Box 1979/49-65.

———. 1964b. "Minutes, SDEC Meeting," October 13. Texas Democratic Party Papers, Archives and Information Services Division, Texas State Library and Archives Commission. Box 1979/49.

———. 1966. "Minutes of the Committee on Platform and Resolutions," September 20. Texas Democratic Party Papers, Archives and Information Services Division, Texas State Library and Archives Commission. Box 1979/49-65.

———. 1983. Minutes of the State Democratic Executive Committee of Texas, July 30. Billie Carr Papers, 1956–2003, MS 373, Woodson Research Center, Fondren Library, Rice University. Box 11, Folder 18.

Stephenson, Charles W. 1967. "The Democrats of Texas and Texas Liberalism, 1944–1960: A Study in Political Frustration." MA thesis, Southwest Texas State University.

Stoler, Susan. 1982. "Armstrong 151 Votes Shy of MAD Endorsement." *Valley Morning Star*, March 7. Moya (Richard) Papers (1969–1986), Austin History Center, AR.2002.024.

Strauss, Robert S. 1974. Letter to Calvin Guest, October 8. Billie Carr Papers, 1956–2003, MS 373, Woodson Research Center, Fondren Library, Rice University.

Stutz, Terrence. 1993. "Cavazos Confirmed to Employment Panel." *Dallas Morning News*, February 19. Irma Rangel Collection (A2003–042), South Texas Archives and Special Collections, James C. Jernigan Library, Texas A&M University–Kingsville. Box 4.019.

Sullivan, Kathleen. 1972. *Robert D. Price: Republican Representative from Texas*. New York: Grossman Publishers.

Sussman, Robert, and Robert Cochran. 1972. *Wright Patman: Democratic Representative from Texas*. New York: Grossman Publishers.

Swartz, Linda. 1974. "A Quiet Revolution in Pharr." *Texas Observer*, August 9.

Tati [Santiesteban] to Texas Senate Committee. 1972. "Platform," March 2. Tati Santiesteban Personal Papers.

Taylor, Robert. 1972. *Richard C. White: Democratic Representative from Texas*. New York: Grossman Publishers.

Taylor, Robert, and Charles J. Brown. 1972. *O. C. Fisher: Democratic Representative from Texas*. New York: Grossman Publishers.

Telles, Edward E., and Vilma Ortiz. 2008. *Generations of Exclusion: Mexican Americans, Assimilation, and Race*. New York: Russell Sage Foundation.

Texas Advisory Committee on Segregation in the Public Schools. 1956. "Report on Segregation in the Public Schools," November 20. Texas Governor Price Daniel Records, Archives and Information Services Division, Texas State Library and Archives Commission, Segregation. Box 369.

Texas Democratic Party. 1948. "1948 Platform of the Democratic Party of Texas." September 14. Texas Governor Price Daniel Records, Archives and Information Services Division, Texas State Library and Archives Commission, State Democratic Party. Box 53.

———. 1950. "Transcript of Proceedings of the State of Texas Democratic Convention," Mineral Wells, September 12. Texas Democratic Party Papers, Archives and Information Services Division, Texas State Library and Archives Commission. Box 1979/49-102.

———. 1952a. "Concerning the 'Loyalty Pledge.'" Texas Democratic Party Papers, Archives and Information Services Division, Texas State Library and Archives Commission. Box 1979/49.

———. 1952b. Texas Delegation to Democratic National Convention Chicago—1952. Texas Democratic Party Papers, Archives and Information Services Division, Texas State Library and Archives Commission. Box 1979/49.

———. 1952c. "Texas Democratic Convention," September 9. Texas Democratic Party Papers, Archives and Information Services Division, Texas State Library and Archives Commission. Box 1979/49-102.

———. 1952d. "Texas State Democratic Convention," May 27. Texas Democratic Party Papers, Archives and Information Services Division, Texas State Library and Archives Commission. Box 1979/49-102.

———. 1958a. Platform and Resolutions Adopted by the State Democratic Convention, San Antonio, Texas, September 9. Texas Democratic Party Papers, Archives and Information Services Division, Texas State Library and Archives Commission. Box 1979/49-135.

———. 1958b. "Platform and Resolutions of the Democratic Party of Texas, State Democratic Convention," September 9. Texas Democratic Party Papers, Archives and Information Services Division, Texas State Library and Archives Commission. Box 1979/96–10.

———. 1964. "Platform of the Democratic Party of Texas, State Democratic Convention." September 15. Texas Democratic Party Papers, Archives and Information Services Division, Texas State Library and Archives Commission. Box 1979/49.

———. 1966. "Declaration of Principles." State Convention, September 20.

Texas Democratic Party Papers, Archives and Information Services Division, Texas State Library and Archives Commission. Box 1979/49-65.

———. 1974a. "Answer of the Democratic Party of Texas and the Challenged At Large Delegates and Alternates of the Texas Democratic Party." Joe J. Bernal Papers, Benson Latin American Collection, University of Texas Libraries, University of Texas at Austin. Democratic Party—Texas: State Democratic Exec. Committee (Party Rules). Box 107.

———. 1974b. 1974 Affirmative Action Plan. Joe J. Bernal Papers, Benson Latin American Collection, University of Texas Libraries, University of Texas at Austin. Box 107.

———. 1974c. Press release, April 5. Texas Democratic Party Papers, Archives and Information Services Division, Texas State Library and Archives Commission. Box 1979/49-123.

———. 1978. "Specific Programs Designed to Strengthen the Democratic Party," November 22. Billie Carr Papers, 1956–2003, MS 373, Woodson Research Center, Fondren Library, Rice University. Box 12, Folder 4.

Texas Democratic Party Affirmative Action Committee. 1974. Transcript. Texas Democratic Party Papers, Archives and Information Services Division, Texas State Library and Archives Commission. Box 1979/49-123.

Texas Democrats. ca. 1976. Billie Carr Papers, 1956–2003, MS 373, Woodson Research Center, Fondren Library, Rice University. Box 11, Folder 20.

Texas Democrats Organizational Report. n.d. Billie Carr Papers, 1956–2003, MS 373, Woodson Research Center, Fondren Library, Rice University. Box 11, Folder 20.

Texas Secretary of State. 1994. Race Summary Report, 1994 General Election, November 8. Online (accessed September 27, 2010): http://elections.sos.state.tx.us/elchist.exe.

———. 1998. Race Summary Report, 1998 General Election, November 3. Online (accessed September 27, 2010): http://elections.sos.state.tx.us/elchist.exe.

———. 2002a. Race Summary Report, 2002 Democratic Primary Election. Online (accessed June 30, 2009): http://elections.sos.state.tx.us/elchist.exe.

———. 2002b. Race Summary Report, 2002 General Election, November 5. Online (accessed September 16, 2010): http://elections.sos.state.tx.us/elchist.exe.

———. 2006. Race Summary Report, 2006 General Election, November 7. Online (accessed September 16, 2010): http://elections.sos.state.tx.us/elchist.exe.

———. 2010. Race Summary Report, 2010 General Election, November 2. Online (accessed January 17, 2011): http://elections.sos.state.tx.us/elchist.exe.

Thompson, Greg. 1978. "Raza Unida Candidate Odd Clements Helpmate," October 16. Dolph Briscoe Papers, 1932–2010, Dolph Briscoe Center for American History, University of Texas at Austin. Box 48.

Thompson, Kyle. 1982. "White Owes Debt to Hispanics." *Fort Worth Star-Telegram*, November 28. Records, Texas Governor Mark White, Archives and Information Services Division, Texas State Library and Archives Commission, "General Hispanics." Box 1991/141–94.

Thompson, Paul. 1970. Editorial. *San Antonio Express*, September 2. Henry B.

González Papers, 1946–1998, Dolph Briscoe Center for American History, University of Texas at Austin. Box 2004-127/395.

Thorpe, Helen. 2001. "Tony the Tiger: Texas Dems Think Laredo Oilman Tony Sánchez Is Their Savior. But Then So Did George W. Bush. Can They Both Be Right?" *Texas Observer*, May 25, 2001.

Tiede, Saralee. 1974. *Dallas Times Herald*, February 17 Dolph Briscoe Papers, 1932–2010, Dolph Briscoe Center for American History, University of Texas at Austin. Box 33.

———. 1982. "Latin American Support Touted by Office Seekers." *Dallas Times Herald*, September 14. Governor William P. Clements Jr. Records, Mexico and Latin American Relations Office [MALAR] Records, First Term, 1979–1983. Box 5, Folder 16.

Times of Texas. 1982 (August/September).

Tony Bonilla Campaign. 1966. Document (no title, undated). LBJ Library, "LBJ Human Rights" HU2/MC 6/7/66–10/12/66. Box 22.

Torrez, G. A. 1956. Letter to Hector P. Garcia, May 28. Dr. Hector P. Garcia Papers, Special Collections and Archives, Texas A&M University–Corpus Christi, Mary and Jeff Bell Library.

Townsend, Claudia. 1972. *Abraham Kazen, Jr.: Democratic Representative from Texas.* New York: Grossman Publishers.

Trejo, Frank. 1981. "Judge Barrera Eager to Make His Benchmark." *Fort Worth Star-Telegram.* August 2. "Barrera, Roy Jr." Vertical File, Dolph Briscoe Center for American History, University of Texas at Austin.

———. 1982. "LULAC Official for Clements." *Fort Worth Star-Telegram*, October 15. Governor William P. Clements Jr. Records, Mexico and Latin American Relations Office [MALAR] Records, First Term, 1979–1983. Box 7, Folder 8.

Treviño, Jesse. ca. 1986. "Tough Pick: Credentials Boost Barrera as GOP Ponders Gubernatorial Race." Undated newspaper clipping. "Barrera, Roy Jr." Vertical File, Dolph Briscoe Center for American History, University of Texas at Austin.

———. 1991. "Berlanga: An Embattled Mystery Man of Texas Politics." *Austin American-Statesman*, April 10. "Berlanga, Hugo" Vertical File, Dolph Briscoe Center for American History, University of Texas at Austin.

Truan, Carlos. ca. 1968. Campaign speech (undated). Carlos Truan Papers. South Texas Archives and Special Collections, James C. Jernigan Library, Texas A&M University–Kingsville. Box 823.009.

———. 1988. "The Mexican American Impact on Politics." Carlos Truan Papers, South Texas Archives and Special Collections, James C. Jernigan Library, Texas A&M University–Kingsville. Box 537.005.

———. 1990. "Senator Carlos F. Truan Senate Select Committee on Legislative Redistricting and House Redistricting Committee," April 6. Carlos Truan Collection, South Texas Archives and Special Collections, James C. Jernigan Library, Texas A&M University–Kingsville. Box 540.001.

———. 1992. "Remarks of Senator Carlos F. Truan to the Kingsville Small Business Development Corporation," September 9, Bonanza Restaurant, Kingsville. Carlos F. Truan Collection, South Texas Archives and Special Collections, James C. Jernigan Library, Texas A&M University–Kingsville. Box 9.001.

————. 1998a. "NAFTA and the European Union: A Vision towards Global Integration in the 21st Century," May 22. Carlos F. Truan Collection, South Texas Archives and Special Collections, James C. Jernigan Library, Texas A&M University–Kingsville. Box 12b.001.

————. 1998b. Oral history interview by José Ángel Gutiérrez, June 17. Center for Mexican American Studies No. 39.

United States Department of Commerce. 1916. *Special Census of the Population of El Paso, Texas* (January 15). Washington, D.C.: Government Printing Office.

Untermeyer, Chase. ca. 1972. "Raza Unida Members Quiz Grover during South Texas Campaign Stop." Unidentified newspaper clipping. Texas Observer Records, 1952–1990, Dolph Briscoe Center for American History, University of Texas at Austin.

————. 1974. "Building Chicano Political Power." *Houston Chronicle*, August 25. Joe J. Bernal Papers, Benson Latin American Collection, University of Texas Libraries, University of Texas at Austin. Box 38.

Upham, Chester. 1981a. Letter to Eddie Aurispa, June 16. Governor William P. Clements Jr. Records, Mexico and Latin American Relations Office [MALAR] Records, First Term, 1979–1983. Box 6, Folder 5.

————. 1981b. Letter to John Gavin, October 27. Governor William P. Clements Jr. Records, Mexico and Latin American Relations Office [MALAR] Records, First Term, 1979–1983. Box 7, Folder 1.

————. 1981c. Letter to Malcom Baldridge, June 10. Governor William P. Clements Jr. Records, Mexico and Latin American Relations Office [MALAR] Records, First Term, 1979–1983. Box 10, Folder 18.

Valdez, O. J. 1967. Letter to Henry B. González, May 5. Henry B. González Papers, 1946–1998, Dolph Briscoe Center for American History, University of Texas at Austin. Box 2004-127/395.

Vara, Luis. 1978a. Memo to David Dean, August 24. Governor William P. Clements Jr. Records, Mexico and Latin American Relations Office [MALAR] Records, First Term, 1979–1983. Box 14, Folder 29.

————. 1978b. Memo to David Dean, August 31. Governor William P. Clements Jr. Records, Mexico and Latin American Relations Office [MALAR] Records, First Term, 1979–1983. Box 14, Folder 29.

Vara, Richard. 1977. "The Governor vs Raza Unida." *Houston Post*. October 30. Dolph Briscoe Papers, 1932–2010, Dolph Briscoe Center for American History, University of Texas at Austin. Box 48.

Vaughan, Vicki. 1979. "Teamwork: Killing HB 227." *Texas Observer*, May 25.

Vela, Pilar Saavedra. 1978. "Irma Rangel—Breaking Down Barriers in Texas." *Agenda/National Council of La Raza* (January/February): 34–36. Irma Rangel Papers, South Texas Archives and Special Collections, James C. Jernigan Library, Texas A&M University–Kingsville. Box 2.001.

Vera, Luis. 1978a. Memo to Nola Haerle, August 9. Governor William P. Clements Jr. Records, Mexico and Latin American Relations Office [MALAR] Records, First Term, 1979–1983. Box 14, Folder 30.

————. 1978b. Memo to press (internal memo), July 21. Governor William P. Clements Jr. Records, Mexico and Latin American Relations Office [MALAR] Records, First Term, 1979–1983. Box 14, Folder 33.

Vertuno, Jim. 2002. "Perry Invoking Name of Sam Houston to Boost Campaign, Slam Sánchez." Associated Press State and Local Wire, August 1. Retrieved from http://www.lexisnexis.com.

Viamonte, Norberto. 1979. "Truan Survives Battles." *Corpus Christi Caller*, June 10. Carlos Truan Papers, South Texas Archives and Special Collections, James C. Jernigan Library, Texas A&M University–Kingsville. Box 1b.002.

Vigil, Ernesto B. 1999. *The Crusade for Justice: Chicano Militancy and the Government's War on Dissent*. Madison: University of Wisconsin Press.

Villalpando, Cathi. 1981. Letter to Eddie Aurispa, May 14. Governor William P. Clements Jr. Records, Mexico and Latin American Relations Office [MALAR] Records, First Term, 1979–1983. Box 10, Folder 18.

Waldrep, Ray. 1971. "New City Controller Leonel Castillo Aims to Be More Than Bookkeeper." *Houston Chronicle*, December 12. Margo Gutiérrez Personal Files, University of Texas at Austin.

Waters, Mary C. 1990. *Ethnic Options: Choosing Identities in America*. Berkeley: University of California Press.

Watkins, Alfred J. 1982. "Nineteen Rights Make a Wrong." *Texas Observer*, July 9.

Watkins, Sharon. 1974. "Candidates Use Racial Issue." *San Antonio Light*, October 30. Dolph Briscoe Papers, 1932–2010, Dolph Briscoe Center for American History, University of Texas at Austin. Box 30.

Weeks, Oliver Douglas. 1930. "The Texas-Mexican and the Politics of South Texas." *American Political Science Review* 24, no. 3: 606–627.

———. 1953. *Texas Presidential Politics in 1952*. Austin: University of Texas Institute of Public Affairs.

———. 1957. *Texas One Party Politics in 1956*. Austin: University of Texas Institute of Public Affairs.

———. 1961. *Texas in the 1960 Presidential Election*. Austin: University of Texas Institute of Public Affairs.

Welch, Andy. 1976. "Guest Could Be Unwelcome One." *Abilene Reporter-News*, July 11. Dolph Briscoe Papers, 1932–2010, Dolph Briscoe Center for American History, University of Texas at Austin. Box 415.

West, Felton. 1982. "Groups Demand Changes in State School Aid." *Houston Post*, December 22. Governor William P. Clements Jr. Records, Mexico and Latin American Relations Office [MALAR] Records, First Term, 1979–1983. Box 3, Folder 1.

Wheat, John. 1978. "Growing Up Chicano." *La Onda Latina*. Online (accessed January 13, 2010): http://www.laits.utexas.edu/onda_latina/program?sernum =000515936&term=john%20wheat.

White, John C. 1974. Speech delivered to members of the State Democratic Executive Committee, June 15. Joe J. Bernal Papers, Benson Latin American Collection, University of Texas Libraries, University of Texas at Austin. Democratic Party—Texas: State Democratic Exec. Committee (Party Rules). Box 107.

White, Mark. 1975. "Remarks of Secretary of State Mark White," United States Senate Subcommittee on Constitutional Rights, Washington, D.C., April 22. Texas Observer Records, 1952–1990, Dolph Briscoe Center for American History, University of Texas at Austin.

————. 1982. "The Governor's Race." *Mexican American Democrat: Official Publication of the Mexican American Democrats of Texas* 1, no. 3 (August).

————. ca. 1982a. "Statement: Rural-Urban Coalition Policy Platform Response." Records, Texas Governor Mark White, Archives and Information Services Division, Texas State Library and Archives Commission, "Hispanics." Box 1991/141–94.

————. ca. 1982b. "Talking Points C.O.P.S." (n.d.). Records, Texas Governor Mark White, Archives and Information Services Division, Texas State Library and Archives Commission, "Hispanics." Box 1991/141–94.

————. 1987. Transcript of interview by Chandler Davidson, June 11. Chandler Davidson Texas Politics Research Collection, 1967–1992, MS 259, Woodson Research Center, Fondren Library, Rice University. Box 12, Folder 1.

Wiese, Art. 1970. "Bush-Eggers Woo Minorities." *Houston Post*, September 13. Dr. Hector P. Garcia Papers, Special Collections and Archives, Texas A&M University–Corpus Christi, Mary and Jeff Bell Library.

————. 1972. "Briscoe's Support of Wallace Cost Him Role of Peacemaker." *Houston Post*, July 14. Dolph Briscoe Papers, 1932–2010, Dolph Briscoe Center for American History, University of Texas at Austin. Box 294.

————. 1975. "Extension of Voting Rights Debated." *Houston Post*, May 4. Texas Observer Records, 1952–1990, Dolph Briscoe Center for American History, University of Texas at Austin.

————. 1978. "Ad Blitz Urged for Tower to Woo Hispanic Voters." *Houston Post*, September 30. Texas Observer Records, 1952–1990, Dolph Briscoe Center for American History, University of Texas at Austin.

Wilcox, Nate. 2008. *Texas Political Strategist Kelly Fero Talks to Nate Wilcox*. (July 11). Online (accessed June 12, 2009) at Netroots Rising: http://www.netrootsrising .com/2008/07/texas-political-srategist-kelly-fero-talks-to-nate-wilcox/.

William C. Velasquez Institute. 2004a. Texas General Election—November 5th, 2002—Exit Poll Results. Online (accessed September 16, 2010): http://www .wcvi.org/latino_voter_research/polls/tx/2002/exit_results02.html.

————. 2004b. *US Population Comparison by Ethnic Group, 1970–2050*. Online (accessed November 4, 2008): http://www.wcvi.org/data/demographic/.

Wirtz, W. Willard, et al. 1967. Press release, June 9. Office Files of White Aides, Office Files of Harry C. McPhearson, LBJ Library. Box 11 (1412) (file: "Mexican Americans").

Wood, Jim. ca. 1966. "Tony Bonilla, González Tangle at Lions Meet." *Corpus Christi Caller* (n.d.). Dr. Hector P. Garcia Papers, Special Collections and Archives, Texas A&M University–Corpus Christi, Mary and Jeff Bell Library.

Wood, Sam. 1958a. "Minority Bloc Has Candidates Ready." *Austin American*, May 29. Dr. Hector P. Garcia Papers, Special Collections and Archives, Texas A&M University–Corpus Christi, Mary and Jeff Bell Library.

————. 1958b. "Minority Bloc Has Candidates Ready." *Panola Watchman*, June 5.

Woodruff, Judy, et al. 2002. "Texas Gubernatorial Candidates Prepare for Spanish Debate; War of Words on War against Terrorism Continues." Cable News Network, March 1. Retrieved from http://www.lexisnexis.com.

Woods, L. A. ca. 1949. "Instructions and Regulations to All School Officers of County, City, Town and School Districts." Texas Governor Price Daniel

Records, Archives and Information Services Division, Texas State Library and Archives Commission, Segregation. Box 57.

Woodward, Kay. 1982. Letter to Sherry Hausenfluck, July 26. Governor William P. Clements Jr. Records, Mexico and Latin American Relations Office [MALAR] Records, First Term, 1979–1983. Box 10, Folder 18.

Yarborough, Ralph W. 1957. Handwritten note to Hector Garcia, January 30. Dr. Hector P. Garcia Papers, Special Collections and Archives, Texas A&M University–Corpus Christi, Mary and Jeff Bell Library.

———. 1969. Letter to Henry Muñoz Jr. October 1. Dr. Hector P. Garcia Papers, Special Collections and Archives, Texas A&M University–Corpus Christi, Mary and Jeff Bell Library.

———. 1982. Transcription of interview by Chandler Davidson, June 26. Chandler Davidson Texas Politics Research Collection, 1967–1992, MS 259, Woodson Research Center, Fondren Library, Rice University. Box 11, Folder 1.

Yardley, Jim. 2002. "Slow Texas Primary for Governor Gains Speed." *New York Times*, January 6.

Zapata, Licha. "Corrido de Irma Rangel." Irma Rangel Papers, South Texas Archives and Special Collections, James C. Jernigan Library, Texas A&M University–Kingsville. Box 236.015.

Index

Lightning Source UK Ltd.
Milton Keynes UK
UKHW012336080722
405560UK00006B/139